Endless Possibilities

Sunny skies and mountains high

Craig Briggs

By the same author

Journey To A Dream

Beyond Imagination

ISBN: 1537230417
ISBN-13: 978-1537230412

In Memory

Geoffrey Kidd
(1941–2006)

Jesus Angel Rodriguez Puentes
(1964–2005)

Nellie (Claire) Merry
(1936–2016)

Judge each day by the seeds you sow,
not by the harvest you reap.

CONTENTS

Acknowledgements

Special thanks go to my wife, Melanie,
without whose help, advice, and incredible memory
this chapter of our lives would never have been written.

Also to Mrs June Viles for her support,
enthusiasm, and encouragement.

I'd also like to thank Louise Lubke Cuss of wordblink.com
for her skill and professionalism in preparing the final edit.

Introduction

In May 2002 my wife Melanie and I decided to sell up and chase our dream. We packed all our worldly belongings, including our dog Jazz, into my ageing executive saloon, and headed off to Spain. Not for us the tourist-packed Costas of the Mediterranean. Our destination of choice was Galicia: a little known region in the northwest corner of Spain.

The contrast in lifestyles from England's industrial north to Spain's rural interior was quite a shock and significantly more traumatic than either of us had imagined. It wasn't as though we hadn't made an effort to prepare ourselves. We'd spent three and a half years studying Spanish at night school only to discover that Galicia has its own language, gallego. A proudly spoken tongue that has more in common with Portuguese than Spanish.

Dubious estate agents and questionable property descriptions turned our search for a new home into a lottery. Clear objectives became blurred and after several failed attempts to buy a property, we were forced to reassess our goals.

Eventually, we found our dream house, a tiny bungalow on the outskirts of the sleepy village of Canabal. Coping with Spain's laidback approach while trying to manage a building project tested our resolve.

What could go wrong did and by Christmas we were ready to throw in the towel and head back to Blighty but Yorkshiremen are made of sterner stuff. A timely visit from my dad re-energised our ambitions. Twelve months and ten days after arriving in Galicia, we moved into our new home and completed the first stage of our *Journey To A Dream*.

Choosing a name for our renovated property proved difficult but eventually we settled on *El Sueño* (The Dream). After the challenges of the first twelve months, we settled into a more relaxed lifestyle. With Melanie's help, I set about transforming our barren plot into a garden paradise. It wasn't all plain sailing and dealing with Spanish bureaucracy proved difficult. As time drifted by we finally started to enjoy a life *Beyond Imagination*.

For the first time in a long time, I had the freedom to take up some hobbies. Little did I know that writing and viniculture would become my pastimes of choice. With help from our neighbour, Meli, I took my first tentative steps on the road to winemaking. The success of my fledgling hobby was left in the hands of Mother Nature. It was she who would decide my fate.

1

Resistance is Futile

It could be the best of wines,
it could be the worst of wines.

For six long months we'd resisted the urge to sample our fledgling plonk. A test of willpower to challenge the most disciplined of individuals, let alone a pair of eager beavers. Long winter nights and freezing temperatures can weaken the strongest resolve, but hope springs eternal and spring brings hope.

'Have you tasted the wine yet?' asked Meli, on one of her visits to the house.

Meli is a close neighbour and our self-appointed winemaking mentor. Last year she'd tutored us in the ancient art of viniculture.

'No not yet,' replied Melanie.

'It's time.'

Her measured reply and wistful gaze required but one response.

'In that case, Meli, let's go and taste it.'

'Why not?' said Melanie eagerly.

My excitement was tempered with an equal measure of apprehension. I plucked a glass tumbler from the cupboard and the three of us marched across to the garden shed. It seemed fitting that Meli should be here for the first tasting of our collaborative efforts.

'Red or white?' I asked, as we huddled together in the confines of the shed.

Standing along one wall, like a pair of squaddies on parade, were two wine vats. The first wore a tunic of brushed stainless steel and the second, shiny chromium plate.

'Not for me,' replied Meli.

'What?'

My surprise triggered an immediate response.

'The doctor told me not to drink.'

'Surely a little sip can't hurt,' I replied.

'No, not for me.'

It seemed a shame but Meli was adamant.

'Red or white, Melanie?'

'Let's try the white first.'

Located two inches from the bottom of each vat is a stainless steel valve. I held the glass underneath and gently twisted it open. A grape skin and several pips spluttered out followed by a cloudy, yellowy green liquid. It looked as appetising as early morning pee. Quickly, I closed the valve and glanced across at Meli.

'That's alright,' she said. 'Throw it away and top the glass up.'

We'd visited many *bodegas* (wine cellars) over the last three years and watched in horror as the owner threw away the first glassful of wine. We now knew why. The floor of the shed is concrete so I stepped outside and tipped the murky brew onto the lawn before refilling the glass. The colour didn't improve but at least the floaters had disappeared.

'Here you go,' I said, offering the glass to Melanie.

'You first,' she said, looking decidedly suspicious.

'That looks much better,' said Meli.

Coming from anyone else, Meli's comment could easily have been mistaken for sarcasm, or as we say in Yorkshire "taking the piss", but not from her.

In my experience, most homemade whites tend to be a little cloudy. Without further ado, I raised the glass, wished all present good health, and drank.

Many years ago, a friend from Portugal told me that the best way to appreciate the subtle flavours of a wine is to swirl a mouthful around on the palate, run your tongue over the front of your teeth and swallow. Breathe in through the nose, let the air circulate and then out through the mouth.

'Well?' asked Melanie.

Meli stared at me, waiting for a response.

Its flavour was like nothing I'd ever tasted before, but in a good way. Our usual teatime tipple is rather bland. Mind you, what can we expect for forty-nine cents a bottle? This, on the other hand, was bursting with character. Slightly more Winnie the Pooh than Pepé Le Pew, but who cared? We'd done it: we'd actually made drinkable wine; I was gobsmacked.

'It's …' I paused, searching for a fitting description.

'Well?' asked Melanie eagerly.

'It's … distinctive.'

'Is that distinctively good or distinctively bad?'

'Put it this way, I'll be drinking it.'

'What did he say?' asked Meli, eager to hear the verdict.

'He said it's good enough to drink.'

Meli looked decidedly pleased with herself, and why not? Without her help I can't image the disaster we would have presided over.

'Let's have a taste then,' said Melanie, reaching for the glass.

The fact that I hadn't keeled over dead seemed to have triggered Melanie's more adventurous side. I handed her the glass and waited with bated breath. Melanie took a sip and swallowed.

'It certainly tastes better than it looks,' she remarked.

To reinforce her statement she downed the lot and handed me back the empty.

'Let's hope the red is as good.'

The red wine was in the smaller of the two vats. Once again I held the empty glass under the valve and twisted. After the initial splutter, an inky red liquid flowed into it.

'Colour looks good,' I commented, as I squeezed past Meli to tip it outside.

The contents left a deep purple patch on the lawn.

If it could do that to the grass, what was my liver going to look like?

I stepped back inside and poured a good glassful.

'Do you want to be first to try this one?' I asked, offering it to Melanie.

'That's very generous of you but I'll pass.'

Her sense of adventure clearly hadn't progressed to the role of King's Taster. Once again, the risk of a pickled liver fell to me.

I lifted the glass to my nose and inhaled the aroma. It smelt incredibly fruity, like a glass of crushed blackcurrants. The omens smelled good. I took a sip and rolled it across my tongue. This too was like nothing I'd ever tasted before, but unfortunately not in a good way. Adjectives such as foul, revolting, even yucky, sprang to mind. Meli was waiting anxiously for the verdict. She'd been so pleased with the white that I hadn't the heart to deliver such a crushing blow.

'Well?' asked Melanie.

Her question caught me on the hop. Searching the depths of my grey matter for a sympathetic description I blurted out, 'Different, it's different.'

'What did he say?' asked Meli.

I stared wide eyed at Melanie. Thankfully, she took the hint.

'He says it's not quite as good as the white,' she replied.

'What do you think?' I asked, handing the glass to Melanie.

Given her explanation to Meli, she could hardly refuse to taste it. Somewhat reluctantly she accepted the offering and took a sip.

'I see what you mean,' she said.

On reflection, we were pretty satisfied with our first attempt at winemaking. We had a vat full of palatable white and enough dodgy red to keep us in sangria for the whole summer.

It's often said that "Life is too short to drink bad wine" – perhaps that's true, but I'm certain that it's far too short *not* to have a go at making it.

Our questionable success was the only incentive I needed to plant more vines: fifteen red, of the Mencia variety, and ten Palomino whites. That brought our total vine stock to fifty-five. It would be three or four years before we reaped the fruits of our labour, but we weren't in a rush.

Planting the new vines proved much easier than pruning the old ones. After last year's tuition from Meli's son, Jesus, I'd hoped to find the task a little easier this year. How wrong could I be?

By the time our neighbours begin pruning, most growers in the area have long since finished. The village of Canabal is situated on the slopes of the Val de Lemos facing northeasterly. This makes it susceptible to late spring frost which can destroy young shoots. For this reason, villagers wait as long as possible to prune their vines, with one overriding caveat: the cycle of the moon.

'You need to prune your vines today. It's a good moon,' instructed Meli. 'Jesus won't be able to help you this year; he's in hospital in Santiago having some tests done.'

'What's matter?' I asked.

'They don't know,' she said, looking quite concerned.

'They're hoping the test will reveal what the problem is.'

'I hope everything goes well, Meli. Give him our love.'

Meli managed a polite smile before heading home.

In these parts, ignoring the moon is tantamount to heresy. Everything from planting vegetables to getting your hair cut is dictated by its cycle. I had no choice but to drop what I was doing and prune the vines. The moon was on the rise and far be it from me to upset Selene, or should that be Luna? I guess that would depend on whether I worshipped the Greek or Roman god. As a lunar sceptic, I'd probably have more success praying to the Clangers.

Despite my cynicism, daily temperatures had certainly picked up since the new moon. The heavy morning frosts and biting chill at sunset had disappeared. Whoever or whatever was responsible, we weren't complaining.

That afternoon I began in earnest. Secateurs in hand, I stood motionless, staring at the first vine. Last year, Jesus made it look so easy and logical: one cane trimmed to six buds, another to two, and all the remaining canes removed. Facing me now was a two-metre-tall trunk topped with a thicket-like mass of last year's fruiting canes. My actions today would determine the quantity and quality of this year's grape harvest. The sense of responsibility was overwhelming. Once I'd made my cut, there was no turning back.

Every snip with the secateurs sent a wiry cane tumbling to the ground. Clear sap formed teardrops on the open wounds. As they dripped to the ground, it seemed as if the vines were weeping for their loss. It took Melanie and me all afternoon to unravel the tangled puzzle of canes. Time would tell whether we'd found the correct solution or not.

Within three weeks of pruning, the first buds had begun to burst open. Spring was in the air. For the most part, last winter had been dry and cold. For us, that's far more preferable to wet and warm. Throughout autumn and winter, work on remodelling our investment property had kept us busy. Its completion and subsequent sale, to our new American friends, Rajan and Mitty, had left us at a loose end. And despite Melanie's concern at the timing of the sale, coming as it did on April Fool's day, the cheque cleared and the funds went into the account. For the first time in three years we had more money coming in than going out.

Feeling rather flush, I thought a holiday might be in order, but where should we go? Perhaps the sunny Caribbean, or romantic Maldives, or maybe somewhere a little closer to home?

'Would you like to go on holiday?' I asked one evening.

'Holiday?'

'I think we deserve one after all the hard work we did renovating the farmhouse, don't you?'

'You haven't forgotten that Bob and Janet are coming to stay with us in a few days' time, have you?'

Bob and Janet are an English couple we met during our second year here. They were searching for a property to renovate and finally found their dream ruin. Unfortunately, not everyone's dream converts into a living reality, and so it proved for them. Trying to organise the renovation from overseas hadn't helped. Broken promises and dubious lines of communication meant that their new life in Spain got off to the worst possible start. At the time we were powerless to help and within the space of six months they'd packed their bags and headed back to Blighty. It seems ironic that we only became friends when they asked for our help to find a local estate agent to sell their dream home.

'No, I haven't forgotten. I thought we could go after their visit.'

'Where to?'

'What about England?' I suggested. 'I'm sure both your granny and your mum would love to see you.'

'You wouldn't have any other reason for choosing England, would you?'

'Like what?' I replied innocently.

'Like a football match for example.'

'I can't believe you would think such a thing.'

Talk about hit the nail on the head. It just so happened that with clever planning I might be able to squeeze Huddersfield Town's final home game of the season into the trip.

'I'm only joking,' she replied. 'England's fine by me.'

'What do you think, Jazz? How does a holiday in England sound?'

On hearing her name, she jumped to her feet and wagged her tail with delight.

'You see, even Jazz wants to go to England,' I added.

'How long were you thinking of going for?'

'What about three weeks?'

'Three weeks!'

'I thought that I might be able to get a new pair of boots while we're there.'

One consequence of being born with deformed feet is that my footwear has to be made to measure. Describing my condition has always proved problematic. The first time I enquired, I was told that I had club feet. As a young boy, the only image I could conjure up was that of Fred Flintstone. I can't remember who it was that told me but they clearly hadn't seen my feet; they're not pretty but they don't look anything like clubs.

I've discovered over the years that society has a fondness for labelling those of us who deviate from the norm. Take me for example. I entered the world as a cripple, a crude and unsympathetic description that had largely disappeared before I could walk. Later in life, I was designated handicapped by the forerunners of political correctness, a description that was relatively short lived. Soon after that I became physically handicapped; heaven forbid that I should be confused with the mental variety. In the 1980s, PC went into overdrive and I transformed from being physically handicapped into being physically disabled. However, this was deemed discriminatory and soon afterwards I was reunited with my mentally handicapped cousins under the all-encompassing banner of The Disabled. Not that I'm complaining; I've been called much worse.

The reality is that being born with a physical disadvantage can often give that person a lifelong advantage, but not when it comes to buying footwear. I'd arrived in Spain with two pairs of boots. After three years' hard labour, one pair was now beyond repair.

It wasn't as though we hadn't tried to have them made in Spain; we had. On hearing about my problem, Meli introduced us to Mano and Anna, owners of a shop selling mobility aids in Monforte, imaginatively called Orthoforte. In turn they introduced me to Isaac, a local manufacturer of orthopaedic footwear based in the city of Ourense. He made plaster casts of both feet, took all the necessary measurements, and made a bespoke pair of boots. Unfortunately, although they'd been made to measure, they felt as if they'd been made to measure someone else. At a cost of 500 euros, I couldn't risk having another pair of ill-fitting boots. This time I had to be sure.

'I bet they'll cost more than 500 euros,' I remarked.

'I'm sure they will but you can't do anything without boots,' replied Melanie.

She was right but that didn't stop me from getting a quote. That afternoon I emailed TayCare Medical, in the UK; within twenty-four hours I'd received a reply.

'I've heard from Philip at TayCare.'

'And?'

'And they'll cost more than double what they did here.'

'What? Over a thousand euros?' said Melanie.

'Seven hundred quid; that's well over a thousand euros.'

'But can they make them while we're in England?'

'Philip said that they still have the lasts; if I give him the go-ahead now, he can have them ready for a fitting by the time we get to England and completed before we leave.'

'You'd better tell him to make a start then.'

The cost of our holiday was starting to mount up and we hadn't left home yet.

'By the way, when do Bob and Janet get here?' I asked.

'It's Bob, Janet and Janet's sister, Sue, and they arrive on Monday.'

'What! This coming Monday?'

'Yep.'

Once again *El Sueño* was opening its doors to visitors from afar, if Nottingham qualifies as afar.

'How long are they staying for?'

'Just four days. They want to make sure their house is OK.'

When Bob and Janet returned to England, they found themselves in a catch-22 situation. Like most building projects, theirs had run a little over budget. This overspend was reflected in the asking price which in turn had limited the number of viewings. Those that had seen the property were presented with an empty and uninviting house, looking out onto a dark and dingy courtyard surrounded by semi-derelict outbuildings. Hardly the most appealing characteristics. Taking everything into account, the prospect of them finding a buyer looked very bleak indeed.

'I really feel for Bob and Janet,' remarked Melanie.

'It's terrible what happened to them. No one deserves to have their dreams shattered.'

'What do you think they should do?'

'I'm not sure. The way the house looks at the moment I can't see anyone wanting to buy it, even if they did reduce the price. If it was up to me, I'd do something with those outbuildings.'

'Like what?'

'Like tear them down,' I replied.

'But that would mean spending even more money.'

'I know, but at least then they'd have other options.'

'What kind of options?' asked Melanie.

'Well, if they didn't want to reduce the price they could

look at buying some cheap furniture and try letting it. At least that way they could start recovering some of their money.'

'Let it to who?'

'Tourists.'

Melanie reflected on my suggestion.

'They could use it themselves as well,' she added.

'That's right, and who knows, they may even decide to return.'

'Why don't you suggest that to them?'

I've learnt through experience that having a good idea is far easier than making it a reality. 'It's not quite as simple as that,' I replied.

'Why?'

'We can't just make suggestions without offering to help.'

Their experiences to date had left them battered and bruised and I had no intention of adding to their misery by making suggestions and then leaving them to it.

'What kind of help?'

'Let's say that they decided to tidy the courtyard and demolish the outbuildings. They couldn't organise that from the UK; we would have to do that from here.'

'We could organise that,' replied Melanie.

'I know we could, but let's say they wanted to buy some furniture and start letting it; we'd have to do that as well or at least offer to.'

'Do what?'

'Do things like cleaning, marketing, taking bookings, and …'

'And what?'

'And everything else that I haven't thought of.'

'We could do that as well,' she replied.

'I know we could, but do we want to?'

Melanie paused for a moment. It had dawned on her that offering advice could have far-reaching implications.

'I see what you mean,' she said.

The room fell silent as we considered the future. Did we want to change our current lifestyle and take another leap into the unknown?

'Let's sleep on it,' I suggested.

The following morning we'd made our decision. If Bob and Janet wanted our advice, we'd give it, and if they asked for our help, we'd provide it.

2

Janet, Sue, and Bob Too

Our visitors arrived at *El Sueño* as planned: Janet, Sue, and Bob too. We hadn't met Janet's sister Sue before but we hit it off straight away. Her happy-go-lucky personality and carefree attitude seemed to rub off on everyone. Within sixty seconds of being introduced, it felt as if we'd known her forever.

Before their arrival, Bob and Janet had arranged to meet up with another expat couple, Rob and Dee, for drinks and dinner. The two couples had undertaken a similar property project, at about the same time. Fortunately for Rob and Dee, their Spanish experience had been very different.

That evening we drove to the agreed rendezvous, a bar in the nearby town of Monforte. By the time Rob and Dee arrived, we'd almost finished our first drink. Right from the start the atmosphere seemed tense. After a brief introduction, Dee made an announcement.

'We won't be joining you for dinner.'

Given her mood, we were quite relieved. Within half an hour, she'd inexplicably changed her mind.

'Where are we going for dinner?' she asked.

Rob looked dumbfounded; we were left speechless.

The night developed into a battle of wills. Dee's desire to wreck the evening against our determination to enjoy it, and poor Rob caught in the crossfire. The fractious dinner date would have long since been forgotten had it not been for one memorable moment.

Having finished our meal, Sue decided to lighten the mood by telling us her favourite joke.

'Right then, who's next?' she said, after the laughter had died down.

One by one, Bob, Janet, Melanie and I told our favourite joke. By the time I'd delivered my punchline, we were laughing uncontrollably, all except for Dee and Rob. She remained po-faced throughout and poor Rob didn't know whether to laugh or cry. It wasn't as if any of the jokes were that funny but once the alcohol-induced giggles had started, there was no stopping us. That's when the evening took an unforgettable turn. Without warning and much to everyone's astonishment, Dee thrust herself into the limelight.

'I know a joke,' she announced.

A stunned silence descended on the table as everyone, including Rob, leant forward and stared at Dee.

'I'm not very good at accents though,' she admitted.

Our surprise changed to curiosity.

Dee and Rob originate from Sunderland, an industrial town in the northeast of England. Consequently, they both speak with a broad Geordie accent.

'I'll let you know when you have to imagine the accent,' she told us.

As Dee began her joke, you could have heard a pin drop.

'Nelson Mandela decided to go to Sunderland for a holiday and rented a house on the outskirts of town.'

Her forced delivery was more chronic than comic.

'One afternoon, while he was watching TV, he heard a knock at the door. When he opened it, there was a little Japanese man standing outside, holding a clipboard.'

She paused and turned to Rob.

'That's right isn't it?'

Rob nodded in agreement. I looked away. If I hadn't, I would have burst into fits of laughter.

'This is where you have to imagine a Japanese accent,' she revealed.

Sue cleared her throat as if struggling to keep calm. I stared across the room searching for anything to distract my overwhelming desire to crack up.

'"You sign! You sign!" yelled the Japanese man.'

She wasn't kidding about the accent. Her man from Japan sounded like an Aussie suffering from sinusitis. Undaunted, she continued.

'Nelson Mandela looked over the man's shoulder and saw a lorry parked in the street full of brand new dashboards.

'"You must have the wrong address," he said. "I didn't order any dashboards," and closed the door.

'The following day, Nelson was watching afternoon TV when he heard another knock at the door ...'

Try as I did, I couldn't imagine Nelson Mandela watching *The Jerry Springer Show*.

'... When he opened it, there was another Japanese man standing outside, holding a clipboard.

'"You sign! You sign!" yelled the Japanese man.'

Dee's ridiculous Japanese accent had developed a South African twang.

'Nelson Mandela looked over the man's shoulder and saw another lorry parked in the street. This one was full of brand new steering wheels.

'"You must have the wrong address," he said, "I didn't order any steering wheels," and closed the door.'

Bob shuffled in his seat and Melanie took a sip of wine.

I focused on a print of Van Gogh's Sunflowers hanging on the wall opposite: quite a hilarious painting when compared to Dee's stand-up skills. She continued.

'The following day, Nelson Mandela was watching TV when he heard a knock at the door …'

Perhaps he was watching the afternoon matinee. *Zulu* is one of my favourites.

'… When he opened it, there was another Japanese man standing outside holding a clipboard.

'"You sign! You sign!" yelled the Japanese man.

'Nelson Mandela looked over the man's shoulder and saw two lorries parked in the street, stacked to the gunwales with car parts. By now, Mr Mandela had just about had enough. He picked up the Japanese man by the scruff of his neck and yelled, "I didn't order any car parts and I don't want any car parts. You've got the wrong address. Who are you looking for?" Feeling quite shaken, the Japanese man stared at his clipboard and said, "You not Nissan Main Dealer?"'

Dee paused and we waited. All of a sudden, it dawned on us that she'd finished the joke and delivered the punchline. At times like this, life would be so much easier with a rewind button. The silence continued. At least I wasn't the only one not to get it. Even Rob looked stunned and he'd heard the joke before. Dee was first to break the silence.

'Nissan Main Dealer,' she repeated.

Nissan Cars is the biggest employer in Sunderland but what did that have to do with the joke?

'Oh yes,' remarked Sue.

Oh yes what?

'Oh, I get it,' added Melanie.

Whatever they'd got, I hadn't. I stared at Melanie searching for an explanation.

'Nissan Main Dealer,' she repeated. 'It sounds a bit like Nelson Mandela.'

Dee's gag brought the curtain down on a testing

evening. Unsurprisingly, from that day to this, our paths have not crossed but the legacy of Nissan Main Dealer will forever hold a special place in our hearts.

It took quite some time to erase the image of Nelson Mandela lapping up *The Jerry Springer Show* but the following morning over breakfast, our attention turned to more pressing matters. Melanie's homemade lemon curd was quickly becoming every visitor's favourite and while Bob and Janet munched on their toast, Melanie broached the subject.

'Have you had many viewings at the house?' she asked.

'There were a few at first but we think they were time wasters curious to see what we'd done with the place, but nothing since then,' replied Bob.

After breakfast, we headed off to check on the house. Running down the side of their property was an unmade track. Bob drove down and we followed. The grassy lane was still damp from the morning dew. Tall metal gates guarded the entrance to a small courtyard. Patches of rust covered the faded paintwork like moss clinging to a weathered boulder. Bob turned the key in the lock and bullied them open. Janet looked on, tears welling in her eyes. Sue wrapped a consoling arm around her elder sibling. The torment of their short time in Galicia was still raw in Janet's emotions. Even entering the courtyard was too painful.

'I'll check the house, love,' said Bob. 'You stay here.'

'Would you like a hand?' I asked.

Bob nodded his approval and I followed him through the gates. Ruinous outbuildings surrounding the courtyard cast menacing shadows. Tall weeds had sprung up through cracks in the concrete surface. A flight of weathered stone steps climbed out of this depressing space to the front door. Bob unlocked the door and we stepped inside. From here on in, everything was brand new.

On the left was a light and airy *galleria*: a long sitting

room typical of Galician country homes. A door on the right led into a beautifully finished kitchen/diner, fitted with hardwood cabinets and all mod cons. Leading off the central hallway was the lounge, complete with a romantic wood burner. The master, en suite bedroom was opposite and at the end of the hallway was the second bedroom and a separate family bathroom.

'Everything seems OK in here,' said Bob, looking around the kitchen.

'And here,' I said, standing in the *galleria*.

Room by room we wandered through the empty house looking for any signs of trouble. Other than a few dead insects, the place was empty.

'I'd better check the boiler room and the *bodegas* while we're here,' said Bob, pulling the front door closed.

The girls had wandered off up the lane. The sight was too upsetting for Janet to face. All their hopes and dreams of a new life abroad had been shattered. In that moment my mind was made up. If we could help them out, we would.

Over the next few days the mood lightened as we visited some favourite places, eating and drinking as if we were on holiday. On their final evening at *El Sueño*, the opportunity cropped up to offer our help.

'What do you think we should do with the house, Craig?' asked Bob.

I ran through the ideas that Melanie and I had discussed.

'Whatever you decide, we're happy to help in any way we can and if you decide to let it out, we'd be happy to manage it for you.'

Our offer seemed to lift a weight from their shoulders. Somewhere in the darkness there was light at the end of the tunnel. They could head back to England, consider the options and decide at their leisure how best to proceed. Their stay had been brief but productive.

Shortly after they left, Melanie received a formally addressed letter from the Xunta.

'I've got the date,' she said, staring at the letter.

'What date?'

'The date for my op.'

'When is it?'

'The 19th of May.'

About a year ago, Melanie's right knee started giving her some gyp.

'It really hurts when I kneel down,' she'd complain.

To which I would reply, 'Well don't kneel down then.' Having used this same line for nearly a year, the joke was wearing a bit thin.

In the main, Melanie had suffered in silence and neither of us had paid it much attention. However, when she woke one Saturday morning with a knee the size of a watermelon, all that changed.

'That needs looking at,' I said.

'I'll go to the doctors on Monday.'

'We'll go to Accident and Emergency right now,' I replied.

They say it's a sign of growing old when policemen and doctors don't look old enough to shave. The young doctor who attended Melanie didn't look old enough to be a student, never mind a qualified clinician.

'Where did you bang it?' asked the doctor.

'I haven't banged it,' replied Melanie.

'Perhaps not today, maybe a few days ago.'

Melanie paused for thought.

'No, I can't remember banging it,' she confirmed.

'Are you sure?'

I tried to recall what we'd done over the last few days but nothing leapt out.

'Yes, I'm sure,' she replied.

Without a probable cause, the investigation moved swiftly on to a physical examination. With an emphasis on the term physical.

'Lay on the bed please,' instructed the doctor.

Melanie hopped onto the bed looking decidedly apprehensive. Whether the doctor was gentle or otherwise, Melanie flinched with pain as she prodded and poked the swollen mass. I watched from afar, feeling as helpless as an anaesthetised patient on an operating table.

'You have fluid on the joint,' she announced. 'I will have to drain it.'

Ouch! I didn't like the sound of that and it wasn't even my knee.

'Wait here a moment. I'll be back in a minute,' she added, before dashing through a gap in the treatment room curtain and marching off down the corridor.

'What did she mean by drain it?' asked Melanie.

I had no idea. More to the point, why did she ask Melanie to wait a moment? Given her present condition, she was hardly likely to do a runner.

'I don't know but she appears to know what she's doing,' I replied.

My words of comfort seemed painfully inadequate.

A few minutes later she returned carrying a kidney-shaped stainless steel bowl covered with a small white towel. She placed the bowl on the bed before whipping off the towel like Waldo the magician. From my vantage point, the contents were hidden. I looked at Melanie for a clue. Her eyes widened and all the colour drained from her face. Whatever the doctor had meant by 'drain it' was hiding in that bowl.

'Don't worry,' she said, noticing the terror on Melanie's face.

Piece by piece she revealed the bowl's contents. She lifted out a pair of surgical gloves and pulled them on with a customary snap. Nothing to fear there, which couldn't be said about her next reveal: the biggest syringe I had ever seen. I glanced at Melanie who looked as white as a sheet. Her final exposé was a fearsome needle the thickness of a pencil lead. Carefully, she attached it to the syringe.

'You might feel a little discomfort,' she said, preparing to thrust this instrument of torture into Melanie's kneecap.

There's nothing like cutting to the chase and getting straight to the point.

Melanie looked away and closed her eyes, making doubly sure that she didn't see a thing. Hesitantly, the doctor thrust the needle into Melanie's kneecap. She squealed in agony. I took that to mean she'd missed the mark. The doctor confirmed my assumption by withdrawing the needle and striking from a different angle. This also failed, as did the third attempt and the fourth. Melanie was in excruciating pain and I was powerless to help. After four attempts she'd managed to remove less than a thimbleful of fluid.

'Just one moment,' she said, before whipping back the curtain and rushing down the corridor.

'Are you alright?' I asked.

'It chuffing kills,' she replied, wiping away a tear. 'What about you, are you alright?'

Watching Melanie being tortured had sent me weak at the knees and left me feeling a little queasy. All of a sudden I felt dizzy and unsteady on my feet.

'I think I'm going to faint.'

'Sit down before you fall down and put your head between your knees.'

I collapsed to the floor and bent my head as low as I could. On leaving the treatment room, the doctor had inadvertently left the curtain slightly open. A couple of staff members, standing nearby, noticed my plight and began to giggle. Melanie was in agony and I was the one about to faint. A few minutes later the junior doctor returned, accompanied by a more senior member of staff.

'Are you all right?' he asked me.

'He's feeling a bit dizzy,' said Melanie.

'Perhaps it would be better if you waited outside.'

I didn't need telling twice.

Moments after I'd taken my seat in the waiting room,

Melanie appeared at the door. The second doctor had quickly removed a bowlful of fluid and a nurse had bandaged up the evidence.

Back home, we racked our brains searching for a cause to the swelling but nothing sprang to mind. Melanie was sure that the pain had started months earlier, coinciding with a return from a trip to England. Since then she couldn't remember doing anything to aggravate it. Thankfully, syphoning the fluid eliminated the swelling. Unfortunately, it hadn't cured the cause. Melanie's knee was still troubling her.

Several weeks later, she stumbled across a probable cause while reading a women's magazine. The relevant article warned readers of the medical dangers of alcohol-fuelled trampolining. That's when the penny dropped and the likely culprit was exposed.

Our last trip to England included a few nights in London. We stayed with my sister Julie, her husband Jem and their two sons, Sam and Jake. They live in a detached property with a good-sized garden. A few years ago, their eldest lad, Sam, was given a trampoline for his birthday. While we were there, Melanie was persuaded to give it a go. The rest, as they say, is history, and in this case, a somewhat painful history.

Thankfully, clinicians in the Spanish health service are a little more tenacious than their English counterparts. Following her visit to A&E, Melanie visited our GP who immediately referred her to a consultant orthopaedist. Dr Xoán Miguéns Vázquez accepted the challenge and set about diagnosing the problem. When an MRI scan failed to detect the cause, he suggested exploratory keyhole surgery.

That was several weeks ago. Luckily for us, the date set aside to perform this hi-tech surgical procedure wouldn't interfere with our latest holiday plans.

'It couldn't have worked out better,' I commented.

Tomorrow, I had it all to do again; a good night's sleep was essential.

'OK.'

The hotel's main reception rooms were combined in one vast space, divided into lounge, bar area, and dining room by screens and strategically positioned furniture. The predominant colour was white and the cathedral-style roof space gave it the appearance of an African colonial-style house. To our surprise, the dining room was surprisingly busy.

'*Bonsoir* (Good evening).'

We'd been approached by a tall, athletic-looking man in his late thirties or early forties. He was enviously handsome with a jet black complexion, dazzling smile, and designer dreadlocks. Every inch of him oozed cool sophistication. If he wasn't a male model, he should have been.

'*Bonsoir. Una mesa para deux s'il vous plaît,*' I replied in my best Franco-Iberian English.

'It's *une table pour deux,*' whispered Melanie, elbowing me in the ribs.

It had taken me the best part of three years to grasp the basics of Spanish; adding French to my linguistic repertoire was a step too far. The last time I'd spoken French I was twelve years old; before I reached my thirteenth birthday the teacher had correctly steered me into woodwork classes. The only French phrase I can remember was spoken by a chimpanzee in a PG Tips advert. In the ad, the chimp takes a tumble while competing in the chimp equivalent of the Tour de France. After falling off his bike he seeks comfort in the arms of an equally hairy maiden and asks '*Avez-vous un* cuppa?' Of all the phrases I could have remembered, I chose the most useless.

Our host replied in the poetically nasal tone that only the French can deliver, captivating to listen to but completely unintelligible. I can't imagine what Melanie and

I must have looked like, staring into his eyes, and listening to his hypnotic mumblings.

After a brief pause he added, *'Anglais?'*

'Si, oui, yes.' By now I was that confused I didn't know what language I should be speaking.

Talk about feeling like a plonker.

'Parlez-vous français?' he asked, looking directly at Melanie.

My Franco-Iberian English had clearly made an impression: the wrong impression.

'Un petit peu,' replied Melanie.

Hark at her, I thought to myself. *'Un petit peu'* indeed.

In a calm and simplified manner, our host conveyed his message to Melanie. I watched and listened, waiting for a break in the narrative.

'What did he say?' I asked.

'They've finished serving and the chef has gone home.'

I checked my watch.

'But it's only eight o'clock.'

'They must eat earlier in France,' she replied.

An elderly couple caught my eye as they left their table and wandered off in the direction of the bedrooms. My forlorn gaze initiated a response from our handsome host.

'What did he say?' I asked.

'He said that if we're happy to eat what's in the kitchen, he'll see what he can rustle up.'

I suspected that Melanie was ad libbing. Nevertheless, I was over the moon. The kindness and generosity of others always amazes me. Our hospitable host had no idea that we'd been on the road all day and were hungry enough to faint. He could just as easily have turned us away, but no.

'Muchas gracias,' I replied.

Melanie quickly corrected me.

Dinner turned out to be one of the best I'd ever had in France. Sandwiched between the main course and dessert was the most marvellous fruit sorbet followed by a fabulous cheese board and our host's choice of wine was a rather nice Bordeaux. By the time we'd finished, there wasn't another guest in sight. We wandered into the bar area where our host was enjoying a fruit juice.

'*Voudriez-vous un verre?*'

'What did he say?' I asked.

'He asked what we want to drink.'

We ordered gin and tonic and relaxed on the squidgy sofa.

Conversation proved challenging but over the next hour or so we discovered that our host was called Philippe Chanlot. He'd bought the hotel after retiring from professional football. Of all the hotels in all the places in all the world, we'd chosen this one, owned by a retired professional footballer. I couldn't believe it. It's at times like these that I really wish I'd paid more attention at school, particularly during French lessons.

'Who did you play for?' I resisted the temptation to ask my English spoken question with a French accent.

'*Je ne comprends pas* (I don't understand).'

If at first …

'*¿Hablas español* (Do you speak Spanish)?' I asked.

'*Un poco* (A little),' he replied.

I repeated the question in Spanish.

'*Je jouais pour de nombreux clubs différents,*' he replied.

'He can't have been very good,' I whispered to Melanie. 'I've never heard of *nombreux*.'

'Tsk!'

'What?'

'He said that he played for a lot of different clubs.'

'Oh.' I turned towards our host, feeling slightly embarrassed: '*Muchos clubes diferente.*'

'*Oui. Vous savez Marseille* (Yes. You know Marseille)?'

'Marseille, *si*, I mean *oui*.'

The harder I tried to remember which language I was supposed to be speaking, the more mistakes I made.

'*Je jouais à* Marseille *quand* Voodel *était là* (I was playing at Marseille when Voodel was there),' he said, proudly.

'Voodel?' I replied questioningly.

'Voodel *de Angleterre*.'

When it comes to the subject of football, I like to think I have a reasonable knowledge but I'd never heard of Voodel.

'Voodel *de Angleterre*?' I asked.

'Voodel, Chris Voodel.'

All of a sudden the penny dropped. Philippe's thick French accent had given one of England's finest wingers a completely new surname.

'Waddle,' I said triumphantly, 'Chris Waddle.'

'*Tout à fait* (Absolutely).'

It turned out that Philippe was quite a journeyman. In a career spanning twenty years he'd played for fourteen different clubs, scoring almost 100 goals in less than 500 appearances. Not bad for a big powerful centre forward. After finishing our gin and tonics, we thanked Philippe for his hospitality and wandered off to bed. Meeting him had been the icing on the cake of a very enjoyable stopover.

3

Not-So-Funny Bone

What could be worse than a six o'clock alarm call, the day after an eleven-hour road trip? I know, a five o'clock alarm call.

By 8:30 am the darkness had lifted and we were counting down the kilometres to Paris. Compared to northern Spain, the scenery through France is tedious to say the least: kilometre after kilometre of flat rural countryside. If it wasn't for the nation's love of modern design, this stretch of the journey would be intolerably dull. Strange-looking road bridges, quirkily designed industrial units, and electricity pylons that look as if they've been plucked from the set of a Hollywood sci-fi movie kept my attention.

With the exception of an unplanned detour around the streets of Versailles, everything went to plan. We arrived at the port of Calais in plenty of time to have Jazz's passport and paperwork approved before rolling on to the ferry. Ninety minutes later, we rolled off in Dover, England.

Back in Blighty, the traffic was hellishly busy. More vehicles passed us in fifteen minutes than we'd seen in the previous two days. Why people are in such a rush to get to the next set of traffic lights before anyone else is a mystery to me.

Our holiday began in London, at my sister's. Four days later, we drove north to Wolverhampton in the Midlands, to stay with friends Carol and Gerry.

We first met Carol and Gerry three years ago in Galicia. Melanie and I were enjoying a quiet drink at our favourite riverside bar when Carol, Gerry, and Carol's brother, Malcolm, blundered in. Before we knew it, we were chatting to each other.

'I've got a house near Escairon,' Gerry had said, in his broad Brummie accent. 'We've been coming here for the last seventeen years.'

'Is that how long you've owned the house?' I'd asked.

'Yes, I'd planned to live here permanently but things didn't work out.'

Gerry had moved to the area intent on setting up a business. As everyone knows, business start-ups have their ups and downs; Gerry's idea was reliant on it. He'd intended to tour the local fiestas with a bouncy castle but quickly discovered that others had beaten him to it. Having jumped in with both feet, within six months he'd rebounded back to Wolverhampton.

Carol's brother Malcolm was born with Down's syndrome. Since the death of their parents, she'd become his guardian. That first encounter ended with me inviting them round for a barbecue. They accepted and we've been friends ever since.

After spending the night with them, we continued north, to the village of Warton in the Lake District. There we met Andy and Helen, friends that we hadn't seen since moving to Spain. We stayed at the George Washington Inn, a traditional English pub offering bed and breakfast. Given the hospitality of Monsieur Chanlot, the landlord had a lot to live up to. We weren't disappointed and the full English breakfast was to die for.

By the time we left Warton, our first week in England was drawing to a close. Next stop, Huddersfield, a place we used to call home. We arrived at my dad's, three days before Town's final home game of the season. It turned out to be a great afternoon of football. A partisan crowd watched The Terriers (Huddersfield Town) thrash a lacklustre Swindon Town 4–0.

The holiday passed quickly; a busy schedule saw to that. TayCare Medical fulfilled their obligation and made me a shiny new pair of orthopaedic boots, on time and only slightly over budget. But two days before we were due to leave, I received a worrying phone call.

Ring ring … Ring ring!

'Can you get that,' shouted Dad from upstairs.

'Hello,' I said, holding the phone to my ear.

'Craig.'

'Is that you, Melanie?'

Earlier in the day, she'd met her mum in town to do some last-minute shopping. I sensed from her tone that something was wrong.

'What's matter?'

'I've fallen and I think I've broken my arm,' she replied.

I could tell from her trembling voice that she wasn't joking.

'Where are you?'

'I'm in town but I don't know where Mum is.'

Her tearful tone had developed into uncontrollable sobbing.

'Don't worry,' I said. 'Tell me where you are and I'll come and pick you up.'

Through a tearful exchange, Melanie explained exactly where she was.

'Just wait there; I'm on my way.'

Dad caught the last part of our conversation.

'What's happened?'

Quickly I explained, before rushing into town.

By the time I arrived, shock and distress had turned to disbelief and exasperation.

'I can't believe I've done it,' she said. 'One minute I'm walking along the pavement and the next I'm in a heap on the floor and my arm is absolutely killing me.'

'Does it still hurt?'

'I'm in agony,' she replied.

'We'd better go to the hospital and get you checked out.'

An X-ray revealed a hairline fracture of the lateral epicondyle, but there's nothing amusing about breaking your funny bone, and the wrist to shoulder plaster cast was no laughing matter either.

'We've made an appointment for you to see the consultant tomorrow,' said the nurse before we left.

The following day, the consultant had the cast removed and replaced by a rather nifty bright blue sling.

'Try that overnight and come back tomorrow,' said the consultant. 'My receptionist will make you an appointment.'

'I can't,' replied Melanie.

The consultant looked at her questioningly.

'We're heading to Spain in the morning,' she added.

'Of dear, I hope it doesn't spoil your holiday.'

'We're not going on holiday; we live there.'

Having cleared up the misunderstanding, he wrote a letter to our GP and gave us the X-rays.

'When you get home, take these to your GP,' he instructed.

Outside in the car park, I took a peek at the letter.

'I'm glad he gave us the snaps,' I said.

'What snaps?'

'The X-rays.'

'Why?'

'The writing on this letter looks like a spider with eight broken legs has limped across the page.'

There was more chance of divine healing than a Spanish GP reading this scribble.

That evening Melanie said a tearful goodbye to her granny, knowing that this might be her final farewell: aged ninety-one and in poor health, the sands of time were slipping through life's hourglass.

A relaxing holiday and a long drive home gave us the opportunity to consider the future. We couldn't have wished for a better outcome to our first renovation project and decided that reinvesting the money in another was the way forward. As soon as we got home, we would begin our search for a new property.

'You might have to start looking on your own,' said Melanie.

'Why?'

'You haven't forgotten about my knee op, have you?'

Given everything we'd gone through over the last three weeks, it had slipped my mind.

'When do you go into hospital?' I asked.

'Next Thursday.'

'Two days after your birthday,' I said in surprise.

'At least you've remembered that date.'

For Melanie, the journey home had been long and uncomfortable. As we drove through the village, *El Sueño* came into view. For the first time ever, I could appreciate the saying, "I had a lovely holiday, but I'm glad to be home."

I am, and will always be, an Englishman. England is the country of my birth and home to many friends and family but from the moment the ferry docked in Dover, I felt at odds with the environment. Everybody was in a rush. Traffic raced from one junction to the next. Congestion fuelled rage and rage made people selfish and insular. Everyone we met was struggling to either catch up, or keep up. For many, the tide of expectation has become a tsunami of debt. Over the last three years, the treadmill of

English life seemed to have stepped up a gear.

Here in Galicia, I feel relaxed and content. Even in towns and cities the pace of life is much slower. People have time for others; they're polite and patient. Life is a gift to be shared rather than a competition to be won and happiness is an emotion to experience, not something to buy.

Melanie unlocked the gates and I pulled the car onto the drive. For the first time in hours, Jazz sat up and looked out of the window.

'We're home,' I said, but she knew that.

Melanie opened the tailgate and Jazz jumped excitedly onto the drive. She darted this way then that, checking her domain for uninvited guests.

'Crikey, look at the lawns,' I said, as I stepped from the car.

Like a classroom of unsupervised children, the garden had descended into horticultural anarchy. In a little over three weeks, the parallel lines of my neatly manicured lawns had vanished. These had been replaced with island clumps of deep green weeds floating in a sea of tall, straw-like grasses.

'And look at the vines,' I added.

All the buds had burst into life and early signs of growth had become metre-long, leafy canes adorned with miniature bunches of grapes that had started to flower.

As I marvelled at the grapevines, Melanie wandered around the side of the house to take a look at the back garden.

'Come and have a look at this,' she called excitedly.

Jazz lifted her head and dashed around the side of the house. I followed at a more sedate pace.

'Look,' she said, as I rounded the corner.

Two years ago we'd planted a Rhododendron bush in a raised flowerbed close to the house. When we saw it in the garden centre, it had been covered in glorious pink flowers. By the time it had been delivered and planted, the colourful petals had withered and died. When it failed to flower the following year, we'd considered digging it up and exiling it to a far-flung corner. In the time we'd been away, it had burst into flower and looked absolutely stunning.

'If you think that's good, come and look at this,' I said.

We were acting like excited kids in a sweet shop. Hardly surprising given that neither of us have green fingers.

'What is it?' she asked.

'Look at that,' I said proudly, pointing at my precious *Chamaerops excleso* (palm tree).

In the weeks leading up to our trip I'd noticed five yellowy green pods developing at the top of the trunk, just below the waxy, fan-like fronds. They'd reminded me of clasped hands at prayer.

'We've got coconuts,' I'd announced one morning.

'Speak for yourself,' Melanie had quipped.

Despite her razor-sharp wit, Melanie was curious enough to come running.

'I don't think they're coconuts,' she'd said, after staring at them for a while.

'Why not?'

'I don't think they grow on this kind of palm tree.'

I'd never seen coconuts growing in the wild but I suspected that she was right.

'If they're not coconuts, what are they then?' I'd asked.

'I don't know.'

Melanie's observation proved correct, which was a real shame. The thought of sipping piña coladas using milk from our own coconuts was very appealing. Instead we'd been treated to a magnificent floral display. The swollen pods had burst open revealing hundreds of bright yellow flowers clustered around a coral-like stem. There were five stems in all, circling the trunk like a Hawaiian floral garland.

Given the three-week time frame, Mother Nature's

achievements were staggering. Having inspected the garden, my thoughts turned to more practical matters.

'I think it's about time you went for a walk,' I said to Jazz.

On all but the wettest days, the *w* word is greeted with uncontrollable excitement. Having spent ten hours in the car, today's walk was long overdue. As if to prove the point, Jazz wagged her tail so furiously I'm surprised it didn't fall off.

'Come on then.'

'Wait for me,' called Melanie.

Jazz trotted in front as we strolled up the lane. Every so often she stopped, when the scent of something interesting caught her attention. At this time of year, the drainage ditches running down both sides of the lane are covered with long grasses a metre high. Beneath this sea of straw grow a profusion of wildflowers. Every conceivable form and all the colours of an artist's palette are represented in their miniature corollas.

Whether outbound or returning home, Jazz insists on leading the pack but never strays too far and always checks that we're keeping up.

'I think a Teatime Taster is in order. What do you think?' asked Melanie as I closed the gate.

'I think we deserve one.'

I'd missed our much-loved ritual while we'd been away. Sitting in Dad's back garden, looking out on a landscape of crumbling textile mills and rows of terraced houses, supping from a can of lukewarm beer, didn't have the same appeal as a glass of chilled white and a Spanish sunset.

As the sun began its final descent, the whisper of musical notes floated up from the village.

'That'll be Anna, Meli's granddaughter, practising on her recorder,' said Melanie.

After listening to the constant drone of traffic on Britain's overcrowded island, Anna's interrupted tune and repetitive notes were a great way to end the day and an ideal welcome home.

I'd like to say that after a good night's sleep I was raring to go, but I wasn't. Two ten-hour days behind the wheel is enough to make anyone's back ache.

'How are you feeling?' asked Melanie as we sipped our morning coffee.

'Stiff.'

'Really,' she replied, with raised eyebrows and a cheeky grin.

'I'm referring to my back.'

'Oh dear.'

Our first job was a visit to the doctor, to get Melanie sorted out. After breakfast we drove up to the health centre in the village of Sober. The receptionist looked up from her computer and smiled questioningly. Melanie explained the reason for our visit.

'Take a seat,' she said, gesturing towards the waiting area.

It wasn't long before our GP, Dr Arean, stepped out of his consulting room, pointed at Melanie and then turned around. We jumped to our feet and marched into the room. He stared at Melanie, prompting her to speak. She explained what had happened and handed him the letter and the X-rays. He opened the letter, studied it carefully and then looked up.

'Do you know what it says?' he asked.

'No,' replied Melanie.

'Is it written in English?'

'Yes, but …' She paused for a moment thinking how best to phrase her answer.

'*Pero él es un medico* (But he's a doctor),' he said, finishing the sentence.

'*Si.*'

I knew the letter would be neither use nor ornament. Fortunately, we had the snaps. He pulled the X-rays out of the stiff cardboard folder and held them up to the light.

'Your elbow is cracked,' he said.

Melanie smiled; there was no answer to that.

'What's that?' he asked, pointing at the sling.

I wasn't surprised that he couldn't decipher the letter; neither could I, but the sling?

'The hospital in England gave it to me,' said Melanie.

'Well only wear it if you are out and about. You need to keep moving your arm as much as possible,' he instructed.

Melanie nodded her agreement

'Hand this to the receptionist; she will make you an appointment to see the trauma specialist,' he added, sliding a handwritten note across the desk.

Melanie handed it to the receptionist who tapped away on her computer.

'You already have an appointment,' she said, 'on the 18th.'

'Yes,' replied Melanie, 'that's for my knee.'

'Your knee?'

'Yes, my knee.'

The receptionist looked confused.

'Not your elbow?' she asked, pointing at the appropriate body part.

'No, not my elbow, my knee.'

She looked at Melanie as if to say: what on earth have you been doing to yourself, girl? Under the circumstances, that was preferable to her staring at me and asking what I'd been doing to her.

Over the next few days, I restored the lawns to their parallel uniformity and tidied the rest of the garden. As for the grapevines, they'd reached the stage when a dusting of sulphur powder was required. I'd yet to be convinced of the merits of sulphur dusting but far be it from me to question established wisdom. The locals seem convinced that it keeps young shoots warm during cold nights but science would have me believe that it's nothing more than an ancient pesticide, and not a very effective one at that.

After last year's eye-stinging efforts using Meli's homemade sulphur shaker, I decided to invest in a proper applicator. The ingenious design combines a cylindrical container, about the size of a pint glass, with a set of hearthside bellows. It looks like the kind of apparatus Heath Robinson might invent. Pumping the bellows ejects a fine mist of sulphur powder from a fanned pipe: simple yet effective.

'I'm going to sulphur the vines this morning,' I said at breakfast.

'Well do be careful.'

The new applicator worked a treat and within the hour I'd created a modern artwork of sugar-coated vines.

'We must call and see Meli,' I said, as I entered the kitchen.

Dusting the vines had reminded me that we hadn't called to see her since we'd returned.

'We must,' replied Melanie.

After lunch we wandered down the lane to see if she was home. I opened the gate and Jazz raced down the driveway, up the front steps, through Meli's open door and straight into the house. We knew she wouldn't mind but that wasn't the point. As we strolled down the driveway, Meli appeared at the door with Jazz at her side. That's when we noticed Jesus, sitting in a garden chair on the terrace, enjoying the afternoon sun. He'd always had a slim frame, but slumped in the chair he looked as if life itself was draining from him. Meli greeted us warmly but her eyes were filled with sorrow. Today was not the time to enquire about Jesus' health. We sat on the terrace and told her about our trip to England. She asked about our family, all of whom she'd met at one time or another.

'Dad and Claire are coming out to stay with us July,' I remarked.

'And what about your vines, have you sulphured them yet?' she asked.

'Yes,' I replied, 'but I'm still not sure what some of the varieties are.'

'I'll call up and take a look,' said Jesus.

However unlikely this seemed, at least his response was positive. Our walk home passed in silence; hope is seldom enough.

4

Happy Birthday

'Happy birthday.'

With Melanie suffering from a broken elbow *and* a dodgy knee, my heartfelt sentiment sounded rather hollow but as the saying goes, "Things can only get better". Mind you, taking into account that she would soon be going under the surgeon's knife, the maxim "Things often get worse before they get better" seemed more appropriate. To lighten the mood, I decided to treat the birthday girl to lunch at the coast; nothing lifts the spirit like sea air and an ocean view.

The seaside town of Baiona, on the west coast of Galicia, is a modern resort with a long history. The earliest settlement dates back to 140 BC. For centuries the town has been dominated by the Castelo de Monterreal, a medieval fortress occupying a prominent position, overlooking the entrance to the bay.

At first sight, Baiona looks like many contemporary Spanish resorts. A sweeping promenade runs along the front. Opposite this is an endless line of souvenir shops, fish restaurants, and fast food eateries, but hidden behind this modern façade is a historic old town with narrow, cobbled lanes, medieval buildings, small squares, and perhaps more importantly, one of our favourite eateries. It's the Spanish equivalent of an English greasy spoon but without the grease. Our favourite is their made-to-order Spanish tortilla.

After lunch we strolled along the beach. Jazz could hardly contain her excitement as she bounded along the sand. Playfully, she ran in and out of the sea, barking at the breaking waves. That alone made the trip worthwhile.

Two days later, Melanie's wait was over. I parked in the hospital car park and we strolled towards reception.

'Are you sure you've got everything?' I asked.

'Toilet bag, nightie, and lots of books. What more could I need?'

In spite of her chirpy remark, I could sense her apprehension. Being unwell in your own language is bad enough; being unwell in someone else's is a different matter altogether.

'Take a seat in the waiting room,' instructed the nurse at the reception desk.

Given the early hour, we were surprised by the number of people waiting. In Spain, trips to the hospital tend to be a family affair, especially when it involves an overnight stay. We found a seat and waited. Every so often, a door in one corner of the room opened. A nurse would enter and call out a name. Before long it was our turn.

'Melanie Jine Bricks!'

We jumped to our feet, rushed to the door and followed the nurse along a corridor. She stopped at the lift and pressed the call button. The three of us waited in silence. A bell *pinged* and the lift doors slid open. We stepped inside. When they opened again, we found ourselves on a large open landing.

'Come this way,' she said, leading the way.

We walked across the landing, through a set of double doors and into the ward. I was surprised to see that all the rooms were private. The nurse led us into a twin bedded room with an en suite bathroom. It looked more like a hotel suite than any hospital I'd stayed in.

'This is your bed,' she said, pointing at the one nearest the window. 'Someone will be with you shortly.'

No sooner had she left than the lady occupying the other bed said hello.

'Hola,' we replied.

'This looks alright,' I whispered.

'It's not what I expected,' said Melanie, quietly.

'Nor me.'

In the UK, we are used to NHS wards being very public spaces, rows of beds whose only privacy is a flimsy curtain. Private rooms are usually reserved for the very sick or those with private insurance. Things had got off to a good start.

Melanie put her overnight bag on the floor and sat on the bed. I sat on a chair in the corner feeling like an able-bodied athlete at the Paralympics.

'You don't have to wait,' said Melanie, but her eyes told a different story.

'Don't be silly,' I replied. 'I don't mind waiting.'

After a quarter of an hour, another nurse entered.

'You need to put that nightie on and get into bed,' she instructed, pointing at a sky blue nightdress at the foot of the bed.

The gown looked to have been starched to within an inch of its life and folded into submission. Melanie picked it up and prised it open. I could tell by the way she was holding it that she wasn't impressed.

'I'll just be a minute,' she said, before disappearing into the bathroom.

When she returned, the cut of her gown aptly demonstrated the disadvantages of being a tall woman in

Spain. Her granny-style nightie looked more like a Mary Quant mini.

'Very stylish,' I commented.

'Look at the state of it.'

With her back to the wall, she shuffled towards the bed.

'What's the matter?' I whispered.

'Can you fasten it up for me?'

Melanie turned, revealing a gaping split in the back of the nightie, from neck to knee. Four sets of cotton cords were designed to tie the two sides together. A difficult task at the best of times but quite impossible with a broken elbow.

'Do I have to?' I joked.

'Not unless you want all and sundry to see my arse.'

'Oh, go on then, cheeky.'

No sooner had I covered Melanie's modesty than the nurse returned. Melanie hopped into bed.

'I need to take your blood pressure,' she said.

Gingerly, Melanie offered her arm. Unaware of her condition, the nurse grabbed it and pulled it sharply towards her.

'Arrh!' cried Melanie.

'What's matter?' asked the nurse

'I've broken my elbow.'

'Your elbow?' replied the nurse quizzically. 'I thought you were having surgery on your knee.'

'I am,' replied Melanie anxiously.

The nurse looked confused.

'Two weeks ago I fell and fractured my elbow,' she explained.

The nurse continued with her test, pumping up the pressure before releasing it. Her silence did nothing to reassure me that she'd understood; even Melanie looked a little apprehensive. She recorded her findings and left.

'Make sure they don't cut your arm off,' I quipped.

'Don't even joke about that,' replied Melanie.

I quickly realised that my attempt to lighten the mood was somewhat misplaced.

'Don't worry,' I said reassuringly, 'I'm sure they know what they're doing.'

Melanie looked unconvinced. Half an hour later, a medic entered the room.

'I'm the anaesthetist,' he said.

It was his responsibility to check that Melanie was who she said she was and explain what would happen tomorrow.

'Do you have some crutches?' he asked.

'No.'

'You won't be able to put any pressure on your knee for two weeks,' he warned.

Melanie glanced across at me. I knew exactly where I could buy a pair.

'Do you have any questions?' he asked.

Melanie had one question that she was very keen to ask.

'It is my knee that you're operating on, isn't it?'

I could see from his expression that Melanie's question created a split second of doubt. That moment of terror just before you remember where you left the house keys. Quickly, he glanced at his clipboard and his panic turned to relief.

'Yes,' he replied, 'your right knee.'

Melanie smiled, reassured that her arm was safe.

'I told you,' I said, after he'd left. 'They know exactly what they're doing.'

'What about crutches?' asked Melanie.

'I'll get some from Orthoforte,' I replied.

I hung around for another half an hour before Melanie insisted I go.

'You get off and see if you can buy some crutches,' she said.

'OK, I'll pop back this evening to see how things are going.'

Later that evening I returned. Melanie had spent the whole day sitting in a chair reading her book. She'd eaten lunch and just finished dinner, both of which had been chosen by the bed's previous occupant.

'I managed to get some crutches; they weren't that expensive.'

'That's good. What colour are they?'

'They're a mobility aid, not a fashion accessory,' I replied.

We chatted for a while but as neither of us had done anything, the conversation soon dried up. Her surgery was scheduled for the following morning, so this would be the last time we'd see each other until after her op. We both knew that the procedure was as risk free as any operation can be but that didn't make it any easier to say goodbye.

'Good luck and I'll see you at lunchtime tomorrow,' I said.

Given the circumstances, "Break a leg" seemed inappropriate.

'Love you.'

'Love you too, bye.'

We kissed and I left.

That night I slept surprisingly well. When I woke in the morning, Melanie's half of the bed was untouched. All that room and I hadn't strayed an inch. I arrived at the hospital just before one. As I climbed the stairs to the second floor I felt quite anxious. My pace quickened as I marched across the landing and through the double doors into the ward. I smiled politely as I passed the nurses' workstation and on into Melanie's room. My concern was ill-founded. Melanie was lying in bed with her eyes closed. No sooner had I taken a seat than she woke. It was almost as if she knew I'd arrived.

'How are you feeling?' I asked.

'Thirsty,' she replied.

'And your knee?'

'I can't feel a thing.'

Quickly, I glanced at the bedcovers.

'What?' she asked.

'Just checking that it's still there,' I replied.

The faintest hint of a smile spread across her face but Melanie was in no state to laugh at my bad jokes. I hung around for an hour or so watching her slip in and out of sleep, and then left.

'I'll see you this evening,' I said, before kissing her goodbye.

When I returned, Melanie was wide awake and tucking in to her evening meal: a plastic tray, neatly segmented with mouse-sized portions of plastic-looking food.

'How is it?' I asked.

'I've eaten worse,' she remarked.

'Do you know when you're coming home?'

'The nurse said that the doctor will assess me in the morning and if he's happy I should be able to leave by tomorrow lunchtime.'

That was great news.

The following day, Melanie was washed, dressed, and dying to get out of there by the time I arrived.

'How are you feeling?' I asked.

'Apart from being fed up, I'm fine.'

Two nights in hospital had been quite enough. The lady in the next bed had insisted on watching TV throughout the night. Consequently, Melanie hadn't slept a wink.

'Just get me out of here,' she pleaded.

'You can go then?'

'Yep. I saw the doctor this morning and he gave me the all clear.'

'Try these,' I said, handing her the crutches.

'Black,' she remarked, 'is that the only colour they had?'

'Black is as good as any colour for getting you out of here,' I replied.

Melanie stood on one leg while I adjusted them to the correct height.

'OK, try that.'

Gingerly, she took hold of the crutches and attempted to move

'Argh.'

'What's matter?'

'My elbow,' she replied, 'I can't use these with a broken elbow.'

It hadn't crossed my mind that in order to take the weight off her knee, she would have to put it onto her elbow.

'Wait there and I'll see if I can find a wheelchair.'

I searched the hospital high and low but couldn't find one anywhere.

'I can't find one,' I said, as I entered the room.

'Well I'm not staying here another minute.'

A dodgy right knee and a fractured left elbow was the worst possible ambulation combination. Determined not to spend another minute in hospital, she forced herself to smile as she hobbled past the nurses' workstation. Outside, on the landing, she was almost in tears.

'What can I do to help?'

'I can't go on; it's absolutely killing me.'

I had no idea what to do.

'Take a seat over there and I'll have another look for a wheelchair,' I said.

'If I stop now I might never get going again.'

After a brief, one-legged pause she continued on. I could see that every step was agonising. Eventually she made it to the entrance.

'You wait here and I'll get the car.'

Half an hour later we were back home and Melanie was resting comfortably in her favourite recliner. It would be ten days before we knew the results of her endoscopy; until then she'd been prescribed complete rest with an emphasis on keeping the weight off her knee. Her patience lasted almost twenty-four hours.

'I can't sit around here all day,' she complained.

'You know what the doctor said.'

'How much would a wheelchair cost?' she asked.

'We're not buying a wheelchair for the sake of waiting a few days.'

'I'm not spending the next nine days doing nothing,' she replied.

Melanie was adamant. I needed to find a solution.

'I've got an idea,' I said.

'What?'

'Just wait there.'

'Where else am I going to go?' she mumbled under her breath.

I went into the spare bedroom, which also doubles as the office. Moments later I returned, pushing the office chair.

'Here you go,' I announced proudly.

'What I am supposed to do with that?'

The chair is a typical, swivel-style office chair with five castors on the base.

'Sit on it.'

'I'm not pushing myself around the house on that,' she protested. 'It's dangerous.'

'Nonsense,' I replied, 'you'll be fine. Just give it a go.'

Reluctantly, Melanie lifted herself up from the comfort of her recliner and hopped toward the chair.

'Make sure you hold it while I get seated,' she said, 'and whatever you do, don't let go.'

Cautiously, Melanie lowered herself onto the chair.

'There, I told you it would be alright.'

'And now what?'

'Push yourself around with your good leg.'

Instead of pushing herself backward as instructed, she tried pulling herself forward, resulting in her banging her ankle on the base.

'Ouch! This is no good,' she moaned.

'You need to push yourself backwards not pull it forwards.'

'But I won't be able to see where I'm going.'

I didn't want to admit it, but that was the least of her problems.

'You'll be fine; just look where you're going before you push.'

Melanie pushed backwards and bumped straight into the wall.

'It won't go where I want it to,' she moaned.

'Give it time; you'll soon get the hang of it.'

I thought it best to leave her to it and set about washing the car.

By the time I'd finished, Melanie was whizzing around the kitchen like R2-D2.

While Melanie convalesced, I began the search for our next restoration project. Since getting back from England, we'd fine-tuned our idea and come up with a plan of action. When we first moved abroad, we'd intended earning an income by letting a second property to holidaymakers. Within months of our arrival, we'd started to doubt the viability of that idea. Galicia is as far removed from the Spanish tourist map as it's possible to be. If it wasn't for the Camino de Santiago, I doubt the region would attract any foreign visitors. Since then, things had changed. Not too much, but enough for us to reassess the possibilities. We now believed that property letting had real potential and if that failed we could always sell the place.

Renovating *El Sueño* had taught us a lot. Since then we'd gained even more knowledge. The most important thing we'd learnt was that price is everything.

Most local properties fall into two main categories: those that need bulldozing and those that don't. We'd been incredibly lucky during our last search to uncover the latter. If we could find something similar, that would be ideal. If not, our tiny budget would only stretch to the former. In reality, this meant buying a pile of stones and the land it sat on. Over the last three years, the cost of that pile had risen sharply. With a limited budget, we had no choice but to find a bargain.

There were other important considerations when focusing on the rental market. Location was a key requirement. Quick and easy access to the road infrastructure was essential and last but not least, our choice had to have the "wow factor" or at least the potential to achieve it. All these requirements had to be accomplished on a budget that Ebenezer Scrooge would find embarrassing.

'Right, I'm off. Is there anything you want before I go?' I asked.

'No, I'll be fine.'

Melanie had a stack of chick lit to keep her entertained and a mobility office chair to get around on; what more could she want?

'Good luck,' she called as I left.

The starting point for my search was the offices of Monfortina, the estate agency where we'd found our last purchase. The owner of the agency, Lucrecia, hardly flinched when I announced the budget. Her husband deals with the initial viewings; her involvement comes later when there's a deal to be struck. She told him which properties to show me and we headed out of the office.

The first place was well within our budget which, given the miserly amount, hardly seemed possible. Its location wasn't too bad, although the outlook could have been better. The main highway was less than two kilometres away and the house itself was down a short track less than fifty metres from a tarmacked road.

Viewing this property brought an entirely new meaning to the phrase "internal inspection recommended". The whole façade had collapsed into the front garden. From the track outside, I could see all the interior rooms. As for the "wow factor", it certainly had that. My first thought was wow, how the hell is this place still standing?

Defects aside, the remaining pile of stones had a

number of advantages. During its long history, mains electrics had been connected. Getting it reconnected shouldn't pose too much of a problem. The property also boasted its own water well. Despite these major selling points there were a few issues of concern. Most worrying of these was waste disposal. The size of the plot wasn't big enough to accommodate a septic tank. Another parcel of land was included in the price but that was in an elevated position, fifty metres away. As everyone knows, shit always flows downhill. Technically, this problem isn't insurmountable; with that in mind, my shortlist had its first addition.

The second property was in a similarly poor condition but on a much grander scale, a fact reflected in the asking price. The other ruins we visited weren't worthy of consideration.

Back at the agency I asked Lucrecia if she had anything else that might be suitable.

'Of course,' she replied.

'In that case, I'll call back tomorrow afternoon if that's OK?'

'No problem.'

By the end of the second week I'd exhausted Monfortina's stock of affordable ruins. I'd visited over a dozen places but none were as interesting as the first two. The limitations of our budget were becoming apparent and my confidence in finding something suitable was starting to wane.

My disappointment at the lack of affordable housing paled into insignificance when compared to Melanie's frustration at not being able to walk. With a bit of luck, in two days' time we'd finally discover what the problem was and, more importantly, how to resolve it.

5

Doubtful Dowsing

At this time of year, lawn maintenance involves little more than a regular cut. As spring drifts into summer, all that will change. Without regular irrigation, lush green lawns quickly deteriorate into dreary dustbowls. Watering with a hosepipe is tedious and time consuming, and inevitably clashes with our Teatime Taster. This year, I was determined to find a less disruptive solution.

'We ought to get a sprinkler system to water the lawns,' I suggested one evening.

'What sort of sprinkler system?'

'Those that pop up out of the ground.'

'Is that something you can do?' asked Melanie.

'I think so; it can't be that difficult.'

Melanie looked unconvinced. 'Where will you get all the stuff from?'

'That big DIY store in Ourense has everything we need. As soon as you're back on your feet, we'll go and take a look.'

'I suppose it can't hurt to look,' she replied.

That weekend, I decided to make a start. I began by taking precise measurements of the garden and drawing a scaled plan of the grounds.

'What do you think?' I asked, showing it to Melanie.

'Lovely,' she replied. 'What is it?'

'A blueprint to success,' I said, confidently.

'That's good then.'

Despite Melanie's scepticism, confidence was high. As soon as she was back on her feet, I could finalise the plan and work out how much it would cost to implement.

On Monday we were up with the larks; the alarm clock saw to that. Melanie had her post-op appointment at the hospital in Monforte and we didn't want to be late.

In many respects, Spain's National Health Service is very different to that of the UK. For starters, they seem to allocate far more resources to clinicians than managers; they certainly spend less on aesthetics and interior design. For me, though, the most noticeable difference is the lack of red tape. How the hospital in Monforte functions without it is anyone's guess.

During our recent visit to Huddersfield's Royal Infirmary, I was struck by the endless lines of two-inch-wide self-adhesive tape. It ran down corridors, through doorways and around corners. Stuck on the floor were lines of red, yellow, and blue tape and running along the walls, green, black, and brown. Patient logistics had taken over the corridors like colourful jungle creepers. Each colour represented a newly implemented system, or the failure of previous ones.

'Melanie Briggs, please follow the red line to treatment room three,' had echoed over the PA.

'Follow the blue line to the X-ray department,' instructed the consultant, following his examination.

'The yellow line will take you to the plaster room,' the radiologist had said, after taking the X-rays.

The service seemed so reliant on coloured tape that I was left wondering how the visually impaired found their way around.

Whatever the differences between the two systems, they have one thing in common: quality care that's the envy of all.

To the uninitiated, the Spanish approach seems quite intimidating. Fortunately, we were old hats. Here in Monforte, the outpatients waiting room is situated on the ground floor. A short corridor leads from the main car park into a subterranean room, devoid of natural light. On the left is a reception office. It's abandoned, and looks like it has been for years.

'You take a seat and I'll wait for the nurse,' I said.

Melanie hobbled off and found a seat in the busy waiting room. I joined a small crowd gathered around a set of double doors. Without warning, they opened; a nurse stepped out. Her sudden appearance initiated a stampede; the waiting crowd surged forward thrusting their appointment slips at her. The throng swelled as the elderly and less mobile leapt to their feet and joined the rabble. The nurse grabbed the slips like a stock market trader before disappearing into her lair. A disorganised game of musical chairs followed as impatient outpatients jostled to find a seat.

It's a strange paradox that the waiting time between consultations seems much longer than the consultation itself.

'Melanie Jine Bricks,' called the nurse.

We followed her through the double doors and into the consulting room, took a seat and waited while Dr Vázquez read Melanie's notes.

'We've discovered the cause of your discomfort,' he said.

We held our breath, hoping for a favourable diagnosis.

'It's the ligaments behind your kneecap, there're twisted.'

Identifying the cause was good news; prescribing a remedy was more important.

The prognosis sounded encouraging. He suggested a course of physiotherapy; if that failed, further surgery would be needed.

'You will have to wait for physio,' he said, 'but as soon as a place becomes available someone will contact you.'

We were relieved to finally discover the culprit and delighted to know that it could be corrected. After a thorough examination he advised her to ditch the crutches. We thought it wise not to mention the mobility chair.

'You can start walking again but *poco a poco* (little by little),' he added.

That was great news.

We thanked him for all his help and headed home.

We couldn't have wished for a better outcome. To celebrate, I thought a trip to Ourense might be in order.

'Would you like to go to Brico Centre this afternoon?' I asked.

'Why not?'

Having been housebound for a fortnight, even a fact finding mission to a DIY superstore sounded fun. I was keen to finalise plans for my automated irrigation system and find out how much it would cost.

'Are you sure you'll be alright?'

'I'll be fine,' she insisted.

Ourense is about forty kilometres from home, down one of the most spectacular roads in the area.

'You can wait in the car if you want,' I said, as we pulled into the car park.

Wild horses couldn't have stopped her. Gingerly she stepped out of the car and limped towards the store.

'I think the plumbing materials are down here,' I said, wandering off down an aisle.

Melanie followed.

Plumbing yes; gardening no.

'Watering systems must be in the gardening section; I think that's over there,' I said, pointing towards the far end of the store.

Wandering aimlessly around an out-of-town warehouse was the last thing Melanie needed.

'You wait here and I'll check,' I added.

'I'm fine,' she insisted.

Thankfully, the garden section had everything I needed.

'These should do the job,' I said, pointing at a display of pop-up sprinklers.

The packaging indicated a three metre watering radius.

'They're not cheap, are they?' remarked Melanie.

Melanie's comment resonated long after we'd returned home. That evening, I set about designing my system and calculating the cost.

'Have you got a compass?' I asked.

'What would I want with a compass?' replied Melanie. 'More to the point, what do you want with one?'

'I need to draw a series of overlapping circles onto the plan to work out how many sprinklers we need.'

Melanie looked at me as if I'd lost my marbles.

'Sorry, I can't help,' she replied.

I would have to improvise.

When drawn to scale, a three metre watering radius became a six centimetre circle. I thought that a pencil tied to a piece of string might do the trick but as I arced it through 360°, my fat fingers got in the way and the circle ended up looking like a hard-boiled egg.

Back to the drawing board.

'You haven't got anything round that measures six centimetres, have you?' I asked.

'Like what?'

'I don't know: a piece of jewellery or kitchen utensil.'

'What about a tin of baked beans?'

Melanie's attempt at humour turned into a great idea. A tin of beans was far too wide but the base of an aerosol might do the trick. I opened the cupboard under the sink and rifled through the cleaning products. The furniture polish was a bit on the small size but the fly spray was perfect.

'This will do,' I said, waving it at Melanie as I raced into the office.

Using the base of the tin, I mapped out the position of each sprinkler onto the scaled plan. Forty-three would do the job: fifteen in the front lawn and the rest in the back. The other items on my shopping list were: 112 metres of forty millimetre tubing, forty-three T-joints, six elbow joints, four pipe connecters, two stoppers, and a computerised control panel.

The following morning, we returned to Ourense. The tubing was sold in tightly banded coils of twenty-five metre lengths which meant buying a bit more than I needed. Taking everything into account, the total cost came to just over 500 euros.

'How much?' exclaimed Melanie.

'Five hundred euros. What do you think?' I asked.

'At that price, I think it had better work,' she replied.

She wasn't kidding.

Joking aside, I couldn't wait to get started.

'Make sure you don't lose the receipt,' said Melanie.

A less than subtle reference to the store's ten day returns policy.

Within five minutes of getting home, I'd changed into workwear and unloaded the car.

'I'm going to make a start,' I said excitedly.

'OK,' replied Melanie.

After careful consideration, I decided to tackle the front lawn first. I'd allocated fifteen sprinklers to this area, arranged in three rows of five. I marked the position of each one by hammering wooden pegs into the lawn. Using a ball of string I joined the pegs together. By the time I'd finished, it looked like a giant join-the-dots puzzle.

The next step was heartbreaking: excavating a thirty-centimetre-deep trench between each peg. All the effort

I'd put into creating this green carpet and here I was, digging it up.

To minimise the damage, I used a hand trowel. Hour after hour, on bended knees, I stabbed at the sandy soil. Lunchtime came and went and still I chipped away. Sweat ran down my nose and dripped into the lengthening trench. The urge to attack it with the pickaxe was overwhelming but I managed to resist.

Halfway through the afternoon I decided to take a break, much to the relief of my swollen blisters. The trench stretched from one end of the lawn to the other and halfway back again, long enough to accommodate seven of the fifteen sprinklers. To alleviate the monotony, I decided to start laying the tubing.

Cutting the bands on the tightly coiled plastic tubing gave it a life of its own. Inadvertently, I released the plumbing equivalent of a twenty-five-metre-long toothless python. No sooner had I buried it than it sprang out of the ground like a character from *Zombie Apocalypse*. Soil catapulted into the air, refilling the trench as it fell to the ground.

'Melanie,' I called from the garden.

'What?'

'I need a hand.'

Melanie had been resting her knee after this morning's exertion.

'Can you hold this end?' I asked, as she rounded the corner of the house.

She lowered herself gently onto the lawn and held the tube in position.

'What are you going to do?'

'I'm going to measure the distance to the next sprinkler and cut it to the exact length.'

I wrestled the python-like tube into submission and marked the cut with a pencil. At times like this, the saying "measure twice, cut once" screams caution. To make absolutely certain, I measured it three times.

'Are you sure that's the right length?' asked Melanie, as I prepared to cut.

As if my own doubts weren't enough, now Melanie was undermining my confidence.

'I'm certain,' I replied, and made the cut.

The shorter section proved much more manageable. I fitted a T-joint to one end, screwed a sprinkler into that, and buried the lot. The only thing visible was the top of the sprinkler. One by one I worked my way down the garden, measuring, cutting, screwing, and backfilling. By the end of the day, I'd installed seven sprinklers. Despite my efforts to minimise the impact on the lawn, it still looked like a family of moles had spent the day tunnelling.

'I'm going to give it a go,' I announced eagerly.

'I thought it had to be plumbed in to the mains,' replied Melanie.

'It does but I can test it by attaching this end to the outside tap.'

'Don't you think you've done enough for one day?'

'It won't take a minute.'

The outside tap was in the back garden mounted to the shed. Three quarters of an hour later, it was ready for testing.

'Do you want to come and watch?' I asked.

With all the enthusiasm of a death row inmate shuffling towards the electric chair, Melanie marked the page in her book and ambled around to the front garden.

'Are you ready?' I called, from outside the shed.

'Ready.'

I opened the tap and dashed into the front garden. Melanie was staring at the lawn looking decidedly underwhelmed.

'Is that it?' she asked.

I didn't know what to say. The first sprinkler had popped out of the ground like an erect penis and the head was spraying an even circle of fine water particles over a three metre radius. The second seemed far less enthusiastic. It had popped halfway up leaving nothing but a damp patch around the base. The third in line had lifted its head less than an inch, producing little more than a dribble. As for the other four, they hadn't popped up at all and the ground around them was as dry as a bone.

'Something's wrong,' I said, stating the obvious. 'I'll just check the tap.'

I sprinted round to the back of the house; Melanie followed at a more sedate pace. I turned the tap off, disconnected the tube and turned it back on. Water gushed out.

'There's nothing wrong with the tap,' I announced.

'Why don't you leave it for today and start again in the morning?' suggested Melanie.

It's simply not in my nature to give up without a fight, a fact that Melanie knew only too well.

'I'll just recheck the sprinklers. When I give you the word, can you turn on the tap?'

Melanie stood at the ready while I returned to the front lawn.

'OK, turn it on,' I shouted.

The result was exactly the same. Back and forth I wandered, determined to make it work. Two hours later, with the light fading, I conceded defeat. I'd excavated every joint and checked every sprinkler; I'd disconnected each one and reconnected them but I still couldn't find a fault.

'I don't know what's wrong. We'll have to get Antonio Roca to come and take a look at it,' I suggested.

Antonio Roca was the plumber we'd used during the initial remodelling of the house. He wasn't the best I'd ever come across but he was the cheapest.

'Does that mean we can have dinner now?' asked Melanie.

First thing the following morning I rang Antonio and explained the problem.

'I'll call round this afternoon and take a look,' he said.

Antonio Roca is a serious man, quietly spoken with an unflappable manner.

Clang, clang, clang, clang!

Woof, woof, woof, woof! Jazz sprang to her feet and darted round the side of the house.

'That'll be Antonio,' I said, jumping to my feet.

'Hola,' I called, as I walked down the driveway.

'*Buenas tardes*,' he replied.

I opened the gate and let him in.

'What's the problem?' he asked.

Revealing DIY blunders to a tradesman is uncomfortable at the best of times. Showing him my half-finished irrigation system was painfully embarrassing. Reluctantly, I explained the problem.

Antonio stared at the snaking tube which ran from the lawn, down the side of the house to the outside tap. His raised eyebrow spoke volumes.

'That tube should be underground,' he said, without a hint of sarcasm.

'I know but I wanted to test that everything worked before I buried it,' I replied.

'So what's the problem?'

'Wait here and I'll show you.'

Hurriedly, I walked across to the shed and turned on the outside tap.

'That's the problem,' I said.

He stared at the lawn in disbelief.

'Is this water from your own well?' he asked.

'We don't have a well,' I replied. 'This is council water.'

'That's your problem. There's not enough pressure from council water.'

The verdict was in; my irrigation system was destined for a watery grave. Antonio's conclusion came as a hammer blow. It wasn't the fact that I'd spent the previous day digging lumps out of the lawn or that the materials had cost a small fortune. My biggest disappointment was that for the foreseeable future I was destined to waste hours of my life watering the grass with a garden hose.

'It would be a different story if you had a well,' he added.

'Why?' I asked.

'The water pressure from your own well is determined by the size of the pump.'

This nugget of information sent my grey matter into overdrive.

'How much would it cost to dig well?' I asked.

Antonio explained that the cost of a borehole is determined by the depth of the water table. The deeper the hole the greater the cost.

'I can do the plumbing work but I can't drill the borehole,' said Antonio. 'You'll have to get someone else to do that.'

'And what about this?' I asked, pointing at all the equipment we'd bought.

'That's no good,' he said. 'You need proper plumbing supplies.'

That evening, we picked over the bones of Antonio's suggestion. We'd suffered supply problems in the past; discussions about drilling a borehole weren't new. In our first summer here, unannounced water restrictions had almost killed our stock of newly purchased plants. Last summer we'd been without water from eight in the evening until eight in the morning.

'What do you think?' I asked.

'It seems a bit extravagant just to water the lawns,' remarked Melanie.

'But it's not just for watering the lawns. We can plumb it into the house as well.'

'Why don't we get a price and then decide?' she suggested.

'That sounds like a great idea.'

'There is one thing though,' remarked Melanie.

'What?'

'What are we going to do with all the stuff we've bought?'

'Let's try taking it back; I kept the receipt.'

The next day we returned to Brico Centre, more in hope than expectation. Customer service in Galicia doesn't always live up to its billing. To our delight, the store honoured their guarantee and gave us a full refund.

Finding a company to quote for drilling the borehole proved easier than we'd expected. After asking around, we invited a local firm, Sondeos Morales.

Clang, clang, clang, clang!

Jazz jumped to her feet and went racing around the side of the house; I chased after her.

Woof, woof, woof, woof!

By the time I'd caught up, she was lapping up the attention of the young man standing at the gate.

'Hola,' he called, 'I'm Roberto from Sondeos Morales.'

'Come in,' I said, opening the gates.

I was pleasantly surprised by the speed of his response. Getting things done at the first time of asking is quite unusual. Roberto listened as I explained what Antonio had suggested.

'We don't have enough pressure to water the lawns,' I explained.

'Pressure to water the grass?' replied Roberto quizzically.

I could see from his expression that he thought I was mad. Drilling a well to water the lawns went against every convention. For locals, owning a borehole is a status symbol, a prized possession to put food on the table and keep livestock hydrated through the long summer months. Using it to water the lawn was akin to collecting hay in the back of a Rolls Royce.

'We'll use it in the house as well,' I added.

Just then Melanie came to see what was going on.

'He thinks we're mad,' I whispered.

'Where would you like it?' he asked.

It's not every day I'm asked where I want my borehole drilled. For that reason alone, I was understandably hesitant. When questions are asked in a foreign language, hesitancy or consideration is interpreted as a lack of understanding. Roberto rephrased his question.

'The well, where would you like it?'

I had an uneasy feeling that my ignorance could have unforeseeable consequences.

'He said …'

Now Melanie was getting in on the act.

Quickly, I interrupted.

'I know what he said but I haven't a clue, have you?'

Melanie's expression was as blank as my mind.

'What about over there?' I said, pointing towards the far corner of the garden.

If nothing else, it would be out of the way. The three of us strolled across the lawn. Roberto looked decidedly unhappy.

'*Es muy complicado*,' he replied, shaking his head.

The last thing I wanted was to make it difficult. Especially as I wasn't bothered where it went.

'And look,' he added, pointing over the wall at a manhole cover. 'There are sewage pipes running under here?'

Other than water, it hadn't crossed my mind what might be buried beneath the lawn. From memory, the waste pipe ran in a straight line from the corner of the house to the manhole cover in the lane.

'The pipes run from there to here,' I said, pointing along the ground.

'And electricity?' he asked.

'That's over there,' I replied, pointing in the opposite corner of the garden.

We ummed and ahed for a while before I made an alternative suggestion.

'What about here?'

Roberto seemed pleased with my new choice.

'Here is good,' he said, 'providing there's water.'

Surely, the only way to find that out is to drill a hole. How wrong could I be? No sooner had he made the comment than he pulled a pendulum from his pocket.

Roberto fancied himself as a bit of a DIY dowser. Instead of using traditional rods, his instrument of choice was a brass pendulum attached to a thin chain.

Melanie and I watched in silence as he marched back and forth across the lawn with his mystical tool dangling before him. Only when he reached the spot that I'd chosen did the pendulum begin to swing.

When artists such as David Blaine employ sleight of hand, the audience is left searching for answers. Roberto's obvious wrist movement required no such questioning.

He looked across at us, satisfaction etched on his face, bemusement on ours.

'Here is fine,' he said confidently, stamping his heel into the turf.

'How much will it cost?' I asked.

'That depends on the depth. The price is twenty-four euros a metre.'

'Have you any idea how deep you will have to drill?' asked Melanie.

Roberto shrugged his shoulders. He hadn't a clue.

Dowsing had its limitations: you can lead an ass to water but you can't fathom its depth.

Decisions, decisions.

Some friends had recently had a well drilled to eighty metres. At that depth, the cost would be somewhere in the region of 2,000 euros. I stared at Melanie; she looked back at me. Roberto could see that we were struggling to make up our minds.

'If we don't find water there's no charge,' he said.

If his remark was meant to reassure us, it had the opposite effect. It would seem that he had less faith in his dowsing skills than we did.

'What do you think?' I asked Melanie.

'Once it's done, it's done.'

There was no answer to that pearl of wisdom.

'How soon can you start?' I asked.

'What about a week on Wednesday?'

The timing couldn't have been better. Dad and Claire were due to arrive in two and a half weeks for a fortnight's holiday. With a bit of luck, the borehole would be drilled, the house plumbed, and the irrigation system installed.

'OK, go ahead.'

6

Mind Your Step

Casting aside her crutches and returning my office chair seemed to accelerate Melanie's convalescence. The small incisions on both sides of her knee were healing well. As for her elbow, the only time that hurt was when she inadvertently knocked it, and despite advice to the contrary, she seemed determined to prolong her discomfort.

'Do you feel up to looking at a few houses today?' I asked.

The weather throughout June had been idyllic, hot sunny days followed by warm still evenings. Today was no exception.

'Why not?' she replied.

After days of searching, risking life and limb tramping through overgrown undergrowth and scrambling around tumbling down ruins, I had a shortlist of two, neither of which were exactly what we were looking for.

'What about the keys?' asked Melanie.

Unsupervised viewings are very unusual. Local agents are paranoid about buyers doing their own deals. For that reason, house keys are passionately guarded. I had hoped that she wouldn't ask; neither property had a standing façade, never mind a front door.

'We're only going to take a look,' I replied.

My uninspiring answer seemed to satisfy her query so I said no more.

We left home after lunch and headed into the Galician countryside. Over the last three years, June has become my favourite month, a four-week period when the vibrancy of spring merges with the heat of summer. Country lanes are deserted and the sound of chirping cicadas fills the warm air.

The first of my two picks was located down a short track.

'Is that it?' asked Melanie, as I pulled up outside.

First impressions weren't encouraging.

'You need to look beyond its current state of repair,' I remarked.

'Beyond! I can see straight through it.'

The front wall of this property had completely collapsed but her comment was a little harsh; the rear wall was still standing.

'It's nothing more than a glorified pile of stones,' she added.

'I know, but it's a gloriously cheap pile of stones.'

It didn't take long to chalk this one off the list and the next one fared no better.

'You've got to be kidding,' said Melanie. 'Are these the best you've seen?'

'Within our budget, yes.'

Given what I'd come across so far, it seemed unrealistic to think that we'd find anything suitable within our price range. Our search for a new project seemed destined to fail.

'What about that bloke at the petrol station? He's

always asking us if we know anyone who wants to buy a house,' I said, on the drive home.

'Do you mean Pablo?'

Pablo is a full-time pump attendant at the Repsol petrol station in Monforte, a position he's held for the last fourteen years. As a young man he worked in London and insists on speaking to us in English. On more than one occasion he's asked us if we want to buy a house or knew anyone who did.

'That's right, Pablo, let's see what he's got to offer,' I suggested.

Melanie agreed, and off we went.

As luck would have it, Pablo was working on the forecourt as we pulled into the filling station.

'Hola,' he called as he walked towards the car.

'Hola,' I replied.

'¿*Cuanto* (How much)?' he asked.

'Forty euros.'

He slipped the pump nozzle into the tank and locked the trigger.

'Do you still have a house for sale?' I asked, trying not to sound overly keen.

'Yes, I have a house for sale. It's a stone house,' he added.

For reasons I am still trying to fathom, stone houses possess a kudos that other materials can only dream of.

'Can we take a look at it?'

'Sure,' he said, 'do you know where the village of Vilatan is?

'No.'

Just then the pumping trigger automatically clicked off. The display read forty euros.

'No problem, meet me here tomorrow at six o'clock and you can follow me there.'

'OK, see you tomorrow.'

The following day we returned at the agreed hour. Pablo was at the end of another long shift.

'Follow me,' he said, hanging out of the window of his sporty Seat coupé.

We drove out of town in the direction of Chantada. From Monforte the road rises steeply. Small hamlets are scattered randomly over the undulating hills. A patchwork of green pastures and leafy forests blanket the landscape. Higher and higher we climbed until we reached the village of Escairon. From here the road begins a gently winding descent. Without warning Pablo began to slow. He indicated to turn right and exited the main road. A signpost at the junction read Vilatan. We'd arrived. Within 300 metres we were entering the village. The road narrows as it squeezes between village houses. Some were old and derelict and others had been beautifully restored. A little way in, Pablo pulled over and stopped.

'I live here, with my parents-in-law,' he said, pointing at a typical Galician country home. 'Wait here and I'll get the keys.'

Pablo disappeared through a downstairs door. Melanie and I waited in the warm evening sun. A few minutes later he returned.

'This is the house here,' he said, pointing at a stone-built property across the lane from his home.

To my surprise it looked in reasonable condition; even the roof looked watertight, quite a find in these parts. Pablo led the way. Five stone steps climbed from the lane into a small pasture.

'Does this land come with the house?' I asked.

'No, not this land but that patch over there does.'

Pablo pointed to a small plot directly in front of the house. In the middle of it sat an old water well, complete with a rusting pail dangling from a worn rope. A tiny walled vineyard occupied the farthest corner of the garden.

The house seemed smaller than it looked when we were standing in the lane. On the ground floor, two weathered wooden doors enclosed what I presumed was the *bodega*. A flight of stone steps led to a narrow covered balcony and the front door. The property was charming, in a Wendy house kind of way.

'Come,' gestured Pablo as he waded through waist high grasses and climbed the steps.

Melanie and I followed.

He unlocked the door, pushed it open, and walked straight in. Viewing properties in this price bracket is usually preceded with a health warning. Something along the lines of watch where you put your feet or you could end up in a plaster cast. Surprisingly, there was nothing wrong with these floorboards.

The upstairs consisted of one room, bigger than I'd expected, but one room nonetheless. The Wendy house charm continued inside. Looking out of the windows involved bending in two. I hadn't had this much fun since playing Twister back in the '80s.

'The windows seem a little low,' I remarked.

Pablo smiled.

'Come look downstairs,' he said, changing the subject.

His reference to the downstairs made me slightly suspicious of the property's past. Since moving to Spain we must have viewed hundreds of properties and downstairs had always been referred to as the *bodega*.

The weathered doors were secured with a rusting chain and padlock. Pablo unlocked it and opened them. With very little light, it was difficult to see anything but there seemed to be two equally sized rooms divided by a thick stone wall.

'What do you think of it?' he asked.

'Has anyone ever lived here?'

'I don't think so.'

Pablo's confession confirmed my suspicion. This property wasn't what it seemed. Traditionally, these types of buildings would have been used to store crops and house livestock. This is why its dimensions were much smaller than you'd expect. That said, it had potential.

'We'll have to think about it, Pablo. Did you say the

owners are asking one million pesetas (6,000 euros)?'

'That's right. It's owned by four brothers and they all want to sell.'

That was good news. Multiple ownership is common in Spain but if one party refuses to sell, the sale cannot proceed.

'You must come and have a drink before you leave.'

It would have been impolite to refuse, besides which, house viewing at this time of year is thirsty work.

'That would be lovely, Pablo, thank you.'

We wandered up the lane and into the courtyard in front of his house. Sitting around a small garden table, in the shade of a chestnut tree, were a young girl and an older man.

'This is my daughter, Sara, and my father-in-law, Ramon,' said Pablo.

They greeted us warmly and we took a seat.

'Would you like a beer?' asked Pablo.

'Yes please.'

'Anna!' shouted Pablo. 'Anna!'

The kitchen window opened and a woman popped her head out.

'¿*Que*?'

'Two beers for our guests.'

Her reply was brutal. Pablo's response was to fetch the beers himself.

'Would you like to see something?' asked Sara, as we waited for Pablo to return.

'Yes,' replied Melanie.

Sara jumped to her feet and skipped across the courtyard to the door that Pablo had disappeared through. It led into a short hallway. Directly in front was a flight of stairs which presumably led to the living accommodation. On the left was another door.

'This way,' encouraged Sara, as she pushed open the door.

A gust of warm odorous air rushed through the open

doorway and hit me in the face like a damp cowpat. It seemed inconceivable that livestock would occupy the same living space as a three generation family but the smell told a different story. We'd heard tales of livestock being stabled below stairs. They help keep the house warm in winter, the story would go. Try as I might, I couldn't imagine how the medieval equivalent of underfloor heating had a place in modern family life.

'Come and look,' beckoned Sara.

It felt like we'd stepped back in time as we entered the dimly lit stable. Overhead, huge chestnut beams supported the wooden floorboards of the living accommodation above. Several low wattage light bulbs dangled from the ceiling on coiled wires. The area was divided into a number of smaller spaces using wooden panels or metal railings. Spread over the floor was a light covering of straw. It looked clean but that didn't prevent me from watching my step. Gingerly, we moved forward. I avoided touching anything for fear of it biting back. Sara had forged ahead without a care in the world and was standing at a wooden pen.

'Look,' she said in a hushed yet excited tone.

Standing in the pen were two cows. In such a confined space they looked absolutely enormous. The first was a Galician Blond, a breed native to the region. Wikipedia will have you believe that the name is derived from their colouring; if that's true, they should be called Galician Latte. As cows go, they are really quite cute. The second beast was jet black. For most people, this scene would be unusual enough, but that wasn't the reason for Sara's excitement.

'Come closer,' she whispered, gesturing us to move a little nearer.

Melanie and I were reluctant to stand too close, especially as both beasts were facing away from us.

Standing on tiptoes, Sara leaned over the wooden pen. Curiosity got the better of us. We must have looked like

Mr and Mrs Kilroy as we placed our hands on top of the panel and peered over.

Laying on a bed of fresh straw was a puddle of latte-coloured flesh and a pair of big brown eyes. This gorgeous little creature was less than two days old. As we peered at her, she stared back at us. Innocent eyes that would melt the coldest heart.

'Ah,' said Melanie, unable to stay silent.

Her remark alerted its mother. She turned her head towards us and started shuffling in the stall. Time to make a hasty retreat.

Running along the opposite wall was another pen. This one was built from brick and rendered with cement. We'd seen this type of enclosure before. The question was, how many pigs did Pablo have? Four little porkers destined for winter slaughter. They were quite small at the moment, playful and noisy, grunting and wagging their tiny tails. Sara leant over and stroked one on its back.

'These will be killed in November,' she said, very matter of fact.

As our tour drew to a close, Pablo appeared at the doorway.

'Beers are here,' he said.

The four of us went back outside and sat around the table sipping ice-cold beer and chatting. Having polished off the first, and politely refused a second, we thanked Pablo for showing us the house and assured him that we'd get back in touch.

'Thanks for showing us the calf, Sara, it's beautiful,' said Melanie as we left.

There's nothing quite like property development for focusing the mind. Over the next few days we concentrated on little else. Ultimately, our decision boiled down to two very different lists: reasons to buy the property, and reasons not to touch it with a bargepole.

Reasons to buy the property

1. Cost. At one million pesetas (6,000 euros) we were unlikely to find anywhere cheaper. Less money spent buying it meant more money for renovations.

2. Location. The village of Vilatan is ideally located for a holiday let. It's an hour from the region's main airport in Santiago de Compostela and central to all the main tourist destinations. The house itself is less than two minutes from a major highway yet far enough away not to know it's there. The property had a pleasant rural outlook and was less than twenty minutes from home. This would make it convenient for cleaning, maintenance, and emergencies.

3. Construction. The property needed a complete overhaul but at least the external walls were standing and the roof was intact. Besides which, it's 'built of stone'.

Reasons not to touch it with a bargepole

1. Size. To maximise our earning potential, we wanted to develop a two-bedroom property. Given its current size, and the small plot it stood on, that seemed unlikely.

'I think we ought to have another look at it?' I suggested.

'This time we'll take a tape measure,' replied Melanie.

The following morning, we set off for Monforte to see if Pablo was working.

'He doesn't start until six,' said one of his work colleagues.

The filling station operates 24/7. If he wasn't at work, there was a good chance he'd be at home, so off we went. Fifteen minutes later we were pulling up in front of his house. No sooner had we opened the car doors than farmyard odours drifted through the cabin.

'That's disgusting,' said Melanie, as she stepped from the car.

'It'll put hairs on your chest,' I remarked.

I couldn't believe I'd just said that. It reminded me of a stupid comment that Dad would make. Why the smell of ripe manure is linked to the growth of chest hair is anyone's guess, and why I'd want to see it growing on Melanie was even more incomprehensible. She treated the remark with the contempt it deserved.

'Tsk.'

We ambled over to the gate and rang the doorbell. A first floor window opened and Anna poked her head out.

'Hola,' she called.

'Hola, is Pablo in?' I asked.

'Just wait a minute,' she replied.

Five minutes later the front door opened and Pablo stepped out. From his dishevelled appearance, it looked as if he'd just got out of bed.

'We didn't wake you, did we?' I asked jokingly.

'Yes,' he replied, 'I'm working nights at the moment.'

So much for trying to be funny.

'I'm sorry for waking you.'

'Don't worry about it. What do you want?'

'Can we take another look at the house?' I asked.

'Sure,' he replied, before heading back inside to get the keys.

Moments later he reappeared, rattling the keys as he walked towards us.

'Come on,' he said, opening the gate.

As we turned into the lane the source of the farmyard odour came into view. Pouring out of a pipe in Pablo's boundary wall was a torrent of animal effluent. The lane had become an open sewer. The likely origins of this septic stream were four little piggies and Pablo's underfloor bovine maternity unit.

This was the worst possible start to our second viewing. Future guests might have to wade through a river of effluent to access their romantic rural retreat. Advertising slogans such as 'Pack Your Wellies and Prepare for Smellies' didn't portray the ambience we were trying to achieve. Pablo could see that we were a little concerned.

'Don't worry,' he said, 'my father-in-law will wash this away.'

His patience was admirable but the global tourist might be less tolerant.

'We can't have people turning up to this,' whispered Melanie, tiptoeing around the larger solids.

She was right. Despite this major setback we took great care to accurately measure the interior of the house. This little property had all the charm and character we were looking for in a holiday let. If there was any chance of making the space work, we could bridge the effluent problem as and when it cropped up. Armed with all the necessary dimensions, we thanked Pablo and left to make our plans.

7

Mind's Eye

Like a heartbroken lover struggling to scribble down his emotions, I tried in vain to squeeze two bedrooms into the tiny Wendy house. Plan after plan tumbled into the waste basket as I screwed up another drawing and threw it away.

'It's no good,' I conceded, 'I can't fit two double bedrooms into such a small property.'

'Perhaps it's for the best,' replied Melanie. 'You know what they say?'

'What?'

'Shit happens.'

'Is that cow shit or pig shit?'

At least the disappointment hadn't curtailed our sense of humour.

'We'd better let Pablo know,' I suggested.

The following afternoon we drove to Vilatan. The midsummer heat felt stifling as we stepped from the air conditioned comfort of the car. I rang the doorbell and waited.

'Try it again,' said Melanie impatiently.

I was just about to press it when the front door opened and Pablo stepped out.

Our decision came as no surprise.

'It's just a bit too small,' I explained.

We chatted for a while before saying goodbye. As I strolled back to the car I had a thought; I stopped and turned.

'I don't suppose you know anywhere else that's for sale, do you?'

It couldn't harm to ask.

'Sure,' he replied.

At moments like this, I doubt I'll ever understand the Spanish mentality. If I hadn't asked, I'm sure he wouldn't have said anything.

'Could we have a look at it?'

'Of course. It's not far.'

The three of us got into the car.

'That way,' he said, pointing through the village.

Slowly, I drove along the narrow lane on the top side of the village.

'Next left,' he said.

I forked left into an even narrower lane lined with majestic chestnut trees. Their leafy boughs provided cool shade from the afternoon sun.

'Slowly now; it's coming up on the left.'

Pablo's tone heightened our suspense.

'Stop here.'

I pulled up and looked to the left. I couldn't believe it. I glanced at Melanie; she looked stunned. Pablo's revelation had rendered us speechless.

'Don't you like it?' he asked.

Pablo had mistaken our silence for disappointment. Nothing could have been further from the truth. He couldn't have shown us a more desirable property if he'd stolen it from my mind's eye. Our search for a second home might finally be at an end.

Access to the house was down an overgrown driveway, lined with dilapidated drystone walls. The weathered granite was encrusted with rich green mosses and mustard yellow lichen. Tall grasses swayed gently in the warm summer breeze, testifying to the property's abandoned state. At the end of the drive, a pair of low metal gates guarded the entrance to a small pasture. Their glossy white paintwork had long since lost its lustre. The lifeless paint was peeling and flaking under a baking sun and patches of rusty iron stippled the surface.

Beyond the gates, tufted patches of green stood out against a backdrop of sun-baked grasses. Thorny blackberries snaked across the unkempt pasture and a few thirsty-looking fruit trees wilted in the afternoon heat.

Sitting comfortably within this parched plot was a romantically appealing farmhouse, typical in design to many local houses. Three tiny windows, framed by huge granite blocks, looked out across the surrounding countryside. Above its ageing ramparts rested a terracotta tiled roof: an undulating collage of rusty reds and earthy browns covered with chequered patches of symbiotic mosses.

'If you're interested, I can ask the owner for the keys,' chirped Pablo.

Pablo's remark shattered my daydream. Any sane person would have said 'No thank you' and walked away, but not us. If the price was right, this was exactly the ruin we were looking for.

'What do you think?' I asked Melanie, trying to sound disinterested.

Melanie played along. 'It can't harm to take a look,' she replied.

'OK Pablo, have a word with the owner and see what you can arrange.'

Two days later, Pablo telephoned. He'd spoken with the owner, Don Antonio Diaz Fernandez, and arranged a viewing.

'He'll meet us tomorrow afternoon at the house,' he confirmed.

Melanie and I could hardly contain our excitement as we made our way to the rendezvous. Today's viewing was as much to meet the owner as look around the house. The place was a ruin. Whatever lay hidden behind the front door was irrelevant. If the owner was willing to strike a deal, the place would be ours; if not, we would have to walk away.

As well as price, there are other issues to take into account when buying a Galician ruin. One of the more important considerations is the quality of the masonry and the structural integrity of supporting walls. That's not to underestimate other factors, water for example. Agents will often eulogize over the existence of a water well but most are little more than shallow pits that dry up during the summer months. A lack of mains electricity could prove problematic but isn't necessarily a deal breaker. Providing other houses in the village have a supply, getting connected shouldn't be too difficult. As for mains sewers, that's as likely as discovering an original Picasso hidden in the loft.

Practical issues aside, when it comes to securing a deal, it's helpful to observe due reverence for family history. Owners will often wander through the abandoned house, reliving childhood memories and extolling the virtues of insect-infested floorboards.

As we drove through the village we came across Pablo. I pulled up alongside and rolled down the window.

'Hola.'

'Hola,' he replied, 'I'm just on my way to the house.'

I parked the car and the three of us walked there together.

'There he is,' said Pablo, pointing at a diminutive figure standing in the overgrown pasture.

Even by Spanish standards, Don Antonio was vertically

challenged. Years of outdoor labouring had left him with a dark tan and a leathery complexion. Perched on his head was a large flat cap, held in position by a pair of elephantine ears. His wardrobe had seen better days. His cotton trousers and tweed jacket would have looked quite dapper, twenty-five years ago. As for his knitted jumper, I'd thrown better away. Through a frayed hole, a once white shirt looked grey and unironed. Looks aside, hiding beneath his shabby attire and hobbit-like appearance was a warm smile and a friendly handshake.

'*Bo dia,*' he said, as we approached

Don Antonio had greeted us in gallego, a language he'd spoken for over eighty years and one he had no intention of changing for our benefit.

'*Buenos dias,*' we replied in our best Spanish.

From now on, we would be in Pablo's capable hands.

Our guided tour began in the *bodega*. Pablo exchanged a joke with him as he pulled out a key the size of a breadknife. The distinctive creak of rusty metal cried out as he pushed open two large wooden doors. Bright sunlight angled in, illuminating the cool, damp room. Dusty cobwebs dangled from thick wooden joists and decades of woodworm infested timbers cluttered the floor. A makeshift cattle pen separated the space.

Reluctantly, we entered. There's never enough light in these dingy cellars for my liking and I haven't yet been in one that didn't shelter something unpleasant. If it's not animal effluent or rotting vegetables, it's dusty cobwebs lying in wait to ensnare the unsuspecting house hunter. Even if we'd wanted to look around, which we didn't, it was far too dark to see anything.

'Can we take a look upstairs?' I asked, eager to leave this dirty cellar.

The entrance was at the top of a flight of stone steps running up the side of the house. Don Antonio led the way and we followed. The front door was nothing more than a hinged barricade, cobbled together from recycled furniture. It didn't even have a handle. Having unlocked it Don Antonio poked his finger through a strategically drilled hole, hooked it around a piece of old twine and tugged. The cord was tied to the door latch which allowed him to shoulder it open. Ingenious if nothing else.

Judging by the thick layer of dust, it looked as if no one had stepped inside for decades. A long corridor ran the length of the building with doorways on both sides. As we tiptoed carefully along the corridor, beams of sunlight angled in through holes in the roof. One by one we pushed open the doors. Most rooms were no bigger than the infested double bed they contained. Halfway along, a thick stone wall shed a little light on the property's past. This dividing wall separated what had originally been two cottages.

At the far end of the house we were surprised to find a bathroom. The 70s-style pea-green suite was the most modern thing in the property but the absence of running water rendered it redundant. We later discovered that the toilet waste flowed straight into the *bodega* below.

Our inspection confirmed what we'd suspected. The property had neither running water nor mains electricity, the roof was completely shot, all the floorboards were rotten, the interior needed completely redesigning, and the grounds required landscaping. On the plus side, the external walls were structurally sound, the place looked charming, and the location was ideal. It was time to get down to business.

'So, how much do you want for it?' I asked.

Don Antonio's opening gambit was three million pesetas (18,000 euros). A reasonable price for this type of property and one we were willing to pay. Pablo had other ideas.

To the unfamiliar, Spanish negotiating can seem aggressive and ill-tempered. Voices are raised, fingers pointed, and fists hammered on table tops. In Don Antonio and Pablo, we had two canny exponents of the art. For the sake of a few pesetas, Melanie and I were keen not to lose the sale but we decided to leave the wheeler dealing to Pablo. After half an hour of hard bargaining, Don Antonio dug his heels in.

'Two and a quarter million; that's my final price,' he insisted.

We stared at Pablo, eager for him to close the deal, but he was having none of it.

'Honestly, Pablo, that price is fine,' I whispered in English.

'No, it's too high. Don't say a word,' he insisted, before turning back to Don Antonio.

'Do you want to sell the place or not?' he asked.

Don Antonio shuffled uncomfortably and stared at the floor.

'Two million (12,000 euros) is a fair price,' said Pablo.

I couldn't believe that Pablo was arguing over 250,000 pesetas (1,500 euros).

'OK two million, but not a peseta less.'

Both protagonists had saved face but the real winners were us.

To seal the deal, Don Antonio spat into the palm of his hand and offered it to me. I glanced across at Pablo; he nodded his head to reciprocate. I spat into mine and we concluded the day's business with a warm damp handshake. Given the surroundings, it felt suitably appropriate. If only all transactions were that straightforward.

'How soon can we meet at the notary and complete the sale?' I asked Pablo.

'When would you like to go?'

'As soon as possible.'

We were determined to strike while the iron was hot or, in this instance, while the palm was sticky.

'Do you have all the papers for the house?' asked Pablo of Don Antonio.

It seemed a strange question but I had every

confidence that he knew what he was doing. Don Antonio assured us that everything was in order.

'When can you go to the notary?' he asked.

Pablo's question initiated a long conversation between the two. Melanie and I listened intently. Although our gallego wasn't up to much, we were able to understand the gist of things.

'Did you understand?' asked Pablo.

'He needs to speak with his son,' replied Melanie.

'That's right, and his daughter-in-law, Pilar. She will ring you with a date. She speaks English,' he added.

We were more than happy with the arrangements. As far as we were concerned, Don Antonio had shaken on the deal.; save for a legally witnessed contract, that was good enough for us.

We spent the weekend at home, lazing around in the garden. At this time of year, Melanie is reluctant to take a dip in the pool but not me. After the initial heart-stopping plunge, the body quickly adjusts to the water temperature. Splashing about sends Jazz into an excited frenzy. Within seconds she fetches a ball, drops it close to the edge and waits patiently for me to throw it. Her reluctance to join me contrasts sharply with her desire to play. I've mastered the art of skimming it across the surface so that it bounces off the far side and rests tantalisingly close to the edge. Jazz sprints around the terrace from one end of the pool to the other and barks constantly until I swim and collect it. Time after time, I throw it from one end to the other, but she never tires of chasing.

Every so often, the ball lands within reach. Seizing her chance, she lays on her tummy with her paws hanging over the edge, stretches out as far as she can and grabs the ball. Prize recovered, she runs to the edge of the garden and gently chews on it for a few minutes. Before long, she brings it back and the chase begins again. Given half a chance, I'm sure she'd play forever.

On Sunday morning I sprayed the grapevines with a solution of copper sulphate. It's a two-weekly routine I'd been following since sprinkling them with sulphur powder in early May. I wasn't completely sure which part of the vine I was supposed to spray so to be on the safe side, I gave the whole thing a generous shower. I must have been doing something right; they all looked really healthy with lots of tiny cluster developing around the leaves. After flowering, these clusters would grow into bunches of grapes.

Moving to Spain has brought a whole new meaning to the phrase "Monday morning blues". In England, it referred to a reluctance to face the stresses and strains of another working week. Now it refers to the colour of the sky.

By mid-morning the mercury was sprinting past thirty degrees Celsius. Not the kind of day to be mowing the lawns without adequate protection. Melanie was sitting on the back terrace enjoying her second coffee of the day.

'Do you know where the suntan lotion is?' I asked.

'Where have you looked?'

A familiar if somewhat annoying response.

'I haven't looked anywhere,' I replied.

'Tsk!'

Melanie jumped to her feet and brushed past me on her way into the house.

'If you tell me where it is I'll …'

'I don't know where it is,' she snapped.

Such was her haste that she'd disappeared from view before I could follow. Within sixty seconds she'd returned.

'That's all we've got,' she said, thrusting a yellow plastic bottle into my hand.

Amazing: I wish I could lay my hands on things that quick when I didn't know where they were.

'Thank you darling.'

The bottle looked ancient. I turned it over and read the label. Use by: Dec 2004. Melanie caught me reading it.

'I know it's out of date but it'll be fine,' she said. 'Just shake it up.'

Vigorously, I shook the bottle. It felt as if half a sausage was flopping up and down inside it. Harder and harder I shook. Melanie glanced across, Queen Victoria etched into her face: "We are not amused".

'It feels a bit lumpy,' I remarked.

I thought it best to make a discreet exit and continue my handiwork inside. After five minutes or so the contents felt slightly more pliable. I flipped open the top and squeezed. A creamy white lotion spurted out, just enough for a light covering.

'It's finished,' I said, stepping back outside.

Melanie glared at me.

'It's been really good. Where did we buy it from?' I added.

'Lidl.'

Lidl is a German owned, European-wide chain of discount supermarkets. They specialise in brands that no one has heard of and sell them at very low prices. In common with the rest of Europe, the locals here can't get enough of the place. Every Monday and Thursday, they offer a limited range of non-food items at discounted prices. So popular are these Special Offer days that large crowds gather in the car park before opening time.

'We'll have to get another bottle.'

'Well we're not going this morning,' insisted Melanie. 'It'll be bedlam.'

She wouldn't hear a complaint from me. Shopping is bad enough at the best of times without having to fight my way through hordes of bargain hunters.

By six that evening we thought it safe to venture into town.

It's two decades since I abandoned my career in retail, but old habits die hard. In common with most shoppers, Melanie wandered around the store looking at the merchandise. I, on the other hand, am drawn to gaps in the display where items are out of stock, or misaligned point of sale tickets, and woe betide if there are dirty strands of mop head caught around the foot of a shelving unit. It wouldn't surprise me if supermarketitis is a medically recognised illness; most personality disorders seem to have a fancy title these days. It's unfortunate, but I just can't help myself.

'That's a good price,' said Melanie, interrupting my inspection.

She'd spotted a bottle of Albariño wine. It's a crisp, fruity white from the Rías Baixas region of Galicia.

'Let's try a bottle,' I suggested.

Melanie took one off the shelf and we moved on.

Running down the centre of the shop was a row of metal plinths containing the remnants of today's special offers. The presentation reminded me of a church jumble sale but one item caught my eye.

'Look at that,' I said, pointing at a gas powered barbecue.

We'd talked about getting one on a number of occasions but the cost had put us off. One of the benefits of living in Spain is the opportunity to enjoy an alfresco lifestyle but lighting a charcoal barbecue for two every evening had become a bit of a chore. A gas barbie would change that: ignition would be instantaneous, the heat controllable, and the food perfectly cooked.

'How much is it?' asked Melanie.

'Seventy-nine euros.'

We stood in silence, staring at the picture on the box.

'What do you think?' I asked.

'Let's go for it.'

Decision made. All we had to do now was choose tonight's menu.

'What about sardines for starters?' I suggested.

We'd become quite partial to grilled sardines. Surprising really; prior to moving here the only fish Melanie would eat came from the chippy: battered cod served with a generous portion of chips, wrapped in last week's news.

'That sounds delicious.'

'And a steak for the main course.'

Galician beef is prized throughout the world. Two thick slices of sirloin would be a fitting way to christen the new barbie.

By the time we headed home, the clock had ticked round to eight and we'd spent well over a hundred euros.

All I had to do now was figure out how to put together our flat-pack barbie. The assembly instructions looked fairly straightforward. A series of helpful diagrams assisted the would-be barbecue builder.

'It's getting a bit late,' said Melanie. 'Perhaps we should leave it until tomorrow.'

'Don't be daft; I'll have it bolted together in no time,' I replied confidently.

What the diagrams didn't show was exactly which way round each piece went. A fact I discovered when the bolt holes for the final two pieces didn't align. The other thing they didn't reveal was if a piece was upside down or not. I found that out after swapping the final two pieces around only to discover that they were upside down.

'How's it going?' asked Melanie.

That was her way of saying, hurry up, I'm starving.

'Nearly there,' I replied.

'I don't think that's right,' she said.

'What?'

'That,' she replied, pointing at the bottom pan.

'What's wrong with it?'

'Well, I'm no expert but when the lid is closed shouldn't the control knobs be at the front?'

She was right. In my rush to put it back together, I'd bolted the pan on back to front. Thankfully, a minor adjustment.

'Right then, here we go,' I announced proudly. 'What time is it?'

'It's just gone eleven.'

Melanie's urgency was understandable. Quickly, I attached the regulator to the top of the gas bottle and flicked open the valve. Gas hissed through the burner as I twisted open the knob. Thumb on the ignition button, I pushed. The burner burst into life. The glowing flame mirrored my sense of pride.

'Right then, let's have the sardines.'

'The first time it's used you have to wait twenty minutes before cooking,' said Melanie.

'What?'

'That's what it says in the instructions.'

I wasn't about to argue; unlike me, Melanie had read them. I slumped into my garden chair and took a sip of wine. The next twenty minutes felt more like twenty hours.

'Time's up,' I said, as I went across to the barbie and lifted the lid.

'The flame has gone out.'

'Gone out! How long ago?'

As frustrating as Melanie's question was, I managed to keep my composure. Did she seriously think that I would have waited twenty minutes had I known the flame had gone out?

'I don't know dear,' I replied calmly.

I thought it wise to turn off the gas and open the lid before reigniting. The last thing I wanted was to blow myself up. After a precautionary pause, I flicked the gas back on, turned the knob and pushed the ignition button. Once again it burst into flames at the first time of asking. Carefully, I closed the lid and waited a short time before opening it to make sure it was still lit.

'It's gone out again.'

'Perhaps it's broken. Can't we phone out for an Indian takeaway?' said Melanie.

If only, I thought to myself.

After several failed attempts, a closer inspection revealed the cause.

'The thingamajig was too far away from the other bit

which meant the slightest breeze blew out the burner,' I said.

Melanie looked a little confused.

'But it's working now?' she asked.

'Yep, won't be long now.'

By the time we'd waited the obligatory twenty minutes the clock had ticked round to a quarter to midnight.

'See, I told you it wouldn't take me long to bolt it together,' I said with a smile.

The sardines were delicious, basted with butter, sprinkled with rock salt and a generous squeeze of lemon, and the steaks weren't bad either. It might have taken a little longer than expected but the results from our new barbie were worth the wait.

8

Lord of the Manor

Melanie's off-the-cuff remark about phoning out for an Indian takeaway had got me thinking. In all our travels through Galicia, I hadn't seen an Indian restaurant but did that mean there wasn't one? I decided to find out and set about my task with relish; after all, how difficult could it be to find some mango chutney and a few poppadoms?

Google's search engine went into overdrive. To my surprise, I found three. Two in the northern coastal port of La Coruña and a third to the west, in the city of Vigo. At distances of 175 kilometres and 135 kilometres respectively, home delivery seemed a little optimistic. But if Muhammad won't come to the mountain, the mountain would have to go to him.

'I thought we might go out for a curry this weekend. What do you think?'

'You are joking?' replied Melanie.

'Not in the slightest.'

After discovering the Indian restaurants, Google and I

found a charming rental cottage situated within the Monte Aloia Parque Natural on the outskirts of the historic town of Tui. My plan was simple: order a takeaway and spend a romantic evening under the stars feasting on Indian food and drinking local wine.

'That sounds like a brilliant idea,' said Melanie. She paused for a moment before asking, 'Is there any football involved in this romantic weekend away?'

'No football, not this time.'

Unfortunately, the season had finished a month ago – shame really.

That weekend we headed west in search of some eastern promise. Jazz leapt into the car, excited to be coming along. First stop, Tui, and the Monte Aloia Parque Natural.

In 1978, the park was the first place in Galicia to be recognised by the local government as an area of outstanding natural beauty. As such, it is now protected against future development. Its peaks rise to over 700 metres above sea level, giving stunning views over the cathedral city of Tui and across the river Miño to Portugal and beyond. This unique landscape is blanketed with forests of Lebanese cedars, firs, cypresses, and the aromatic aroma of eucalyptus.

Within two hours of leaving home we'd reached our destination: a charming cottage nestled within its own landscaped garden. The owners greeted us warmly and took great pride in showing us around their rustic creation. Jazz followed, sniffing in every room. This was exactly the type of rural retreat we were hoping to create in our holiday rental property.

The cottage was constructed from large granite blocks, interspersed with smaller stones. The windows were small, keeping the interior cool in summer and warm in winter. Running along the front of the cottage was an unusual *galleria*, extending from the ground floor to roof level. In front of this was a tiled terrace. Within minutes of our arrival we were back in the car and heading for the city of Vigo.

To most people, the Taj Mahal is instantly recognisable as one of the Seven Wonders of the World. A magnificent mausoleum sculptured from white marble. It represents the personification of one man's love for his wife and the overwhelming grief he felt at her passing. Unfortunately I've never been, but for a curry-starved Yorkshireman living in Galicia, the next best thing is the Taj Mahal Indian restaurant on Calle Vázquez Varela in Vigo.

One look at the menu and I was tempted to order it all.

'What would you like?' I asked Melanie.

'Let's share some starters.'

'OK, I'll start with a portion of onion bhajis.'

'And I'll have chicken pakora.'

'Do you want to share a few samosas as well?' I asked.

'Why not?'

'Vegetable or meat?' asked the waiter.

Melanie and I looked at each other. The answer was obvious.

'One of each please,' replied Melanie.

'I'll have chicken kahari with pilau rice for my main course.'

'And for madam?' asked the waiter.

'Chicken dopiaza and chapattis.'

'What about a peshwari naan?'

'An Indian meal wouldn't be complete without one,' remarked Melanie.

'Will that be all sir?'

I paused for a moment and then remembered the appetisers.

'Four poppadoms, mango chutney and a portion of raita.'

While our order was being prepared, Melanie and I wandered the streets of Vigo.

'Do you think we've ordered too much?'

'Probably,' replied Melanie.

That evening we sat on the terrace sipping a modestly priced Albariño and watching the sun disappear over the distant horizon. Half an hour later we began preparing our night-time feast.

Ping!

'That'll be the starters,' said Melanie, as the microwave finished its cycle.

By the end of the night we were full to bursting. Jazz polished off the last chapatti but other than that, we'd devoured the lot. Staring into the star-studded heavens we savoured our spicy treat. This was one Indian takeaway that had definitely delivered on its eastern promise.

On our return home, Melanie checked the answer machine for messages.

'Pilar has been in touch about the house. Can you give her a call back?'

'Pilar?'

'Don Antonio's daughter-in-law,' replied Melanie.

'I'll do it now,' I said, excited and anxious in equal amounts.

After a brief wait, Pilar answered.

'My husband and I will be in Monforte next Thursday,' she said. 'Can we meet at the notary office to complete the sale?'

That was great news. By this time next week, we would have our prize.

'What did she want?' asked Melanie.

'To meet at the notary next week and sign for the house.'

The following week seemed to drag. It's often the case when you're waiting for something. That Thursday we drove into Monforte, parked in the college car park and made our way along the riverside footpath into the heart of the town. In our eagerness, we arrived a little earlier than expected.

We were fast becoming familiar faces at the notary.

This was our fourth visit in four years, three times to buy and once to sell. Despite that, both of us were feeling a little nervous.

As usual the office was a hive of activity. Small groups of people were huddled together whispering secretly, each party clutching a tatty folder of private papers. The office is reminiscent of a 1960s GP's waiting room. Facing us as we entered was a Formica-topped reception counter. Sitting behind that were two receptionists and a busy office junior who scuttled around photocopying forms and despatching them to their correct station.

On the left of the waiting area are the notary's offices. It's here that contracts are signed and transactions concluded. On the right, a narrow corridor led to the administration office where the contracts are prepared.

By the time Don Antonio arrived, the office was heaving. On spotting us, he barged his way through the throng without so much as a by your leave.

'*Bo dia*,' he called above the chatter, 'this is my son, José, and his wife, Pilar.'

'*Encantado* (Pleased to meet you),' I replied.

'Good morning, how are you today?' asked Pilar in her best English.

Unlike her father-in-law, Pilar was immaculately dressed, confident and authoritative. She seemed determined to speak to us in English, spurred on by the fact that neither Don Antonio nor her husband, José, could understand a word.

'I work as an estate agent in Vigo,' she said.

'*Muy bien* (Very good),' I replied.

'Before we can see the notary, the administrator will have to prepare a new *escritura*,' she explained. 'Do you know what an *escritura* is?'

'The sale contract,' I replied.

She turned to her father-in-law and told him in Spanish what he needed to do. As if to make a point, he responded in gallego.

'You must speak Spanish,' she insisted.

Don Antonio puckered his lips with a look of indignation.

A disorganised queue had formed at the door of the administration office, stretching the length of the adjoining corridor and into the waiting area. Unlike the English, Spaniards are dreadful at queueing. People jostled for position and voices were raised. After two hours we'd shuffled three metres to the front of the queue. As the party in front left, we rushed into the office.

Throughout our wait, Don Antonio had been clutching a tatty folder containing a wad of grubby papers. Finally, he loosened his grip, placed it on the desk, and slid it towards the clerk. She stared at the shabby bundle with a puzzled expression. This wasn't what she'd expected to see. Gingerly, she fingered through the papers, pausing occasionally to quiz Don Antonio, his face a picture of blissful ignorance. Pilar looked furious as the clerk gathered up the papers and handed them back to him.

'What's matter?' I asked, struggling to keep up with Pilar as she fought her way back along the corridor and into the waiting room.

'We will have to get the contract drawn up somewhere else,' she said abruptly. 'I know just the place.'

Pilar was on a mission. Melanie and I were being swept along on a tide of impatience and we weren't the only ones. Don Antonio and his son, José, were struggling to keep up as well. We marched along the street and into another office.

'What's happening?' whispered Melanie.

'I've no idea. Let's just see what happens.'

Pilar spoke with a young lady who was sitting at a computer and then turned to us.

'She can make a private contract for the house,' explained Pilar.

'¿Nombres?' asked the receptionist.

'What is this for, Pilar?' I asked.

'She needs your name and identity number for the sale contract,' she replied.

'Is this a private sale contact?'

'Yes,' replied Pilar, 'but don't worry, this is quite normal.'

Private contracts are not uncommon but if anything should go wrong, they offer the buyer little if any legal protection. Pilar and her husband had travelled quite some way to finalise this deal and they seemed determined not to leave empty handed.

For the first time today, I knew exactly what was going on.

'We don't want a private contract, Pilar; we would prefer to go through a notary.'

Pilar was disappointed but understood our concerns. The notary's reluctance to draw up an official *escritura* threw into question Don Antonio's legal ownership.

'I will find out what my father-in-law needs to do and get back to you as soon as possible.'

Pilar's response was reassuring. Everyone had built up their hopes only to have them dashed by bureaucracy. If anything, the events of this morning had made us more confident that we'd found the right place. All we had to do was remain patient and wait a little longer.

That weekend we had an email from Bob and Janet, the contents of which took us by surprise. Since their visit to Spain in April, we'd exchanged a number of emails and even stayed overnight with them during our visit to England. In all that time, they'd not mentioned anything about their plans for the house. Bob's email changed all that.

From: "Robert Xxxxxx"
To: Craig Briggs
Subject: Re: Hello
Date: Sun 26 June 2005 20:51:40

Hi Both,

From your story about your trip to Tui it sounded very good, glad you enjoyed it.

Also glad to hear that Mel is on the mend now.

Thanks for the offer regards helping with the house, it is much appreciated and we may well take you up on it. We are looking to come over soon at the beginning of September when the flights are a more reasonable price. When we come over we want to have a look round to find and price up some furniture and fittings so that we can possibly rent out next year as well as using it ourselves.

Hope to hear from you soon

Love Bob and Janet (and Sue) xxx

'We've had an email from Bob and Janet,' I said as I stepped into the garden.

'What does it say?'

Melanie was relaxing in the morning sunshine with a mug of coffee and her latest romance novel.

'Come and take a look.'

She put her mug on the table and followed me into the office.

'I'm really pleased,' she said, after reading the email. 'It would have been such a shame for them not to use it.'

'I know, but there's an awful lot to do before they can think about letting it.'

Even if they did furnish the place, renting to tourists was out of the question. The outbuildings were a dangerous eyesore and the courtyard looked like a council tip.

'Like what?' asked Melanie.

'The courtyard for one. They can't have tourists wandering around there; someone is likely to do themselves a mischief.'

'Perhaps you ought to make some suggestions on how best to proceed,' said Melanie.

The property's current problems were due in part to a lack of planning and supervision during the original restoration. We were determined that things would run a little smoother for them from now on. Over the next few days I put together an action plan. If nothing else, it would give them some ideas on how to move forward.

I'd been so busy making plans for Bob and Janet's house that I'd almost forgotten about our property project. That Friday we received an email from Pilar.

From: "Pilar Xxxxxx"
To: Craig Briggs
Subject: Re: Casa
Date: Fri, 1 Jul 2006 09:02:07

Buenos dias Mr and Mrs. Craig:

Next monday we are going to Lugo to get the Certificate. Then we will take it to the notary and ask for an appointment to sign since we see things more clear now... and i understand everything will be ready sooner than I thought.

I will keep you informed, and if everything is ok I will call you from Monforte.

Have a nice weekend...

By the way we will be at San Fiz de Cangas on Saturday since there is a Fiesta just for eating after the mass which is all outside, so my father in law invites you to came and stay with us all if you want, it will be something different.

Please came and join us.

Hope you do.

Pilar

'Melanie, come and look at this,' I called from the office.

Melanie read the email.

'What do you think?' I asked.

'I think she means come,' replied Melanie.

'Don't knock it. Her English is a lot better than my Spanish.'

'Just kidding. It sounds like it might be fun.'

That evening I rang Pilar to thank her for the invitation and confirm our attendance.

'I'm so pleased you'll be coming,' she replied. 'Do you know where my father-in-law lives?'

I had a fairly good idea how to find the village and Pilar explained where his house was.

'It's right next door to the church,' she said. 'You can't miss it.'

'What time should we arrive?'

'After midday mass will be fine.'

The following day we left home at twelve. Pilar's instructions were easy to follow. As we drove up the lane towards the village, a weathered signpost pointed towards the church.

Galicia is blessed with a multitude of historic treasures hidden down leafy lanes and dusty tracks. Grand manor houses and medieval chapels nestle comfortably in the shadow of ancient cypress trees. The church at San Fiz de Cangas and the adjacent manor are typical examples.

'Is that where Don Antonio lives?' asked Melanie.

'It must be.'

Talk about hiding your light under a bushel. Melanie and I were gobsmacked. The manor house was enormous and although it had seen better days, hiding beneath its unloved façade was an architectural treasure.

'It looks like people are parking over there,' said Melanie, pointing into a field.

I pulled in and parked alongside a dozen or so other vehicles. Within seconds of leaving the car, a battery of aerial incendiaries exploded overhead making both of us jump.

'I don't think I'll ever get used to that,' said Melanie.

'It sounds like the festivities are underway.'

As we strolled towards the manor, we noticed a small crowd of exquisitely dressed people milling around the church entrance.

The medieval church looked as though it had recently been restored, which was more than could be said for Don Antonio's manor house. They did have one thing in common: outstanding views over the Val de Lemos.

By the time we reached the entrance to the manor the crowd had disappeared inside the church. Everywhere seemed eerily quiet. Huge wooden gates guarded the entrance to the manor, one of which was slightly ajar.

'What do think we should do?' asked Melanie.

'Go in I suppose; there's bound to be someone inside.'

We squeezed through the gap in the gates which led into a covered courtyard. Stone steps climbed to the front door. This too was wedged open. I poked my head through and peered inside.

'Hola,' I called, having caught sight of José, Don Antonio's son.

José looked up and called us inside. To our surprise he was sitting in a wheelchair with both feet in plaster casts.

'What have you done?' asked Melanie.

He'd fallen off his motorbike and learned the hard way that flimsy sandals don't offer much protection in such circumstances.

'They're all at mass,' he added. 'Shouldn't be long though.'

The only people in the manor, besides him, were his sister and two of Don Antonio's granddaughters. They were busy preparing lunch.

We hadn't been waiting long when the faithful returned. A fashion parade of immaculately presented Spaniards strolled through the hallway. Excited children laughed and played, running noisily between designer-clad guests. Midway through this elegant catwalk appeared the diminutive figure of Don Antonio. On noticing us, his face lit up.

'*Bo dia*,' he called, barging his way past family members.

'*Buenos dias*,' we replied.

His greeting was warm and sincere. He shook my hand and Melanie stooped to kiss his cheeks.

'Hello, how are you?' asked Pilar, who had come to greet us.

Of everyone here, Pilar stood head and shoulders above them all. Every aspect of her appearance was flawless and she commanded the room like royalty.

'Would you like to look inside the church?' she asked.

Who could refuse a guided tour from the princess of San Fiz?

'We'd love to, wouldn't we?' I turned to Melanie.

'Yes.'

Pilar led the way, gliding along the hallway as if on roller skates. Melanie and I scampered after her. As we reached the front door she took a set of keys from a hook on the wall.

'You have the keys?' I enquired.

'My father-in-law has a set. If you ever want to look inside the church with your family or friends, just knock on his door and ask him.'

Pilar always refers to Don Antonio as her father-in-law. The practice is quite common in Spain but seems a little strange when spoken in English.

We entered the church through a side door which led directly into the nave. Inside it was dark and cool.

'Wait here a moment,' said Pilar as she walked into the darkness with assured familiarity.

The echoing click of a light switch illuminated one section of the chapel followed by a second and then a third. The building dates back to the 13th century but the site's origin can be traced back to a Benedictine convent in the Visigoth era. The floor was paved with granite slabs with a rectangular slot chiselled through the thick stone.

'These are tombs,' said Pilar, pointing at the slabs. 'Each one contains an important person of the village.'

'Really?'

'Not any more of course; these are centuries old,' she added.

The chapel had become a depository for religious artefacts, salvaged from other churches in the area which had been ruined through the passage of time. There were several stone baptismal fonts strategically positioned around the walls. The focal point for the congregation was a 13th century calvary or sculptured depiction of the crucifixion. This example had been lovingly carved in different types of wood giving it a polychromatic appearance. The recent restoration had unearthed another historic treasure. While cleaning one of the internal walls the builders had discovered a medieval fresco.

Slowly and reverently we followed Pilar towards the apse, through the transept and into an annex to the left of the high altar. The annex contained a number of tombs of once brave knights, lying in eternal slumber, encased in granite sarcophaguses. One sculpture, depicting a kneeling warrior, was so well preserved it was hard to believe that it was 400 years old. Pilar did her best to translate the inscription but the passing of time had rendered some passages obsolete.

Our absence had come to the attention of Don Antonio who had decided to come looking for us.

'There you are,' he said, wandering through the church. 'It's time for vermouth.'

Back in the manor, all of the guests had congregated in the main reception room. Occupying the centre of it was a long dining table, with settings for twenty or more. Along one wall stood two grand dressers, packed with framed family photos: births, deaths, marriages, and christenings; all had been recorded. Faded black and white wedding prints stood alongside more recent colour photos. Angelic images of children attending their first communion nestled on dusty glass shelves.

Bright sunlight angled into the room through two open doors which led onto a narrow, iron-railed balcony. Ripening grapes were hanging tantalisingly overhead on rusting training wires and the laden branches of a nearby peach tree swayed gently within arm's reach. The view was outstanding, a patchwork of golden pastures and vivid green forests melting into a mountainous canvas of pastel blues and greys, overlapping into infinity and topped with an endless azure sky.

Lovingly prepared and carefully arranged hors d'oeuvres were brought to the table as an accompaniment to a traditional aperitif of iced vermouth. Lunch followed.

'Come sit next to me,' insisted Pilar.

We were hoping to practise our Spanish but Pilar was intent on speaking English. I wasn't too bothered; after a few hours speaking nothing but Spanish, my brain tends to shut down.

Within minutes of taking our seats, the first course was brought to the table. Two large oval platters piled high with freshly fried prawns and baskets of thick chunks of crusty bread. As these emptied, a third one appeared. A seemingly endless stream of *ensaladia* followed the prawns: a mixed salad of diced vegetables (boiled and cooled) and tuna, served with lashings of mayonnaise.

'Wine?' asked the man opposite, holding a bottle of homemade red.

'Por favor,' we replied.

Melanie and I chinked our glasses together and took a sip. I'm no expert but if Spain had a medal for bad wine, this would win best in show. I glanced down the table watching others take their first drink. The verdict was unanimous. Don Antonio was a great host but a lousy winemaker.

As the plates of *ensaladia* emptied, noise levels rose and

the room filled with chatter. Without warning, an annoying, high-pitched whistle sliced through the hubbub. As if in unison, everyone leant forward and stared at Don Antonio sitting at the head of the table. He was fiddling with his hearing aid, oblivious to the distraction. As the whistling faded in and out his family broke into song: the catchy jingle from the national radio station. Don Antonio took it in good heart.

Normal service was soon resumed when the main courses were brought to the table: carved leg of roast pork accompanied by roast potatoes and fresh tomato salad. The pork was delicious but not quite as good as the oven baked lamb which followed.

The desserts were equally bountiful. Homemade apple tart set in creamy jellied custard, *flan de café* (coffee flavour crème caramel), anise flavoured *rosca* (ring-shaped cake), and wedge-shaped slabs of traditional sponge cake. We finished the meal with tiny cups of thick black coffee and Don Antonio's homemade liqueurs, which were significantly better than his wine.

'You must stay for dinner,' insisted Don Antonio.

Melanie and I looked at each other.

'We have a dog that needs feeding,' replied Melanie.

'Go feed the dog and come back.'

'OK,' we replied.

We left the manor at about seven o'clock. Jazz was delighted to see us. By the time we got back to the manor, three hours had passed. Most of the family had strolled the short distance to the village green. Melanie and I joined them. The fiesta of San Fiz de Cangas is a popular affair. The green was busy with people listening to a touring pop group and dancing to the latest hits. At eleven, the band took an hour-long break, just enough time for everyone to go home for dinner.

Back at the manor, we enjoyed another stomach bursting feast before returning to the village green to dance the night away. Our day of festive fun ended at three in the morning when the lord of the manor finally retired.

9

Thar She Blows

Before our move to Spain, friends would often ask, 'What are you going to do with all your spare time?' If truth be known, I hadn't a clue but the premise that I would miss the daily trudge along the treadmill of life lacked imagination and aspiration. Three years on, I'm still none the wiser. The question I now ask myself is, how did I ever find time to do a proper job?

'What time does your dad's flight arrive tomorrow?' Melanie asked over breakfast.

'About eleven.'

'And what time will we have to leave home?'

'About eight.'

Dad and Claire were coming to stay with us for a fortnight and were flying in to Porto. Since returning from our Indian takeaway, we hadn't stopped. Melanie had cleaned the house from top to bottom and I'd mowed the lawns and polished the car.

Clang, clang, clang, clang!

Jazz leapt to her feet and sprinted around the side of the house.

Woof, woof, woof, woof!

I hurried after her.

Roberto was standing at the gate looking particularly pleased with himself. Since his theatrical dowsing performance, we hadn't seen neither sight nor sound of him. The start date for drilling the borehole had passed without so much as a phone call.

'Hola,' I called, as I rounded the corner of the house.

'Hola,' he replied, 'I can start work next Tuesday if that's OK with you?'

Just our luck. Slap-bang in the middle of Dad's holiday. Hardly ideal but I had no intention of postponing; it could be months before we got him back. Dad and Claire would just have to put up with the disruption.

'That's fine.' I replied, and off he went.

The round trip to Porto Airport passed without a hitch.

'Is there anything you'd like to do during your stay or anywhere you want to go?' I asked.

'Don't feel you have to do anything on our behalf,' replied Dad.

Dad and Claire were happy to relax at home, laze in the sun and enjoy the alfresco lifestyle. Even the prospect of a drilling crew descending on the house didn't seem to bother them.

'You're having a borehole drilled just to water the grass,' remarked Dad.

The implication being that we had more money than sense.

'Not just to water the lawns,' I replied.

Dad looked unconvinced.

'What then?'

'We're having it plumbed into the house as well. Council water has been rationed during the last two summers,' I explained, 'and we do have a pool to keep topped up.'

'Oh yes, mustn't forget to top the pool up,' he joked.

'Anyway, they'll be here in the morning to make a start.'

'And how long will it take?'

'That depends on how deep they have to go.'

'You mean they could end up in China,' he replied.

His mischievous grin said it all. I refused to rise to the bait.

Clang, clang, clang, clang!

For a split second I thought I was dreaming.

Woof, woof, woof, woof!

Jazz reminded me otherwise. Through frosted eyes I stared at the alarm clock: 8:25 am. Who on earth could that be at this ungodly hour?

'It's Roberto!' shrieked Melanie.

'Roberto!'

I jumped out of bed and tugged my trousers on.

'He didn't say anything about starting at the crack of dawn,' I said.

Melanie pulled her dressing gown on and dashed to the front door.

'Hola,' I heard her call as she scampered towards the gates.

Moments later I joined her. The morning was damp and overcast, making it feel decidedly cool.

'Hola Roberto, how are you this morning?' I asked.

'I'm very well,' he said, with a cheeky smile.

Knocking us up seemed to have amused him; it certainly wasn't the weather that had perked up his morning.

Parked in the lane was a convoy of vehicles. It looked as if the circus had come to town. Roberto's white Peugeot led the way, emblazoned with the company logo. Given its age and condition, it seemed reasonable to assume that he wasn't making a fortune from drilling holes. The same couldn't be said of the following vehicle, a very tidy purple Mercedes van sporting the same Sondeos Morales livery. Bringing up the rear was the main attraction, a bright orange tractor towing an enormous diesel-powered generator. Vivid images of a giant African elephant towing a tarpaulin covered tiger cage flashed through my mind.

The tractor was very different to the museum-like specimens we see ploughing the fields. This was a modern, purpose-built machine designed specifically for boring. The drilling rig was mounted on the back behind the driver's cab. Its front wheels were at least a metre in diameter and the back ones double that. Secured to both sides of the engine compartment were storage racks filled with two-metre-long sections of drill shafts. These are added to the drill head one at a time as it sinks deeper into the ground. The angle at which they were stacked reminded me of a battery of surface-to-air missiles waiting to be launched.

Roberto wasted no time. He marched across the lawn, whipped out his pendulum, and began dowsing. Melanie and I glanced at each other and smiled.

'Right here,' he announced, digging his heel into the turf.

While Roberto perfected his party trick, his two crew members had manoeuvred the huge generator into next door's field and parked it adjacent to the boundary wall. A more suitable pair of workers I could not have imagined: heavy blokes handling heavy equipment.

Roberto called out to one of them and pointed at his chosen spot. He climbed into the tractor cab and powered her into life. A plume of sooty smoke ejected into the air as he pulled into the middle of the lane. Taking great care, he edged this huge machine between the gateposts and into the driveway. Dad emerged from the kitchen wearing striped pyjamas and a navy blue dressing gown just in time to witness this tricky manoeuvre.

'I wondered what all the noise was about,' he said.

Roberto shouted instructions to the driver as he reversed the beast across the lawn.

'No, no,' shouted Roberto, 'go forward and try again.'

The huge tractor moved back and forth, each turn of the deeply treaded tyres ripping out chunks of turf. Finally, he stopped.

'That's made a mess of the lawn,' remarked Dad.

What had taken two years to create had been destroyed in less than two minutes.

Having positioned the tractor over Roberto's divining intervention, the two roughnecks set about readying the rig for drilling. Using a combination of brute force and precision, they attached the three-metre-long drill head to the turntable. Within minutes, they were ready for action. Ignition pressed, the generator roared into life, ejecting diesel infused fumes into the atmosphere. Slowly, the enormous drill head began to rotate and hydraulic rams lowered it towards the ground. Before it had even touched the lawn a blast of compressed air, running through the centre of the drill shaft, ripped a hole in the turf. Clumps of grass shot across the lawn in all directions.

'I'm going to get a cuppa,' shouted Dad above the racket.

'We'll be with you in a minute,' replied Melanie.

Effortlessly, the foot-wide drill head wormed its way into the ground. With relentless inevitability the slow turning drill sank lower and lower, a monotonous and ear-splitting process. Every two metres the drill stopped and a new section of shaft was added before continuing on its slow descent. Had it not been for the financial implications of these brief pauses, the noise reduction would have been greatly appreciated. As it was, every two metre drop was costing us fifty euros. Talk about a money pit: we were drilling our own.

The action of the drill head was similar to that of an alchemist's pestle, grinding the rock into a fine grey powder. High pressure created by the noisy generator forced this dust to the surface. As the depth increased, a volcano-like mound of ejected debris developed around the well head. Every so often one of the roughnecks shovelled it away, tossing it haphazardly over the lawn. We watched for a while, hoping that water would be discovered just below the surface, but alas no. Deeper and deeper they bored.

'Let's go and get a cuppa,' I said after a while.

'What?' shouted Melanie.

'Cuppa, let's go and get a cuppa!' I screamed above the din.

'Good idea.'

It didn't matter where we were sitting, there was no escaping the booming noise. After what felt like a week but was closer to four hours, the garden fell silent. Had they finally found water?

I glanced at the clock: 1:00 pm, lunchtime. I strolled round to the front, more in hope than expectation. My suspicion was confirmed; the workers had gone for lunch leaving behind an apocalyptic landscape of biblical proportions.

The lush green lawn had been replaced by a wasteland of grey ash. At some point during the morning they'd attached a three-metre-long plastic pipe to the drill head. This had diverted most of the dust into the far corner of the garden. The tubing had acted like a giant air cannon, ejecting dust and debris across the garden at high velocity. Such was its power that it had stripped the cement render off the boundary wall and created a mountainous pile of grey dust.

'¡*Madre de Dios*! What a mess!'

Melanie was speechless.

'I'm going to start moving some of this muck before they get back from lunch,' I added.

I fetched a wheelbarrow and shovel, and started loading.

'Where are you going to tip it?' asked Melanie.

'In the field next door.'

'Do you want a hand?' asked Dad.

'I'll be fine thanks.'

Load after load I wheeled across the lawn, along the driveway, down the lane and into the field. The early morning mist had long since lifted leaving behind a bright sunny day. By the time the workers returned from lunch, I was ready for a break. Within five minutes, they'd slipped into their overalls, fired up the generator, and restarted the drill.

After a relaxing lunch I was itching to see what progress they'd made.

'I'm just going to see how it's going,' I said.

To a Yorkshireman, drilling for water is the financial equivalent of anaesthetic awareness. I knew exactly what was going on but I was powerless to intervene. Every two metres drilled equated to fifty euros spent, and so it went on.

I walked through the house and onto the driveway. One of the roughnecks caught my eye and smiled. A few seconds later his mate noticed me watching and gave me the thumbs up. He was clearly trying to tell me something, but what? That's when I noticed the debris around the top of the drill head. It had changed from grey ash-like dust to a damp cement-like paste. Unless one of them had relieved themselves after their lunchtime refreshments, this could only mean one thing. My heart skipped a beat but I had to be sure.

'*¿Es esta agua* (Is this water)?' I asked, pointing at the glutinous grey paste oozing from the top of the drill.

'*¿Que?*' shouted the drill operator, lifting one cup of his ear protectors.

'*¿Es esta agua?*' I bellowed.

'*Claro* (Of course),' he replied.

At a depth of seventy-two metres, they'd finally hit water. Given the expense, I was half hoping for oil.

'They've hit water,' I announced, as I burst into the kitchen.

'Not before time,' remarked Melanie.

Twenty minutes later the thunderous noise was still echoing around the house.

'I thought you said they'd found water,' said Dad.

'They had.'

Dad's comment demanded further investigation. I went back outside and managed to catch the attention of one of the drillers.

'I thought you'd found water.'

'*¿Que?*'

I repeated my enquiry at the top of my voice. His response was an even broader smile. I suspected that I wasn't the first customer to ask this question. He led me to the far end of the drive where the noise was a little less deafening and explained.

Striking water was one thing but to ensure a constant supply they had to drill down a further ten to fifteen metres. If not, when the water table dropped the well would run dry. Drilling a little deeper now would reduce the risk of future problems.

'Well?' asked Dad, as I went back inside.

'It's an extended warranty,' I remarked.

'What are you talking about?' he asked.

'By extending the hole we're reducing the risk of future problems.'

'What on earth are you babbling on about?' said Melanie.

I explained in a little more detail and the four of us went outside to keep an eye on proceedings. A few minutes later the drill stopped and the generator fell silent.

'We've finished,' called one of the roughnecks. 'You might want to get your camera.'

Throughout the morning I'd been snapping away; it's not every day that one has their own borehole drilled.

'Quickly,' he added.

I dashed inside and snatched the camera off the dining room table.

'Don't stand there. Come over here,' called one of the drillers, as he opened the gate and strolled into the middle of the lane.

Melanie and I chased after him. Dad and Claire kept their distance.

'Are you ready?' he asked.

'Yes,' I replied, pointing the camera at the rig.

'OK,' he called to his co-worker.

His mate pulled a lever on the side of the rig and disappeared behind the tractor. His action released the downward pressure on the drill resulting in a spectacular discharge of water, bursting to the surface and ejecting into the sky like a giant geyser. In less than a minute half the lawn was inches deep in water and still it flowed, gallon upon gallon flooding into the garden.

'When will it stop?' asked Melanie.

The driller shrugged his shoulders and smiled, and still the water kept flowing.

'Is it safe?' she asked.

Apart from the lawn getting a good watering, how dangerous could it be?

No sooner had that thought left my mind than another hit me like a demolition wrecking ball. Positioned in the top corner of the lawn was the subterranean junction box for the domestic electricity supply.

'There's an electricity box in the corner,' I shouted at the driller.

'Electricity box, where?'

I ran through the gates and pointed at the box cover.

'There.'

Fortunately, the garden inclines slightly away from the danger area but inch by inch the water kept creeping up. The ground couldn't absorb it quick enough. As it mixed with the dust, the crystal clear water turned into a pale grey soup, gobbling up the lawn.

'One minute,' said the driller before wading across the lawn to speak with his mate.

The two discussed the problem in a typically Spanish fashion with plenty of expletives, and the occasional thumping on the side of the tractor. By now the water was within a metre of the box and still rising. I stared at them anxiously.

'What are you doing?' asked Melanie as she grabbed my arm.

'I'm going to have a word with them. If they don't do something soon we're going to short out the whole village.'

'Forget the village. If something goes wrong and you're standing in all that water, you're likely to put your own lights out.'

She had a point. No sooner had I changed my mind than they came up with a solution.

'We need to knock a hole in the wall.'

If his statement was meant as a question he was too late. His mate had taken matters into his own hands, picked up a sledgehammer and whacked a hole in the wall. Thankfully, not a moment too soon. Like a scene from *The Dam Busters*, a torrent of grey water burst through the hole and into the adjacent field.

Disaster averted, they began raising the drill head, a slow and laborious job. In total they'd used forty-two sections of shaft at a cost of 2,100 euros. Having removed the head, they set about lining the well with plastic pipe. Remarkably, they managed to coax eighteen five-metre lengths down the hole, cutting the final length off a metre above ground. By 7:30 pm they'd completed the job and capped the well. We thanked them for their efforts and said goodbye.

The lawn looked beyond repair but that was a task for another day. As for the metre length of grey tubing sticking out of the ground, that reminded me of a one fingered salute.

The remainder of Dad and Claire's stay passed without incident but the return trip to the airport began with a most unwelcome sight. As we drove down the lane towards the village, we noticed that Meli's house was encircled with parked cars. Such congestion is attributed to two events, fiestas or bereavement. We feared the worst; Meli's tightly closed *persianas* (window blinds) confirmed our fears. Her youngest son, Jesus, had passed away quietly, surrounded by those he loved. He departed this world from the home in which he entered. At the age of forty, he left behind his wife, Cinda, and their three children: eldest son Brice, fifteen, daughter Anna, ten, and youngest son Jesus Junior, just five years old.

On our return more cars had gathered outside; relatives and friends had arrived to pay their respects. Melanie and I headed home. There would be plenty of time to pass on our condolences.

Since moving to Canabal, Meli had taken us under her wing, giving us help and support whenever we'd asked. Jesus had taught me everything I knew about grapes and viniculture and become our knight in shining armour when everyone else had failed to secure a telephone line.

For over 600 years the bells of the village church of San Pedro have called the faithful to pray for the soul of the passing. The *quietus* or death knell is a medieval ritual. Its peel is hollow and empty, a toneless clang followed seconds later by an equally dispiriting dong. These equidistant chimes repeat over and over, a monotonous sound that eats into the conscience. On that day the bells tolled for Jesus, a young man taken in the prime of life. The *quietus* reminds us all of our own fragile mortality and the value of living life to the full.

The funeral service was held within four days of his death. The 13th century church was packed and hundreds more gathered outside. Four pallbearers carried his coffin through the crowd. His wife Cinda followed, supported by Brice. Halfway to the church she collapsed, crying out in anguish. Brice helped her to her feet, a young man shouldering more responsibility than his years deserved.

After a traditional Catholic service, the priest emerged. The pallbearers carried Jesus to the waiting hearse and the congregation gathered outside for the slow and solemn walk through the village. The funeral procession, led by the priest, ambled past *El Sueño* and on to the walled cemetery. The sepulchres are built in ordered rows, three storeys high. As his father and elder brother were still alive, Jesus was laid to rest in the lowest. The graveside blessing was mercifully brief.

'May his soul and all the souls of the faithful departed through the mercy of God rest in peace.'

Within minutes the crowd had dispersed and Canabal fell silent.

This was our first Spanish funeral but given the age of our neighbours, it wouldn't be our last.

10

Time is of the Essence

Spain's annual shutdown was fast approaching. In less than two weeks, every industry not associated with tourism would be closed for a month. If we didn't get the water plumbed before then, by the time we did, summer would be drawing to a close. On Monday morning we raced into Monforte to speak with Antonio Roca.

'We've had a borehole drilled,' I announced.

Antonio looked stunned. All that expense just to water the lawns.

'Can you give us a quote for installing an irrigation system and connecting the supply to the house?' I asked.

'Sure, I'll call round later today and see what needs doing.'

That afternoon he turned up as promised. I'd spent the weekend trying to clear up the mess in the garden. For all my efforts, the lawn still looked like someone had dumped the sludge from a cement mixer over it.

'Where's the water meter?' asked Antonio.

'Over there,' I said, pointing into the opposite corner of the garden.

'I'll have to cut a channel across the driveway,' he said.

Antonio's vocal tone and facial expression never altered, which made reading him very difficult.

'Is that a problem?' I asked.

'No, no problem.'

Having worked out how to plumb the water into the house he turned his attention to the irrigation system. He began by pacing out the dimensions of the lawns, front and back. I suspected he'd forgotten to bring a tape measure.

'That's all I need for now. I'll get back to you in a few days with a quote.'

True to his word, he returned a few days later. Taking everything into account, 2,160 euros seemed a fair price.

'How soon can you start?' I asked.

'I'll have to order the pump.' He paused for a moment to consider his options. 'How about this Friday?'

'That's great.'

It seemed Antonio was as keen as us to get this job done before the holidays.

'I'll be here at half past nine,' he confirmed, '*mas o menos* (more or less).'

On Friday morning Antonio Roca turned up as arranged, accompanied by two others.

'This is my son,' he said, directing his comment to the younger of the two men.

I'm sure Antonio possesses many admirable qualities but finesse is not one of them. Within minutes of their arrival he'd instructed his lackey to begin excavating trenches for the pipework. It almost brought a tear to my eye watching his mattock-wielding labourer attack the lawn. Where I'd spent hours removing neat strips of turf and carefully excavating narrow channels, he went at it as if he was digging up spuds. Mercifully, most of the new trenches were around the edge of the garden. While he hacked up the lawn, Antonio and his son set about installing the water pump.

'How low do you want this?' asked Antonio, pointing at the metre-tall phallus-like pipe sticking out of the middle of lawn.

It's often the simplest questions I find most difficult to answer. Why would anyone want a length of grey plastic pipe poking out of their lawn? This questions brought into question my understanding of the first question. Had I misunderstood and if so what had he actually asked?

Not for the first time, my dithering made me look like a complete imbecile.

'Do you want it below the lawn or above?' he asked impatiently.

'Below,' I replied quickly.

No sooner had the word left my lips than I began to doubt my decision. Knowledge is gained through teaching or experience; on the subject of capping boreholes, I had neither. Antonio prepared to make his cut.

'Err ... Is it possible to have it level with the lawn?' I asked.

Both Antonio and his son stopped in their tracks, looked up, and stared right at me.

'Level?'

Antonio's response was one of astonishment.

'So that there aren't any obstacles to mow around when I'm cutting the grass,' I explained.

'There'll be a lid on it, like a manhole cover.' replied Antonio. 'That will be level with the lawn.'

Ignorance is bliss, unless you're the ignoramus.

As I'd already made a fool of myself, this seemed like the ideal time to get something else off my chest.

'Where will the pump go?' I asked.

'What?' asked Antonio, with such astonishment you'd think I'd called him a chump, not asked about the pump.

'The pump, where will it go?'

Rephrasing the question brought a smile to Antonio's face.

'It's a submersible; it goes down the hole,' he replied.

I didn't know such things existed. I'd been taught that water and electricity don't mix, yet here they were, tossing an electric pump into a water well.

I'd assumed that it would be housed in a small brick-built shed, next to the well. It's a common sight in many of the surrounding fields. Even the house we sold to Rajan and Mitty had one in the adjacent field. Antonio explained that the depth of the borehole made it easier to push the water to the surface rather than draw it.

'You'd need a pump the size of your house to suck it up,' he joked.

My steep learning curve felt more like an educational oscillation; every answer raised another question.

While Antonio tackled the protruding pipe, his son unloaded the pickup truck. Most of the bed was taken up with two 100 metre coils of 40mm black polypropylene tubing. Behind that was a box of copper fittings, a reel of nylon rope, and the pump: a two-metre-long stainless steel torpedo, heavy enough to need both of them to carry it.

When Antonio cut the ties on the coiled tubing, it catapulted into the air like a Jack-in-the-box. After a lengthy battle, he finally managed to secure one end to the pump. Next job was to tie the nylon rope to it. If anything went wrong, that was the only way to retrieve this expensive piece of equipment. Antonio wrapped the rope around his waist like a rock climber's anchorman and carefully eased the pump into the top of the borehole. For such a calm and unflappable character, he looked decidedly anxious as he began lowering it. Sweat oozed from his brow as he took the strain, and his son grappled with the tubing as he fed it into the hole. Metre by metre it disappeared underground. At a depth of eighty metres they tied it off.

Antonio wasn't one for hanging about. No sooner had

they secured the pump than he started mounting a box on the garden wall to house the electrics. By the end of the day the bulk of the work had been completed. The lawn in the back garden looked like an army of toy soldiers had been digging defensive trenches around the edge; as for the front, the less said about that the better.

'See you on Monday morning,' said Antonio as he pulled the gate closed.

Melanie and I said goodbye and watched as the pickup disappeared from sight.

'Have you seen the state of the lawns?' remarked Melanie.

'They'll recover. It's the sprinklers I'm worried about.'

'Why?'

'Well look,' I replied, pointing at one of them.

'They do seem a bit high.'

'A bit high! That one must be three inches above the lawn.'

The reason for fitting pop-up sprinklers was so that when the system was off, they would retract flush with the ground, enabling the lawnmower to ride over the top.

'So what are you going to do?'

At times like this, my mind echoes back to the past. Long before we moved to Spain, we suffered a nightmare experience at the hands of Bill, known affectionately as Bungalow Bill due to the fact that he had nothing upstairs. Bill was a self-appointed tradesman we found lurking in the small ads. He too lacked finesse and coincidentally called himself a plumber. Having successfully tendered for the installation of a new bathroom suite, we instructed him to proceed. I'd like to say that he won the tender based on his excellent references and competitive price but as the only person to submit a quote, we had little choice.

After five days of disruption that included flooding the bathroom and the staircase, driving a nail through a floorboard into a water pipe, and grouting everything except the tiles, we finally asked him to leave. I spent the following two weeks correcting his mistakes and finishing the job. Drawing comparisons with Antonio was a little unfair, although some of the parallels were uncanny.

'I'll have a word with him on Monday,' I replied.

I spent the weekend sitting on my hands, anxious to rectify Antonio's shoddy workmanship but reluctant to start without giving him the chance to do it himself. First thing Monday I relayed my concerns.

'Sand.'

'Sand?' I replied quizzically.

'Sand.'

His suggestion was to create a small hillock around the sprinkler head using sand. The suggestion sounded ridiculous. As if a small mound of sand would protect a plastic sprinkler from a stainless steel lawnmower blade powered by a three and a half horse power petrol engine, spinning at over 2,500 revolutions per minute. The word that sprang to mind rhymed with hillock but began with a *p*. It seemed that Antonio Roca and Bungalow Bill may well have evolved from the same gene pool after all.

Antonio spent the morning putting the finishing touches to his handiwork, and the afternoon showering himself with water while testing and adjusting his creation. To his credit, by the time he headed home we had a fully functioning automatic irrigation system that despite appearances worked pretty well. We also had a domestic supply plumbed into the house.

'Can we drink the water?' asked Melanie.

'Antonio said we should wait a week or so before drinking it.'

'What about cooking?'

'Providing we boil it, there's no problem. We'll leave it a week and then get it tested,' I added.

A week later I went to the *farmacia*, bought an empty water sampling bottle, took a sample, and returned it to them for testing.

'How long will the results take?' I asked.

'About four days,' replied the chemist. 'We have to send it to a laboratory in Monforte.'

A week later I returned.

'Hola, I'm here for the results of my water test,' I said to the chemist.

My innocent request received a few raised eyebrows from a number of the queueing customers.

'One minute.'

Moments later she returned and handed me an envelope. Eager to read the results, I opened it straight away.

ANALISIS BACTERIOLOGICO

Determinación		Unidades	V. Paramétrico
Recuento de germens aerobios totales (37°C)		UFC/1 ml	20
Recuento de germens totales (22°C)		UFC/1 ml	100
Enterococo………………………………		UFC/100ml	0
Coliformes totales………………………	6	UFC/100ml	0
Escherichia coli…………………………	0	UFC/100ml	0
Clostridium perfringens (inclu esporas)		UFC/100ml	0
Salmonella spp…………………………		/100ml	Ausencia

CALIFICACIÓN

La muestra se considera
SANITARIAMENTE **NO APTA** PARA EL CONSUMO HUMANO

"*No apta para el consumo humano*": I didn't like the sound of that.

'Excuse me, could you explain what this means?' I asked, holding out the analysis sheet and pointing at the appropriate section.

'The laboratory couldn't approve your sample for drinking,' she replied.

I drove home disappointed.

'The water's not fit to drink,' I said, as I entered the kitchen.

'Why not?'

'I'm not sure. I'll have to look on the internet.'

Over the next few hours I found out more about public water quality than it's healthy to know. According to the test results, the sample I provided had six coliforms per hundred millilitres. Drinking water should have less than one. I also discovered that my less than scientific method of collecting the sample might be to blame.

My first mistake was handling the sample bottle. Breaking the seal on the cap, unscrewing it and taking a sniff inside is not advised, quite the contrary. Needless to say, cross contamination hadn't been uppermost in my thoughts. As for the actual water sample, that too was hardly the cleanest. I simply filled the bottle from the outside tap. What I should have done was run the water for at least fifteen minutes before taking the sample.

'Shock chlorination,' I announced confidently, as I walked onto the terrace.

'Excuse me.'

'That's what we need to do to the well.'

'And what exactly is that?'

'It's the bacterial equivalent of an atomic bomb.'

'Bomb!' replied Melanie, alarmed by the suggestion.

'Metaphorically speaking.'

'And where do we get this metaphoric warhead from?'

'I'm not sure. Maybe the swimming pool shop in town can help. If not, they might know someone who can.'

That afternoon, armed with our *Analisis Bateriologico*, we set off for the swimming pool shop in Monforte. As we arrived, the shop owner was about to leave.

'How can I help you?' he asked.

'Do you sell chlorine?'

'What is it for?'

I knew he was going to ask that and I hadn't a clue what the Spanish term for shock chlorination treatment was. As per usual I made it up and hoped for the best.

'*Un golpe de clorinación.*'

'*¿Que* (What)?'

'It's like a bomb,' I replied, 'of chlorine.'

'*Una bomba*,' he repeated.

'Show him the paper,' urged Melanie.

Good idea. I pulled the envelope out and handed him the analysis.

'*¿Que pasa* (What's matter)?' he asked, after reading the results.

'The conclusion states that the water is not drinkable.'

'You mean this,' he said, pointing at the number of total coliforms.

'Yes.'

'Bah, you don't need to worry about that,' he replied. 'Six coliform per hundred millilitres, that's nothing.'

'Nothing!'

'*Nada, nunca, nada.*'

He could see from our expression that we weren't convinced.

'Is it a well or a borehole?' he asked.

'A borehole.'

'And how deep is it?'

'Eighty-four metres.'

'Eighty-four metres!' he repeated. 'You won't have anything to worry about at eighty-four metres. *Nada, nunca, nada.*'

His insistence, and my internet research, persuaded me that we had nothing to worry about. I felt quite relieved. The thought of nuking our water with gallons of chlorine seemed at best a little extreme and at worst downright dangerous.

'Are you sure it'll be safe?' asked Melanie on the way home.

'I'll tell you what, I'll try it for a few weeks; if I survive then we know it's safe.'

'And if not.'

'If not … Make sure I give you the passwords before I pop my clogs.'

Needless to say, I lived to tell the tale and Melanie is still waiting for the passwords to the bank account. Having suffered no visible side effects, Jazz soon joined me in our watery experiment; a week later, Melanie decided it was safe to give it a go.

'See, I told you there was nothing to worry about.'

'*A ver* (we'll see),' she replied.

'Talking about water, when do Richard, Yvonne and the kids get here?' I asked.

Richard, Yvonne, and their kids, Mason and Erren, spent a memorable holiday with us last summer. When they'd asked to visit again this year, we were delighted to welcome them back to *El Sueño* and I for one was looking forward to the inevitable chaos. As for Melanie, she couldn't wait to see how tall her goddaughter Erren had grown.

When it came to watering the lawns, Mason proved to be a willing helper and revelled at the chance of spraying Uncle Craig with the garden hose. Such a shame; the new sprinklers would end all that.

'This Tuesday,' replied Melanie.

I couldn't believe it. Time was passing at an alarming rate.

'Let's get some more inflatable toys for the kids.' I said.

Last year we bought them a blow-up reptile and christened it Gary Gator. At the time, Melanie thought I was mad. 'You can't buy a four-year-old child an eight-foot-long inflatable crocodile. You'll scare the living daylights out of him,' she'd said. Having once been a four-year-old boy, I knew different and the surprise on Mason's face when I pulled it out of the shed and sent it skimming across the pool was a picture.

That weekend I found the perfect addition to our inflatable collection.

'Look at this,' I said, showing Melanie the picture on the front of the box.

'Lovely,' she replied, with a hint of sarcasm.

'They'll love it, and it's only twelve euros.'

'How much?'

'It must be inflation.'

The latest addition to our swimming pool inflatables was Stinger, a bright red dinghy with yellow go-faster stripes down both sides and a chequered flag attached to the stern. That evening, our Teatime Taster was delayed due to a lack of puff.

'It's bigger than it looks on the box,' I remarked, gasping for air. 'You can give me a hand if you like.'

'You seem to be managing just fine,' replied Melanie.

Within half an hour, Gary Gator and Stinger the dingy were ready for action. After catching my breath, so was I.

Three days later, the Kershaw family descended on *El Sueño* like a domestic coup d'état. It certainly looked that way when a nine seater minibus pulled onto the driveway.

'Don't worry,' called Yvonne as she stepped down from the cab, 'we asked for a six seater and this is all they had.'

By the time she'd finished her explanation, Mason had slid open the side door, flung himself into the arms of Melanie, hugged me, and ran through the house dragging his carry-on behind him.

'Mason, slow down!' called his mother, but he was on a mission and no amount of parental guidance was going to get in his way.

Erren, now two and a half, had changed from a tottering, unintelligible cherub into a proper little person. No sooner had Yvonne released her from the security of her car seat than she leapt from the bus and threw herself into the arms of Aunty Mel, followed swiftly by an equally warm embrace for yours truly. By the time we'd unpacked the luggage and made our way into the back garden,

Mason was paddling on the top step of the pool wearing nothing but his birthday suit. Two minutes later, Erren had joined him.

'Come and have some suntan lotion put on,' called Yvonne.

'Do we have to?' moaned Mason.

'Yes.'

'Just a minute.'

It's strange how kids can always find something better to do for sixty seconds.

'No, now.'

One by one they sauntered over to Mum who daubed them generously with factor fifty.

'Mum,' complained Erren, wriggling like a freshly landed trout.

'Mason, put your hat on,' called Yvonne as he took Stinger out on its maiden voyage.

'Do I have to?'

'Yes.'

'Do I have to as well Mum?' asked Erren.

'Yes darling, you have to as well.'

Launching Stinger sent Jazz into an excited frenzy. She dashed around the pool barking uncontrollably at the bright red dinghy.

Woof, woof, woof, woof!

'Jazz, calm down.'

My calls fell on deaf ears.

'What's she barking at Uncle Craig?' asked Erren as she donned her cap.

'She's just excited,' I explained.

'Dad, are you coming in?' called Mason.

'Yeah, go on Dad,' pleaded Erren.

'In a minute,' replied Richard.

It's strange how dads can always find something better to do for sixty seconds.

'Come on Dad,' called Mason.

'In a minute.'

This pandemonium continued all afternoon, punctuated briefly by chicken nuggets and baked beans. Refuelling complete, normal service was resumed. I hardly moved from the safety of my garden chair but by bedtime I felt exhausted.

'Can Uncle Craig read us a story?' asked Erren, staring at me with wistful eyes.

Where everyone else had failed, Roald Dahl's *The BFG* succeeded in bringing peace and tranquillity back to *El Sueño*. I restricted my narration to one chapter, much to the consternation of my audience.

'If you go to sleep, I'll read you another chapter tomorrow,' I promised.

Their four-night stay passed in the blink of an eye. We managed to fit in a trip to Portugal and a cruise down the river Miño; Yvonne was determined to expand their horizon beyond the limits of our swimming pool. All too soon we were wishing them a safe journey home and adjusting back to a more peaceful life.

During their stay, Melanie had worked tirelessly to make sure everyone got fed and watered, on time and in sufficient quantity. A night off from the kitchen would give us both a break.

'Let's go out for dinner,' I suggested.

'That's a great idea.'

'La Maja?'

'Sounds good to me.'

Soon after its opening, the restaurant La Maja in Monforte had quickly become our favourite. A delicious combination of Italian bistro meets traditional gallego. The restaurant was packed when we arrived so we stood in the entrance scouring the room for a spare table. That's when I spotted them.

'Look, Carol, Gerry, and Malcom,' I said.

We walked over to say hello. They'd arrived from the UK earlier in the day for their annual Galician getaway. I greeted Carol with a customary kiss on both cheeks and Gerry with a firm handshake. Like many people with Down's syndrome, Malcom wears his emotions on his sleeve and was eager to greet us. In the middle of the crowded restaurant, he sprang to his feet; wrapped his arms around me in a loving embrace and kissed me repeatedly on the cheek.

'Malcolm, leave him alone,' insisted Carol.

It would be easy to feel embarrassed in such circumstances but Malcolm had a way of turning what would otherwise be an awkward moment into a memorable one. As for the other diners, the sight of two middle-aged men embracing each other in a busy restaurant, with one repeatedly kissing the other, didn't seem to bother anyone.

'Malcolm, that's enough. Sit down!' Carol pulled him away and gently persuaded him to take his seat.

'You must come round for lunch,' suggested Melanie. 'How does Thursday sound?'

We agreed a time and left them to finish their meal.

The following morning, we received some great news.

Ring ring … Ring ring!

'I'll get it,' said Melanie, rushing to the phone.

Within seconds the conversation was over.

'Who was that?' I asked.

'The hospital, calling about my physiotherapy appointment.'

We'd been so busy since Melanie's exploratory knee surgery in May that I'd almost forgotten about the physio. Mind you, it wasn't me that had to put up with the discomfort.

'That's good. When will you be starting?'

'The day after tomorrow.'

'Crikey! They don't mess around once they get started but isn't that when Carol, Gerry and Malcolm are coming for lunch?'

'The appointment is for first thing so we should be OK.'

On the morning of her appointment, Melanie drove herself to the hospital while I made preparations for lunch. Within three hours, she was pulling back into the driveway.

'Well?' I asked.

'Well,' she said, pausing for a moment, 'that was the easiest physiotherapy session I've ever had.'

Melanie's response surprised me. From personal experience, I've always found physiotherapy to be less like therapy and more like medieval torture.

'What did you have to do?'

'Lay on a bed with a circle of magnets around my knee.'

'Magnets?'

'Magnets. The most difficult part was trying to read the Spanish magazine the nurse gave me to pass the time.'

'And what's it supposed to achieve?'

'I've no idea, but it's a very popular treatment.'

'I'm not surprised. So what happens next?'

'Well,' she paused again, 'as patients were leaving they kept saying *hasta mañana* (see you tomorrow) to the nurse, so when I left I asked if I needed to come back tomorrow; she said yes, you have to come every day.'

'Every day!'

'Except weekends.'

'And how long do you have to go for?'

'She didn't say.'

I couldn't believe it. Ten years earlier I suffered a similar knee injury. Back then my GP referred me to an orthopaedic specialist. After a thirteen-month wait, I finally got to see him. The consultation lasted two minutes, just long enough for him to ask what was wrong and refer me to a physiotherapist. Their assessment afforded me four half-hour appointments spanning four weeks. On my final visit the physio sent me away with a sheet of printed instructions and told me to exercise at home. Contrast that to Melanie's experience.

She saw a consultant within two months of being referred by her GP. He conducted a thorough physical examination before requesting a series of X-rays. When these failed to reveal the problem he sent her for an MRI scan. After a second consultation and a further MRI scan proved inconclusive, he recommended exploratory keyhole surgery to diagnose the problem.

His determination to identify the cause of Melanie's discomfort was matched by his desire to resolve it. She would undergo a course of daily physiotherapy treatment for an undefined period of time. If that proved unsuccessful, the consultant would surgically repair the damaged ligament.

Within two hours of Melanie returning home, Carol, Gerry and Malcolm arrived for a long, lazy lunch at *El Sueño*. Malcolm is a man of routine and we were privileged to be included in his holiday habits. Taking a dip in the pool was now part of his must-do holiday experiences. Given the look on his face as Melanie and Gerry supported his descent into the water, you might not have thought so. Neither Jerry Lewis nor Jim Carrey could come close to Malcolm's exaggerated facial expression as the cool water rose up his alabaster frame. But once in, he revelled in the experience and the attention.

11

Action Plan

Throughout the summer, breakfast on the back terrace had become another much-loved ritual.

'Coffee's ready,' called Melanie.

'Coming,' I replied.

I'd been in the office, checking the emails.

'You're not going to believe this,' I announced, as I stepped into the sunlight.

'What?'

'We've had another email from Pilar about the house.'

'And?'

'You'd better take a look after breakfast.'

Some things are too important to interrupt; breakfast in the sunshine is one of them. After soaking up the rays and supping our kick-starter coffee, we wandered through into the office.

From: "Pilar Xxxxxx"
To: Craig Briggs
Subject: latest news

Date: Fri, 29 July 2005 00:25:02

Hi Mr. Briggs:

Sorry for not replaying before, but i was away on a short holiday... yesterday we went to Lugo... and sincerely there is not much news about the papers... we found that the certificate they gave us before was for half of the house... and there is no number for the garden.

We decided to go to Lugo, since the woman from the Notary told us that they should give us in the catastro a negative certificate and with that they could do all the papers... but once there we found that this was not all true since they only give you this certificate with for a house town not for a village... you could imagen how upset we were... all the journey for nothing... they gave us another solution which was to take almost an architect to measure the house and the garden, and once signed take it back to Lugo.. and we did it yesterday... so as soon as we have this papers with the measures done we will take it again to Lugo.. sincerely i never thought this will give us so much trouble.. but once on it we will get to the end...

As you can see with all this difficulties we can not give you a date... these type of papers take more time than one can imaginen, since they work very slowly...

We are doing our best, so once we have news we will let you know.

See you soon

Pilar

'She likes her full stops,' remarked Melanie.
'Grammar aside, what do you think?'
'What can we do? We'll just have to wait.'
Melanie was right. The hold-up was annoying but we'd found the property we wanted and had no desire to start searching for another. We had little choice but to wait for

the slow turning wheels of Spanish bureaucracy to run their course.

'We've also had an email from Bob; they've booked their flights and would love to take us up on our offer to stay here.'

'When are they coming?'

'The 7th until the 13th of September.'

'That gives us plenty of time to tidy up,' remarked Melanie. 'Do you want another coffee?'

'Why not?' It's wasn't as if we had anything planned.

We ambled back outside and slumped into our garden chairs, contemplating the day ahead.

'Can you smell that?'

The unmistakable aroma of woodsmoke drifted across the garden. For many, this alluring fragrance is associated with cosy winter nights snuggled in front of an open fire. During a Spanish summer, it conjures up very different images.

'There's a fire somewhere,' replied Melanie.

We stood up and scoured the horizon searching for a telltale sign. The long hot summer was starting to take its toll on the Galician countryside. Forest fires were breaking out all over the province. Giant conflagrations were destroying millions of hectares of forestry. Reports suggested that more fires had been fought over the last seven months than in the previous ten years. Many are started by thoughtless smokers tossing burning cigarette butts from speeding vehicles but their number and frequency had led to rumours of disgruntled council workers starting them deliberately. Whatever the cause, a raging fire and a strong wind are a terrifying combination.

'Over there,' said Melanie, pointing east.

Beyond the immediate hill, a funnel-like cloud mushroomed into the atmosphere. As it climbed, the charcoal black cloud softened to a pastel grey.

'Wow! Did you see that?'

In the blink of an eye, the base of the funnel doubled in

size, sending thick black smoke billowing into the air.

'How far away do you think it is?'

'Too far to trouble us,' I replied.

Melanie looked unconvinced. The strengthening breeze brought a heavy scent of burning wood, and ashen flakes floated through the air like dusty snowflakes.

'What's that?' asked Melanie, holding out the palm of her hand and catching one.

'It looks like ash.'

'Ash!'

'Don't worry, it's miles away.'

Even I was beginning to doubt my optimism as we stared out across the fields at the expanding cloud, and then I heard it.

'Listen.'

'What?' asked Melanie.

'Can't you hear it?'

'What?'

'An aircraft.'

'Is it a fire plane?' asked Melanie, sounding relieved.

'I expect so.'

In less than a minute the single-seater aircraft came into view.

'There it is,' I said excitedly, pointing into the sky.

As it flew overhead, I could hear every ignition stroke of its slow revving engine. Moments later, a second plane appeared on the horizon following a similar flight path.

'And look over there,' I added, pointing to the south.

Melanie diverted her gaze southward as the unmistakable whirring of a jet propelled helicopter filled the air. Hanging beneath its fuselage, like a giant teardrop, was an enormous sack filled to capacity with fire-quenching water. Our aerial saviours had arrived.

On reaching the seat of the fire, the first plane circled the menacing cloud calculating his perfect angle of attack. Confident in his aerial ability, he banked sharply to the left and dived into the cloud. We waited with bated breath as it disappeared into the dense smoke. A few seconds later it reappeared, climbing steeply through a mixture of smoke and steam like a mechanical phoenix. Payload delivered, he headed back to base to collect more extinguishing agent. Having watched his colleague, the second aircraft began its approach. Once again the plane hurtled headlong into the dense smoke, reappearing moments later. Next into the fray was the helicopter, looking slightly more Steady Eddie than Dashing Dan. Time after time they returned to deliver their lifesaving load. After an hour or so, they'd tamed the raging inferno and reduced the billowing funnel to little more than a smoke signal.

'There's another over there,' I said, pointing in the same direction.

Hiding behind the nearest smoke cloud was another, further away but bigger than the first. Throughout the day the distant drone of the aerial firefighters drifted in and out on the warm breeze. Come dusk, the sky fell silent: aircraft and aviators grounded by the fading light. Aerial advantage had been lost but the battle raged on. Hopes now rested with the local *bomberos*, a small band of brothers, many of whom are part time. Foot soldiers in the fight to halt the advancing inferno.

As dusk succumbed to darkness, a distant glow fringed the horizon. Tall trees silhouetted against the raging blaze flickered like insects caught in the glare of headlights. The fire seemed much closer in the darkness but I felt sure we had nothing to worry about.

'It's about time we were turning in,' I suggested.

I had hoped the fire would be out before we hit the sack but it wasn't.

'It looks awfully close,' said Melanie.

'It's miles away and anyway, I'm sure we'll get plenty of warning if it does move this way.'

Eventually we managed to nod off. The lateness of the hour and a good bottle of red will take its toll on the best of us.

When we woke the following morning, the only signs of the previous day's drama were the speckled remnants of ash laying on the floor of the swimming pool.

'Guess what I'll be doing this morning?' I said, staring into the pool.

'I can think of worse jobs,' replied Melanie.

A week later we welcomed Bob and Janet to *El Sueño*. Their arrival coincided with our Teatime Taster. We sat at the far end of the garden, soaking up the last rays of sunshine and catching up on news. What better way to unwind after a long day travelling?

In contrast to their visit earlier in the year, they seemed upbeat and positive and after a good night's sleep were keen to get things moving.

'So, how do you think we should proceed?' asked Bob over breakfast.

'It's funny you should ask that; since your last email I've been busy putting together an action plan.'

Bob smiled as if to say, I thought you might. I handed him a copy and we worked our way through it.

1. Clear the courtyard and outbuildings of all the rubbish.
2. Get a quote for demolishing the outbuildings, landscaping the courtyard, and finishing all the outstanding building work.
3. Furnish the house and dress it for guests.
4. Create a marketing campaign for holiday letting.
5. Manage the bookings and look after ongoing maintenance.

'What do you think?' I asked.

Most of my ideas aligned with theirs. Our involvement gave them the opportunity to fulfil these goals.

'It looks like you're going to be busy,' joked Janet.

'We can make a start on clearing the outbuildings as

soon as you've gone,' I replied.

'*We* can, can *we*?' said Melanie with a cheeky smile.

'We might need to hire a van to get rid of everything,' I added.

'That's fine,' replied Bob. 'Just let us know how much it costs.'

'As for furnishing the place, there's a shop in Ourense that sells budget furniture.'

'Perhaps we can go and take a look later today,' suggested Janet.

'Why not?'

'What about the demolition work?' asked Bob.

'I think we should ask Manolo to give us a quote.'

Manolo had been recommended to us by our neighbour, Mariano. We'd used him on a couple of jobs and he'd proved to be hardworking, personable, and very competitively priced. He describes himself as an *albañil* or general builder: Jack of all trades, master of none.

'We're happy to go along with your suggestion,' replied Bob.

'As for marketing and managing the holiday let, there's not a lot we can do until all the other work is finished.'

'Are you sure you don't mind looking after the place for us?' asked Janet.

'We'd be happy to,' replied Melanie.

That afternoon we drove the forty kilometres into the city of Ourense. Bob and Janet were on a tight budget and we knew just the place to find bargains: EcoMoble, a shop specialising in affordable furniture. Within the space of an hour, they'd ordered a kitchen table and six chairs, a two-seater settee and a three-seater settee for the *galleria*, two three-seater settees (one of which converted into a sprung double bed) for the lounge, three small coffee tables, a TV cabinet, a large mirror, a double bed with headboard, two bedside tables, a double wardrobe, two single beds with headboards, one bedside table, and a double wardrobe for the guest bedroom.

'I can't believe we've furnished the entire house for a little over 2,000 euros,' said Janet.

Buying furniture was one thing but transforming their abandoned house into a warm and inviting home would take a lot of imagination and a bit more cash. Sourcing inexpensive home furnishings wasn't going to be easy. Finding those extra special bargains would take time and effort. With that in mind, we agreed a modest budget and they left us to work our magic.

Their stay at *El Sueño* seemed all too brief. The weather had been excellent and with the exception of our shopping trip to Ourense, they'd managed to take full advantage of it.

'I can't believe we're leaving already,' said Janet, on the morning of their departure.

'When you're next here, you won't recognise the place,' I said.

'I can't wait to come back,' she replied.

'Keep in touch and let us know how things are going,' said Bob, as he loaded their luggage into the back of the car.

'Will do,' I replied, 'and as soon as we've emptied the outbuildings and tidied up the courtyard, I'll ask Manolo to prepare a quote for the rest of the work.'

'OK, see you both soon.'

We strolled into the lane and waved goodbye as they trundled off through the village.

'How much work is there to do in the courtyard?' asked Melanie, as we ambled back inside.

'I'm not too sure. I haven't really had a good look.'

'Well don't forget that your sister is coming at the end of the month to help with the grape harvest.'

'It won't take us that long to clear them out.'

'She'll be here in a fortnight.'

I could tell from her tone that she wasn't convinced.

'I tell you what, after lunch we'll go and take a look.'

The temperature read thirty-two degrees Celsius as we drove down the lane en route to Bob and Janet's. Their house is situated on the outskirts of Ferreira, the village we'd lived in during our first year here. It lies at the end of a short, unmade track in the middle of a small hamlet. Two-metre-tall gates guard the entrance to a small enclosed courtyard. I reversed down the lane and parked outside the gates.

'What's matter?' asked Melanie, as I fought to turn the key.

'There's something wrong with the lock. Hang on, I think I've got it.'

The key turned but the gates still wouldn't open.

'Now what?' asked Melanie.

'Something's not right,' I moaned in frustration. 'The chuffing things are stuck.'

'Well how did you open them before?'

'I didn't, Bob did. Just stand back.'

'Do be careful.'

Holding the gate handle down, I stepped back as far as my arm would reach and launched myself into the iron gate. As it sprang open, my momentum sent me hurtling into the courtyard. Unprepared for this sudden entry, I tripped over the stone threshold and flew head over heels.

'Are you alright?' asked Melanie, looking rather concerned.

'I'm fine, but those bloody gates are no good. We can't have holidaymakers fighting their way in.'

New gates shot to the top of my "Things to discuss with Bob" list. Slowly, I picked myself up and dusted myself down.

'You've got to be kidding me,' said Melanie, scanning the surrounding outbuildings.

'What?'

'Look at all this, this …'

'Clutter,' I interrupted.

'That's not the word I was thinking of.'

Barging open the gates revealed the enormity of the task. The surface of the courtyard was little more than a wafer-thin skim of cracked and flaking cement, colonised by metre-tall weeds. On the left was the recently renovated house. Opposite that a derelict barn, filled to the rafters with junk. Another barn occupied the right hand side of the courtyard and opposite that stood the remnants of a lean-to which had been partially demolished to make room for a narrow breakfast terrace, accessed from the kitchen.

'The first thing we need to do is get rid of these weeds.'

Melanie looked at me as if I'd lost my marbles.

'That's all well and good but what on earth are we going to do with all this … clutter?'

Good question; what were we going to do with it?

'I've got an idea,' I said.

'What?'

'Let's ask the Romanies if they want it.'

'The Romanies?'

'Why not? There's lots of timber in there. That must be worth something to them.'

'And how we supposed to get it to them?'

Melanie had a point. It wasn't as if we could load it into our little hatchback; there was far too much of it.

'I know,' I said, 'we'll get them to collect it.'

I could tell from Melanie's expression that my madcap idea might actually work, although she did have some reservations.

'Do you think that's wise?'

I knew exactly what she meant. Rightly or wrongly, Romanies have acquired an unenviable reputation for unreliability. Despite this, I felt we had nothing to lose by asking.

'It can't harm to ask. Let's see if they're interested.'

'Right now?'

'Why not? If they agree, we can start tidying the place up first thing in the morning.'

'OK, let's go.'

Tucked away down a dusty track on the outskirts of Monforte is the council's recycling centre. Within a walled and gated enclosure are a number of steel containers each with their own designation. The centre is manned three days a week and kept secure the rest of the time. Surrounding this guarded enclosure is a ragtag community of Romany families. They exist on the fringe of society in temporary dwellings built from used breeze blocks and corrugated tin sheeting.

We first encountered them when we were clearing out the *bodegas* of the house we sold to Rajan and Mitty. That initial encounter was quite intimidating. As we'd neared the entrance to the recycling centre they'd circled the car, curious to see what was on board. Thankfully, they were far more interested in our rubbish than us. Over the course of the next week or so we had got to know them quite well and welcomed their interest. The more they dragged from the car, the less we had to haul into the skips.

As we drove slowly down the dusty track towards the centre, half-clothed kids were playing in the dirt with undernourished hounds. Most of the men were busy cannibalising two beat-up white vans in an attempt to get a third one running. I pulled up outside a shack where a gaunt man was sitting on a makeshift bench watching the men working on the vans.

'Hola,' I said as we stepped from the car.

'¿*Que* (What)?' he asked, viewing us with suspicion.

'I have some wood at my house if you want it. It's free,' I added.

'Wait here.'

The man walked down the lane to the next shack, kicking up dust as he dragged his feet. He shouted someone's name and a young woman came to the door.

'What?' she asked.

'This man has some wood he wants rid of,' he said. 'It's free.'

The woman called into the house and a young man appeared. It looked as if she'd woken him but given everyone else's appearance, it was difficult to tell. After a brief explanation he sauntered across to us.

'You have some wood?' he asked.

'That's right.'

'Can't you bring it here?'

'There's too much to bring in the car,' I replied.

'Where do you live?'

I tried to explain but he hadn't a clue where I was talking about.

'Come here tomorrow at one o'clock and I'll follow you there,' he said.

His request seemed reasonable and at least, this way, we knew he'd turn up.

'*Hasta mañana* (See you tomorrow),' I said, as we readied to leave.

He reciprocated with a grunting sound that could have meant anything.

The following morning, we drove up to Bob and Janet's. The more we could do before we met our Romany friend, the better. We started by clearing the weeds.

'There's stuff everywhere,' said Melanie.

By mid-morning we'd managed to clear a broad pathway to the main barn, which stretched the width of the property.

'There's loads of wood in here, good looking planks as well,' I said.

'No!'

'No what?'

'The only good looking plank I need is you,' replied Melanie.

By midday, we'd either pulled up or hacked down all the weeds surrounding the courtyard and tossed them into the adjacent plot.

'It's about time we set off to meet your new mate,' said

Melanie, checking her watch.

Twenty minutes later we were trundling down the dusty track to the recycling centre. No sooner had we pulled up than our would-be wood recycler stepped out to meet us. A woman, who we presumed was his wife, followed him.

'Hola,' I called from the car.

He acknowledged my greeting with a nod; then he and his missus climbed into the cab of a tatty old box van.

Before long we were driving up the main road heading out of the Val de Lemos. The steepness of the climb slowed the van's advance. At one point I wondered if it would make it. Thankfully, it did.

'It's the last house,' I said, pointing down the track.

I parked at the top while our friend reversed down. Having unlocked the gates, his wife jumped from the cab and guided him through. With great precision he manoeuvred the van to within a metre of the barn.

'All this?' he asked, with a broad sweep of his arm.

'Everything,' I replied.

He flung open the back doors and began loading planks of chestnut.

'Would you like a hand?' I asked.

'No.'

At least I'd offered. Our man of little words worked without pausing, sliding plank after plank into the back. Half full, the vehicle let out a squeal of complaint as the suspension sank lower and lower.

'He'll have to stop soon,' I whispered.

'Look at the tyres,' said Melanie.

The back tyres looked as if they would explode at any minute but still he loaded. Only when it was physically impossible to slide another board inside did he stop. Despite his efforts, he'd hardly scratched the surface.

'Do you want the rest of it?' I asked.

'I'll call back.'

'Today?'

'Tomorrow,' he replied.

151

He wouldn't be the first Romany to give that assurance and I'm sure he won't be the last. At least we knew where to find this one.

In its heyday, his 1990s Renault Master had a load capacity of over 1,500 kilos. Packing twice that amount into the back hardly seemed the wisest decision. If he could coax it to the top of the track, the rest of his journey was downhill.

He jumped inside and fired her up. With a cough and a splutter, and a plume of thick black smoke it reluctantly turned over. Slowly it moved forward, creaking as it squeezed through the gateway and crept up the track. I felt relieved to see it turn down the lane and disappear out of sight. I'd had visions of the three of us trying to push it.

Three days later he still hadn't returned. We'd used the time wisely and managed to empty all the outbuildings. We'd sorted the rubbish into two piles, flammable and inflammable.

'We'll have to go and see if he still wants it,' I suggested.

Save for a few flea-bitten dogs, the recycling encampment seemed deserted as we drove down the track. No sooner had I parked than a door opened and the wood man's wife stepped out.

'He's not here,' she called.

'Do you still want the wood?'

'He's busy with the grape harvest.'

Hardly the answer I was looking for but casual workers are at a premium at this time of year.

'When will he be finished?'

She didn't know. We needed to find a new solution.

'What are we going to do now?' asked Melanie.

'We'll have to hire a van and shift it ourselves.'

'And where are we going to shift it to?'

'What about Sergio?' I suggested. 'There's more than enough wood to keep him warm this winter.'

'That's a great idea.'

Sergio lives in the village with his wife and two young children. He describes himself as an artisan. At least that's what the hand-painted sign at the end of the pathway leading to his house states. He manages to earn a meagre living from making handicrafts and selling them at local markets and fiestas. It's fair to say that Melanie and I have chosen a less conventional way of life; as for Sergio, his lifestyle can only be described as unconventional.

When we asked if he wanted the wood, he jumped at the chance. Hiring a van added a cost element to the job so we spent the next two days working our socks off. We delivered all the wood to Sergio and took everything else to the recycling centre. By the time we dropped off the hire van, we were knackered. In less than a week we'd tidied up the courtyard and cleared out every scrap of unwanted rubbish.

'We'll speak to Manolo tomorrow and ask him to quote for demolishing the barns,' I said on the way home.

We knew from experience that the best time to speak with Manolo was between 1:30 pm and 3:00 pm, as he never misses lunch at home.

'Can you take a look at what needs doing and prepare a quote for us?' I asked.

'Where is the house?'

Having repeatedly said *a la izquierda* (on the left) instead of *a la derecha* (on the right), Manolo looked as confused as I'd sounded.

'I'll call at your house and follow you up there,' he suggested.

Feeling slightly red faced, I agreed.

'When?' I asked.

'As soon as I can,' he replied.

He was in the middle of fixing someone's roof and didn't want to break off until it was watertight. For the time being, we would have to wait. Everything was going to plan and a short delay gave us the opportunity to get ready for this year's *vendimia* (grape harvest).

12

Dead Centre

Life in a rural Spanish village is immeasurably different to that of an industrial town in northern England. Here in Canabal, each new day begins with the melody of birdsong; anything else is unusual and unwelcome.

'What on earth is that noise?' moaned Melanie.

I hadn't a clue but the teeth-tingling sound was getting louder and louder. Curious to discover the culprit, I whipped back the duvet, mooched across to the window and flung open the shutters. A large earthmover was creeping slowly out of the village and heading our way. I'd never seen anything like it. Mounted on the front of the vehicle was a large steel blade. The driver was following the line of the drainage ditch running down the side of the lane. While one side of the blade gouged out the ditch, the other scraped along the asphalt, creating an unholy racket.

'It looks like they're clearing out the drainage ditch.'

'Do they have to do it at this time in a morning?' complained Melanie.

By the time we'd got out of bed, the earthmover had driven past *El Sueño* and disappeared out of sight. An hour later it scratched its way down the other side of the lane and back into the village. Its presence caused quite a stir. Villagers gathered in the lane to see what was going on and offer the driver some words of advice. As usual, everyone had an opinion and they were determined to air it.

'They're going to resurface the lane,' said Meli, as she wandered past the house on her way to the cemetery. 'A waste of money if you ask me.'

Given the traffic flow, Meli had a point; it's rare to see more than five vehicles a day passing the house.

'How long will that take?' asked Melanie.

'I've no idea,' she replied.

Over the next few days a small team of navvies worked tirelessly to prepare the lane for resurfacing. Three days into the work, a pickup truck stopped at the entrance to the cemetery. The truck was liveried with the Xunta de Galicia (Council of Galicia) logo. Two men jumped out and began digging a hole at the side of the road. Curious to know what they were doing, I kept a discreet eye on them. An hour later, they'd installed two metal poles, three metres high and two metres apart.

'What's going on?' asked Melanie.

'I'm not sure.'

'Perhaps we're getting a new village sign,' she suggested.

'I doubt it. It's probably one of those council notices explaining how much the work has cost.'

After a quick nicotine break, the two men dragged a two metre square board off the bed of the pickup and secured it to the poles.

'That's a bit of an eyesore,' remarked Melanie.

That was an understatement; it stuck out like a sore thumb.

Within half an hour they'd packed away their tools, and driven off.

'I'm going to see what it says,' I said. 'Are you coming?'

Melanie and I wandered up the lane to the entrance of the cemetery and stared at the board.

'It hardly seems appropriate,' remarked Melanie, trying not to laugh.

'You're not kidding.'

The message read "We are working to improve the quality of your life. Please excuse the disruption".

We weren't the only ones to spot the faux pas. By the end of the week the local newspaper had got wind of it and sent a photographer out to capture the image. The day after their exposé, the notice mysteriously disappeared. As for the lane, that looks terrific.

Another season of tending the vines was drawing to a close. Word filtered through that the *Zona de Amandi* had started harvesting. This most prestigious of grape growing areas is located on the steep valley slopes of the canyon of the river Sil. It benefits from a very unusual microclimate that helps the grapes mature earlier than the surrounding areas. Tradition dictates that growers in Canabal start their *vendimia* two weeks after the pickers in Amandi. It's the equivalent of the Cold War four-minute warning, except we have two weeks to prepare.

During a very long and dry summer, the last thing you'd expect to see are channels of water flowing down the village streets. When preparations begin, that's exactly what you'll see. Over the last few years, many of our neighbours have abandoned their decades-old oak barrels in favour of stainless steel vats. It's a minor concession to tradition that's had a significant impact on the quality of homemade wines. However, not everyone has embraced this change. Many still clean their wooden barrels in the street, a practice that involves filling them half full with water, rolling them back and forth a few times, and tipping out the contents. As for sterilisation, that's a process that milk goes through, not mouldy old barrels.

'I'm going to clean the vats this morning,' I said after breakfast.

'Do you want a hand?'

'No, I should be fine.'

It's fair to say that last year's wine didn't win any awards but we'd managed to drink most of it. The white proved to be our favourite, despite its urine like hue. We mixed most of the red with vodka, brandy, ice, and lots of fruit chunks to make a rather nice and extremely potent sangria-style punch.

'What are you going to do with the red that's left?' asked Melanie.

'I thought I'd try making port,' I replied.

'Really, and how are you going to do that?'

'By adding *aguardiente* and sugar.'

Melanie looked sceptical; she had every right to be. I didn't know the first thing about making port but anything seemed preferable to throwing it away. I began by pouring a specific volume of aguardiente into a wine bottle and adding a set amount of sugar. After topping it up with wine, I gave it a quick shake and laid it to rest. I repeated the process using different quantities of the two ingredients and labelled each bottle. If by some miracle I managed to concoct anything remotely drinkable, I wanted to know exactly how to repeat the process. By the time I'd finished, I had eighteen bottles of clearly labelled experimental port.

By sheer coincidence, the timing of this year's harvest coincided with a visit from my sister, Julie. She didn't know it yet but we'd already decided to pressgang her into helping, a fitting punishment for the annoying catchphrase she'd coined. For reasons known only to herself, she'd developed the habit of starting our conversations with the only four Spanish words she knew.

Ring ring … Ring ring!

'I'll get it,' I called.

I dashed into the lounge and picked up the phone.

'Hello.'

'Hola, loco, kettle.'

'It's not kettle, it's *que tal.*'

She'd rung to ask if we could visit Santiago de Compostela after we'd picked her up from the airport. Actually that's not strictly true. Julie doesn't ask, she tells. When it comes to her visits, we rarely have to think of anything to do. She has her "must-do" itinerary, and woe betide anyone or anything that gets in her way.

'I want to go to Santiago on our way back from the airport,' she said, ignoring my remark about the kettle.

'You do, do you?'

I didn't want to admit it but that was a great idea. The cathedral in Santiago is the second most visited tourist site in Spain. We'd lived in Galicia for nearly three and a half years and still hadn't seen it.

'If that's OK,' she added.

'That should be fine,' I said, 'as long as you don't forget to pack your wellies.'

'Are you expecting rain?' she asked.

'No, but we'll be harvesting the grapes while you're here so you can give us a hand.'

'So why do I need wellies?'

'For crushing the grapes.'

'I thought you were supposed to stamp on them barefoot.'

'We don't want your bare feet anywhere near our grapes, thank you very much.'

'Does that mean I'll have to do some work?'

'There's no free ride at harvest time.'

'Oh OK, see you both on Thursday, bye.'

I put the receiver down and turned to Melanie.

'Julie?' asked Melanie, before I'd opened my mouth.

'Yes,' I replied, 'she wants to go to Santiago on our way back from the airport.'

'She does, does she.'

'Don't you want to go?'

'I'd love to go,' she replied. 'I just don't like being told that I am going.'

Two days later, on the 29th of September, we drove to Santiago Airport. We couldn't have asked for better sightseeing weather: calm, bright, and warm. After a brief wait Julie walked into the arrivals lounge pulling her Friesian patterned carry-on. The Briggs family have never been one for huggy, kissy reunions; today was no different. We said hello and wandered off to the car park.

'Can we go to Santiago?' she asked.

'I don't see why not.'

From the airport we headed for the town centre following the brown road signs with the words Casco Antiguo written in white text.

'There's a car park,' said Melanie.

I hadn't a clue where we were so this seemed as good a place as any to park.

'Where now?' asked Julie as we emerged from the car park onto the pavement outside.

'Centro Historico looks a safe bet,' I said, pointing at a sign on the opposite side of the road.

Within the space of twenty metres, a cityscape of modern buildings was replaced with a visual feast of medieval and Renaissance architecture. We entered the Rúa de San Francisco, a wide, stone paved thoroughfare. On one side of the street is the Facultade de Medicina e Odontoloxia (Medical School), an elegant 18th century building of neoclassical design. Opposite this is a row of small independent retailers.

Given the city's standing as one of Spain's most popular tourist destinations, the dozen or so shops looked surprisingly low key. There were a few souvenir shops, cashing in on the footfall by offering visitors pilgrim-themed keepsakes, and a number of local confectioners.

The city is famous for producing a sweet almond cake

called *tarta de Santiago*. It's decorated with a dusting of icing sugar masking out the Cross of Saint James (*Cruz de Santiago*). Less well known are the city's *piedras de Santiago*, (stones of Santiago): irregular-shaped pieces of milk, plain, or white chocolate containing whole almonds. Shop assistants patrol the pavement tempting customers into their establishments by offering delicious samples. Julie was in her element.

'Thank you,' she said, picking a piece of cake off the plate.

'It's gracias,' I said.

Having devoured her sample, she nodded her appreciation.

The next shop along was offering samples of *piedras*.

'*Grazie*,' said Julie, plucking a piece of chocolate off a white plastic tray.

'I've never been, but I think you'll find that's Italian,' I said.

Julie stared straight through me, refusing to bite. The same couldn't be said for the chocolate which she popped into her mouth and munched with delight.

'They're delicious,' she said, directing her comment at Melanie. 'Tell her that they're delicious.'

Melanie relayed her enthusiasm to the shop assistant.

'Can I try one of the dark chocolate ones?' she asked.

'I think the idea is to sample one piece and then go inside and buy a box,' I replied.

'I might want to buy two boxes.'

Melanie asked to try the dark chocolate; the assistant was more than happy to oblige.

'We'll call on our way back,' said Julie to the assistant, who turned to Melanie for clarification.

To my embarrassment, Julie had the cheek to stop at the next shop and sample their chocolates. I wandered past pretending not to know her and looked on from a discreet distance.

'Are you two finished?' I asked, as they walked past.

'For the time being,' replied Julie.

As we neared the end of the shops, I caught sight of the cathedral's twin towers rising above the rooftops.

Rúa de San Francisco leads into Plaza del Obradoiro, a vast, cobbled square fronted on one side by the cathedral. Scattered around the square were small groups of people, wandering this way and that. Many were tourists, fascinated by the magnificence of the surrounding buildings. Others were modern-day pilgrims, relieved to have reached their goal after hiking along the Camino de Santiago.

'Let's go over there,' I suggested. 'We'll get a much better view of the cathedral.'

Opposite the cathedral stands the Pazo de Raxio (Rajoy Palace), a four storey, 18th century palace of enormous proportions. Its façade measures more than eighty metres long (260 feet), and spans the western side of the square. On the ground floor, elegant porticos run its entire length. The building's perfect symmetry is centred upon a large triangular pediment supported by eight granite columns, typical of the neoclassical style.

'It looks like Huddersfield train station,' remarked Julie.

'Hardly, and besides which, there isn't a bronze statue of Harold Wilson striding out across the cobbles,' I joked.

Either by design or divine intervention, I was able to squeeze the whole cathedral into my viewfinder from the opposite side of the square.

To a lapsed Baptist, the baroque façade looked a bit over the top. Two ornate towers topped with a crucifix, pointing towards the heavens. Standing between these monastic monoliths is a statue of Saint James (Santiago), dressed as a pilgrim and holding a staff. Even by modern standards it's an impressive building. I can only imagine how intimidating it must have appeared to those early pilgrims.

When it comes to medieval architecture, Julie's attention span is as short as a door lintel, which might well have something to do with being married to an architect.

'Is it time for a coffee?' she asked, after a short time.

'What about over there,' I replied, pointing towards the outside terrace of the city's Parador.

'Will they let us in?' she asked.

'I don't see why not. They're open to the public.'

Parador Hotels are a national chain of state owned luxury hotels. Most, but not all, are housed in buildings of historical significance, saved from ruin and sympathetically restored. The one in Santiago dates back to 1486 and is believed to be the oldest continually operating hotel in the world. Melanie and Julie wandered towards it, leaving me to snap away.

Digital photography has been a godsend to Happy Snappers such as myself. My occasional success is based on the premise that if I take enough photos, one of them might be half decent. After a few dozen shots of the cathedral, I raced to join them.

'What's matter?' I asked, having caught up.

For some reason, they'd stopped a short distance from the entrance and their attempt to appear inconspicuous had failed spectacularly.

'Are you sure it's open to the public?' whispered Julie.

'As far as I know,' I replied. 'Why do you ask?'

'There's a guard on the door.'

Standing outside the entrance was a uniformed security guard.

'Come on,' I said, encouraging them to follow, 'there's only one way to find out.'

Confidently, I marched towards the door. As I neared, an elderly couple pulled it open from inside. The guard leapt to their assistance and held it open. Without breaking stride, I looked him in the eye, smiled, and strolled past with Julie and Melanie following in my wake. Their relief was tangible.

'See, I told you it was open to the public.'

The entrance lobby seemed disproportionately small,

given the enormous size of the building. A gold painted sign pointed the way to the cafeteria.

'This way.'

The sign directed us into a long lounge. Elegantly dressed residents reclined in comfortable-looking armchairs. Underfoot, the lush carpet pile reminded us that we were wandering through one of Europe's top hotels. At the end of the lounge we turned right and then left into the opulently decorated cafeteria. I stared around the room searching for the door to the outside terrace.

'Over there,' said Melanie, pointing at another gold stencilled sign.

The terrace is situated in the western corner of the Parador. It offers its patrons an enviable view of the cathedral and the square. A sizeable portion of the terrace is allocated to a contemporary observation room. This all-glass structure allows unrestricted views across the square to the cathedral. Roman blinds run across the ceiling, shielding its occupants from the sunlight, and a folding glass curtain enables year-round use. The wrought iron tables and chairs, and cotton tablecloths, reminded me of a Victorian English summerhouse. We took a seat and Julie perused the menu.

'Is it too early for a glass of wine?' she asked.

'It's never too early for a glass of wine,' replied Melanie.

As the designated driver, I ordered a non-alcoholic beer.

The unmistakable sound of a solo piper drifted on the warm air as we looked out across the square. We watched as a steady stream of pilgrims trudged through, weighed down with huge rucksacks. Some were barely able to walk while others seemed far less troubled by their ordeal.

There are many routes to the city along the Camino de Santiago. By far the most popular is the Camino Francés: a 769 kilometre trek from Saint-Jean-Pied-de-Port in the French Pyrenees. Those completing the pilgrimage are entitled to a certificate. Back in medieval times, obtaining one was seen as a sure-fire way of booking your seat in heaven. The scheme still operates today although modern-day pilgrims need only walk a hundred kilometres to gain theirs.

In stark contrast to these dedicated ramblers, a luxury coach drove slowly into the square and stopped at the entrance to the Parador. The driver opened the door and stood to attention outside as, one by one, a group of stereotypical Japanese tourists stepped from the coach. As if oblivious to their surroundings each person bowed respectfully at the driver before scurrying into the sanctuary of the Parador.

For the best part of an hour, the three of us looked on as a kaleidoscope of humanity passed before our eyes.

'Are we going to look inside?' I asked, gesturing towards the cathedral.

'Do we have to?' replied Julie impassively.

Julie is much happier nibbling on free samples of chocolate and sipping Albariño than looking around medieval cathedrals.

'It was your idea to come,' I reminded her.

'I'm only joking,' she added.

We paid the bill and strolled back through the hotel and into the square. The doors to the cathedral are more than three metres above the level of the cobbles. We climbed two flights of stone steps and followed the crowds through an open door. Visitors are immediately drawn to an ornate altar at the far end of the cathedral. Such are the excesses of its embellishments that my first thought was of a Buddhist temple rather than a Catholic church. After a brief wander around we exited through the south entrance into the Praza de Platerias.

'Did you see that?' I asked.

'What?' asked Julie.

'The gift shop, inside the cathedral.'

'I wonder what Jesus would have made of that,' she remarked.

13

A Vinicultural Symphony

After a good night's sleep, I was eager to get started on the grape harvest. The same couldn't be said of Julie.

'This is delicious,' she remarked, munching on a piece of toast lavished with Melanie's homemade lemon curd.

'Aren't you ready yet?' I asked, in an effort to instil a little urgency into the morning's proceedings.

'What's the hurry?'

'The grape harvest,' I replied.

'How long will it take?'

Her question was asked with equal measure of ignorance and curiosity. I doubt she'd given the matter much thought since I'd mentioned it on the phone. Even if she had, I'm sure it wouldn't have involved hard work.

'That depends on how soon you stop lazing around,' I replied. 'Did you remember to bring your wellies?'

'Yes, I left them outside the front door.'

'Why?' I asked.

'They're a little muddy.'

'Don't tell me you've brought dirty wellies all the way from England.'

'You didn't say anything about them being clean.'

Her remark hardly justified a response, so I bit my tongue. Moments later she picked up her empty plate and wandered back into the house to get ready.

The timing of this year's *vendimia* was a little later than last year. I'm not sure why as the weather had been much better. At the moment, I'm happy to follow tradition and wait for Meli to give me the nod. On the run-up to Julie's visit, the weather forecast had looked poor. As it turned out, we couldn't have wished for a better day. If anything, I would have preferred it a little cooler.

I checked the shed to make sure everything was ready. The vats were clean and the buckets used for harvesting were stacked in the corner, ready to go. Unfortunately, I only had one pair of secateurs although I couldn't see Julie wanting to do much work. I picked them off the workbench, grabbed a bucket, and headed into the house.

'Have you seen these?' asked Melanie, as I walked into the kitchen.

'What?'

'These wellies – look at the state of them.'

Julie's wellies looked like she'd been line dancing in a filthy farmyard.

'Who in their right mind would pack them looking like this?'

Just then Julie appeared at the doorway.

'You haven't seen my wellies, have you?'

'They're here,' said Melanie, holding them up with her fingertips, 'but they're no good in this state.'

'I can do that,' she said, as Melanie began scrubbing them.

'They're done now.'

'Right, I'm going to make a start in the front garden,' I said, pushing open the French doors.

'What do you want me to do?' asked Julie.

'When you've put your shoes on, you can come and watch me.'

'What about my wellies?'

'They're for crushing not picking.'

I left Melanie to explain the difference and marched outside.

Harvesting grapes is a time consuming endeavour and requires more physical effort than one might think. If it wasn't for the time pressure, this would be my favourite part of the winemaking process. From the moment the first cut is made the clock is ticking. The quicker the grapes are harvested and crushed the better.

I quickly realised that there's more to collecting succulently sweet bunches of plump grapes than wielding secateurs. To ensure a quick and trouble-free harvest I should have taken greater care with my husbandry. Most of the bunches were hanging perfectly below the training wires, begging to have their stems cut. It was the ones that weren't that were slowing me down. What I should have done was reposition them earlier in the year, or remove them altogether. These untrained and untidy bunches had developed around the training wires. Even after snipping their stalks they wouldn't fall. Tugging them free sent plump fruits cascading onto the ground. Others had grown together, creating super-bunches too awkward to handle.

'What do you want us to do?' asked Melanie, as they came outside.

'Give me two minutes and you can take this bucket away and start crushing,' I said, directing my instruction to Melanie. 'You might want to get the wheelbarrow; it's too heavy to carry.'

'And what about me?' asked Julie.

'I only have one pair of secateurs so if you want to pick some grapes you'll just have to wait a minute.'

Two minutes later I lifted the first bucket of grapes into the wheelbarrow and Melanie marched off round the back.

'Here you go,' I said, handing Julie the secateurs.

'You'll have to show me what to do.'

'Hold the bunch firmly in one hand but don't squeeze, then cut the stalk. Mind the training wires though; we don't want to cut them.'

Julie's progress was painfully slow, made worse by me having to watch.

'I'm ready for the next lot,' said Melanie, as she rounded the corner of the house.

'Perhaps you'd be more suited to crushing,' I suggested to Julie.

'What are you trying to say?'

Diplomacy was never my strong point. 'At this rate we'll be here until next week.'

Julie thrust the secateurs in my direction, picked up her quarter-full bucket and plonked it into the wheelbarrow.

'I know when I'm not wanted,' she said jokingly.

By midday, I'd picked all the grapes at the front of the house and made a start in the back. I even found time to take a few snaps for the family album. Julie cut a comical figure stomping the grapes wearing tailored shorts, polo shirt, straw hat, and wellington boots.

'How many more are there?' she moaned.

'Not many now.'

Despite having roughly the same number of vines in the back garden as the front, those in the back had suffered the most during the house renovations and were still not as productive as I would have hoped.

'Can you manage on your own for a while and I'll make a start on lunch?' Melanie asked Julie.

'Do I have a choice?'

Within the hour, all the grapes had been picked, crushed, and deposited in the vats. Melanie and I were delighted with our record-breaking haul of 160 kilos of white grapes and 100 kilos of red. From here on in, Mother Nature would take over, at least until the fermentation process had finished.

After lunch Julie was able to tick another activity off

her "must-do" agenda by spending an afternoon in the pool. Given the length of time she spent in there, I'm surprised she didn't dissolve. At least it gave Melanie and me the chance to enjoy some well-deserved R&R.

'I'd like to have a barbecue for dinner,' she said, having finally stepped out of the pool, 'and I want to go to that castle in Portugal tomorrow to buy some towels, and then I want to have dinner at that nice Italian restaurant in Brighouse.'

The castle she was referring to in Portugal is Valença, a fortified medieval town on the banks of the river Miño. The old part of the town has become a major tourist attraction with many of the houses having been converted into shops. Most sell nationally produced fabric products such as clothes, tablecloths, and towels.

On this occasion, Julie's expectations aligned very nicely with ours. Melanie and I were planning to visit the town to buy the linen and towels for Bob and Janet's holiday let, but I wasn't going to let her know that.

As for Brighouse, that's Julie's nickname for the nearby town of Monforte de Lemos. Along with hola, loco, kettle, and calling Jazz Dog, this is one more example of her idiosyncratic nature. One can only wonder what Brighouse, a small town sandwiched between Huddersfield and Bradford in the industrial north of England, has in common with an historic rural town in the heart of the Ribeira Sacra in Galicia, Spain.

'You do, do you,' replied Melanie, 'and what if we have something else planned?'

If we had, it was news to me.

'You don't, do you?' asked Julie, unsure if Melanie was teasing or not.

'No,' she replied.

'Well then,' realising that her request might have seemed like a demand, she added, 'can we have a barbecue tonight?'

'I don't see why not,' replied Melanie.

Clang, clang, clang, clang!

Jazz, who'd been lying quietly in the sun all afternoon, jumped to her feet and sprinted around the side of the house.

Woof, woof, woof, woof!

'I'll go.'

Standing at the gates was Manolo, the builder. I could tell from his smart appearance that he'd come to take a look at the work that Bob and Janet wanted doing. Manolo always gets washed and changed before going to quote on a job.

'Hola,' he said as I approached, 'is it convenient to take a look at the work you want me to quote on?'

Convenient or not, I didn't want to miss this opportunity. The sooner he quoted, the quicker he could begin. Fifteen minutes later we were pulling down the track outside Bob and Janet's. It took the best part of two hours to explain everything that needed doing. The list of work was extensive. Manolo made notes and took measurements as we went along.

'How long will it take to prepare the quote?' I asked, as we readied to leave.

'About a week,' he replied. 'I'll call round when it's done.'

I thanked him for his time and we both headed home.

That night we had to endure another of Julie's eccentricities, dining by the light of the pool. Don't get me wrong, I'm all for romantic candlelit dinners for two, which by definition excludes Julie. However, trying to eat a plate of food in pitch blackness, with nothing more than the distant blue-green glow of the swimming pool lights, is not my idea of fun. To make matters worse the new moon was only a day away and the radiance from the two tealights was as bright as a glowworm wearing pyjamas.

'Do we have to?' I moaned.

'What?' asked Julie.

'I can't see a thing.'

'I like it with the pool lights on.'

'So do I but not while I'm eating.'

Just then a gust of wind blew out one of the candles.

'Where are the matches?' I asked.

'I don't know,' replied Melanie. 'I can't see a thing.'

'Oh go on then, put the lights on ... but only until we've finished eating.'

By the end of her three nights' stay, we'd managed to tick off all her "must-do" activities and despite her being fairly high maintenance, we'd all had a great time.

'Oh no,' I blurted out, on our way home from dropping her off at the airport.

'What?' asked Melanie.

'Guess what I forgot to do this morning.'

'What?'

'Check the progress of the wine.'

'Oh no.'

Julie's flight was scheduled to depart at eleven. That meant getting to the airport for nine thirty which meant leaving home by eight. After an indulgent night at our favourite restaurant, we'd all been a bit bleary-eyed first thing. In the rush, I forgot to check the fermenting grape must.

Last year's fermentation had been so rapid and violent that the bubbling must had escaped the confines of the vat, cascaded down the outside and spilled across the floor of the shed. As soon as we arrived home, I sprinted through the house, across the terrace, and into the shed. Thankfully, everything looked under control.

A multitude of tiny fruit flies had settled around the rim of the partially closed lid. I hinged it open and peered into the vat. This action sent a cloud of flies filtering into the air. Fermentation had begun. A thick cap of grape skins had formed on top of the must. At this stage, it's vital to break the cap into pieces and mix it with the liquid. The frequency of this action is determined by the speed of the fermentation. From now on, I would need to push the cap down at least twice a day to release as many flavours as possible into the young wine. Thankfully, I had just the tool for the job. Last year, our neighbour Meli gave me a much treasured family heirloom in the form of a *pala de mosto*: a carefully selected and lovingly sculpted piece of oak. The chosen branch has three offshoots which when crafted form a three-fingered claw at the base of the stick.

'Is everything OK?' asked Melanie, poking her head around the door.

'Come and take a look.'

As Melanie moved towards the vat, the swarm of flies took flight like a biblical plague.

'What are they?' she asked, picking a half-dead fly off her bottom lip.

'Fruit flies.'

'It's terrible,' she replied, swiping her hand in front of her face. 'I think I'll leave you to it.'

Melanie made an about-turn, closing the door behind her.

The fermentation process is the vinicultural equivalent of a symphonic musical score. Within two days of crushing, these succulent fruits are literally singing with joy. The performance begins *andante*, slow and calm, but quickly progresses to *allegretto* before racing on to *allegro*. It's a performance influenced by the environment: too cold and the concert descends into a moody dirge, too warm and the stylus skips across the disc. The lateness of this year's harvest had provided the perfect conditions for a balanced anthem. Within a week, the melody had changed. Nature's conductor calls for *calando*, and the final fade to silence.

The end of the fermentation often coincides with the beginning of autumn; it's almost as if the grapevines know that their work is finished. As if by magic, their autumn colours reflect the wines they will produce. The leaves of the white varieties, such as Palomino and Godello, turn a golden brown while the foliage of the red varieties, Garnacha Tinta and Mencia, become inky purple.

Like most of Meli's winemaking tips, determining the exact point at which the fermentation has ended seemed irrelevant and unimportant. However, once it has, the wine needs to be cleaned. A process that involves separating the liquid from the solids. Unfortunately, Meli's winemaking knowledge didn't extend to the actual mechanics of doing this.

Last year, after hours of frustration, Melanie came up with the idea of using a frying pan and a colander. Using a stepladder, I reached into the vat, scooped out the must with a frying pan, tipped it into a colander, and pressed it into a bucket. I doubt the method will ever catch on but until someone suggests an easier way, this is how we'll proceed.

As well as being time consuming and messy, the biggest drawback of using a kitchen colander is its poor filtration. They might be ideal for draining pasta or boiled vegetables but hardly refined enough for wine. What we needed to do was filter the wine twice, once through the colander and then through something finer.

'What about coffee filter papers?' I suggested.

'They're much too small,' replied Melanie. 'It would take forever.'

She had a point. The job took long enough as it was.

'There must be something we can use.'

'I know,' said Melanie, 'I've seen some muslin sieves for sale at the Happy Men's.'

The Happy Men is our nickname for one of the best stocked *ferreterías* in Monforte, so christened because the owners and staff are always smiling.

'That's a great idea.'

Our method of double filtration proved a great success. If anything, the muslin sieves were a little too efficient. They quickly became coated with particles of must which, after a few seconds, restricted the flow of wine to a fine trickle. Nevertheless, we persisted and after the best part of a day, we'd cleaned both the red and white wines.

Ring ring … Ring ring!
By the time I'd wiped the sleep from my eyes, Melanie had jumped out of bed, rushed through into the lounge and answered the call.

'Hola,' I heard her say.

I would have eavesdropped but I had a call of my own to answer.

'Who was that?' I asked, returning from the bathroom.

'EcoMoble,' she replied. 'They want to deliver Bob and Janet's furniture.'

'When?'

'In about an hour.'

'An hour!'

After yesterday's exertions cleaning the wine, I was really looking forward to a lie-in – no such luck.

Within the hour we were washed, dressed, and out. By the time we arrived at Bob and Janet's, the delivery van was already there, waiting in the track outside the house. Quickly I opened the gates as the two delivery men began unloading the furniture.

'Where do you want this?' asked one of the men, balancing one end of a sofa on his knee while his mate held the other end.

'In here,' I replied, directing them into the lounge.

People often criticise Spain for a lack of customer service but when it comes to furniture, they're the tops. Back in the UK, I've passed many a frustrating hour deliberating over the technical construction of a piece of flat-pack furniture. Here in Spain, the delivery drivers double as flat-pack furniture engineers. They wouldn't dream of leaving until everything is correctly assembled and all the packaging is removed – bravo España!

We spent the rest of the week dressing the house: new light fittings in every room, pictures and mirror hung on the walls, and blinds at the windows. By the end of the week we'd transformed this hollow, empty property into a home worthy of the title "Luxury accommodation for the discerning traveller". I went from room to room taking photos of our creation to email to Bob. All we had to do now was ensure that the outside spaces reflected the look of the interior.

Clang, clang, clang, clang!

Jazz jumped to her feet and ran to the French doors, pressing her wet nose up against the glass and excitedly wagging her tail.

'Manolo's here,' called Melanie.

'Hola,' I called, walking towards the gate.

'Hola, I have the quote for your friend's house.'

I opened the gate and invited him in. One by one he explained each item on the quote, making sure I understood.

'If they decide to go ahead, how soon could you start?' I asked.

I was conscious that time was at a premium. To have any chance of advertising the house in time for next year's holiday season, I needed to be marketing it as soon as possible. To do that, I needed at least one alluring photo of the house's façade. At the moment it looked as appealing as a city break in a shanty town.

'Not until the new year at the earliest,' he replied. 'I have so much work on at the moment.'

'I'll email the quote to them and let you know what they decide,' I said, as we walked back to his van.

That evening I wrote to Bob and sent him the quote and the photos I'd taken. Two days later, he replied.

From: "Robert Xxxxxx"
To: Craig Briggs
Subject: Re: Builder's quote
Date: Sun, 09 Oct 2005 20:10:19

Hi Craig and Mel

Thanks for all the photos you sent on Friday. They were really brilliant, it is looking so good. Guess what – Janet cried when she saw them, she couldn't believe how great the place looked.

Thanks for the quote. We have tried to ring you tonight but you are obviously not in. We will try and ring you tomorrow if pos.

Anyway just to briefly say, we are very happy with the quote, like you we think it is a fair price for the work that needs doing. We would rather get it all done in one go and not have to mess about again in the future. At least that way it should all be done by the time we get any bookings.

Janet's son Daniel came round this afternoon and we showed him the photos, he thought the place was looking really good, a lot different from when he saw it over a year ago. He thinks we are doing the right thing by keeping the place.

Thanks once again for everything, hope to speak soon.

Love and best wishes

Bob and Janet

p.s. Janet has got an interview at work tomorrow to be made permanent (to get some money for all the work – ha ha!!). Still only working 4 days though.

I dashed into the lounge to give Melanie the news.
'Bob's emailed. He's given the green light to get the work done.'
Somehow I had to conjure up an attractive image of the house's façade and then I could begin marketing it to potential holidaymakers.

14

Weighing up the Options

Living next door to the village cemetery has its advantages. As well as benefitting from quiet neighbours, we often return home to discover a carrier bag stuffed with fresh fruit or vegetables hanging from the gate. Most of the villagers have a *huerta* or vegetable plot. Throughout the summer they produce far more than they can eat. In years gone by, this excess would have been fed to their pigs but as the village population ages, fewer are being reared. The logical solution would be to grow less but old habits die hard. That's where we come in: the non-vegetable-growing English couple living on the outskirts of the village. I just hope they're not fattening us up for a winter slaughter.

At the start of summer, Melanie mooted the idea of cultivating her own *huerta* on a plot of waste ground at the back of the house. At the time, I managed to parry her suggestion by insisting that the baked earth was far too difficult to work. I realised then that the matter wouldn't end there. My reluctance to encourage her green fingered enterprise stemmed in part from an uninspiring childhood memory.

Aged eleven, I decided that it would be fun to grow my own vegetables. Mum and Dad supported my initiative by securing a short-term tenancy on a council owned allotment. At the time, growing your own veg was an unpopular pastime undertaken by scruffy old men in wellies. It could be said that I was years ahead of my time, if not decades. However, my enterprise was short lived and my enthusiasm quickly waned. I learned an important lesson. The thrill of eating home grown vegetables is far outweighed by the effort of growing them, and so began my lifelong love of supermarkets.

'Now we've finished the work at Bob and Janet's can we make a start on the *huerta*?' asked Melanie one morning.

I suspected that her reference to we actually meant me.

'I still have to do the website marketing you know,' I replied.

My feeble excuse was unlikely to pass muster.

'I thought you couldn't start that until you'd taken a decent photo of the outside,' she replied.

'OK, I'll make a start this morning.'

Converting a stony patch of scrubland into a parcel fit for planting would be no mean feat. After breakfast I readied myself for a morning of hard graft.

Last summer, I encountered a man-eating python on this very same plot. Since then, I hadn't set foot on it. Locals would have me believe that it was nothing more than a metre-long viper but I know a man-eater when I see one. Thankfully, the reptile was more terrified of me than I of it, but that wasn't the point.

'What on earth are you doing?' shouted Melanie from the kitchen door.

She'd been watching me from the window, standing in the middle of the lawn, lobbing bricks over the boundary wall into the undergrowth.

'Checking for snakes.'

'There won't be any snakes at this time of year,' she replied.

Since when did she become a herpetologist, I thought to myself. Besides which, it wasn't her who'd stared death in the face and lived to tell the tale.

'Well I'm not taking any chances.'

Confident that my anti-snake bombardment had done the trick, I wandered into the scrubland and started digging. Painful memories flooded back of preparing the garden for seeding the lawn. Then, as now, my attempts to thrust the garden fork into the ground ended with a stony collision and a seismic vibration travelling through the fork handle, up my arm, and rattling my fillings. After an hour's bruising combat, Melanie popped her head out of the kitchen door.

'Coffee?' she called.

'Yes please.'

My fingers were so sore I could barely grip the coffee mug.

'How's it going?' she asked.

'Slowly,' I replied.

In a little over an hour, I'd managed to prepare a square metre of land. At this rate, it would take until next summer to dig it over. I'd tipped at least ten wheelbarrow loads of rocks down the ravine. That alone was taking up half my time.

'Can I help?'

The ground was unforgiving. Melanie would be the first to admit that she had neither the strength nor the patience to work this unyielding patch of wasteland.

'If I throw the stones into a pile can you pop outside every so often, load them into the barrow, and tip them down the ravine?'

'No problem.'

Rather than stand around in the cold, waiting for me to dig out the stones, Melanie kept popping out of the house every twenty minutes or so. She would quickly fill the barrow, tip the contents down the ravine, and rush back inside to keep warm. By the time she called me in for lunch, I'd de-stoned about three square metres of ground and there was another sizeable pile of rocks ready to be loaded. All this effort only reinforced my belief that vegetables come from supermarkets. After lunch I prepared myself once more for battle and headed outside.

'Are there any more stones ready to tip?' asked Melanie.

'At least another barrow,' I replied.

Melanie fastened up her coat, slipped on her gardening gloves, and followed me outside. No sooner had I thrust my fork into the stony ground than Melanie let out a bloodcurdling scream. Instinctively, I turned to face her. She'd recoiled backwards from the pile of stones, stumbling over clumps of grass in her attempt to retreat.

Listening to her terrifying scream conjured up images of last year's reptilian encounter. Terror gripped my muscles, paralysing me to the spot. Like a trident-armed gladiator, I raised the garden fork ready to strike at the first sign of danger.

'What's matter?' I called, in a girly, high-pitched tone. 'What is it?'

Melanie had been reduced to a mumbling, quivering wreck, unable to speak or act.

Without warning the culprit appeared. A tiny grey field mouse hopped from the pile of stones, scampered past me, and dived over the ravine. My relief was such that my muscles turned to jelly; the fork fell to the ground, missing my foot by inches.

'It's only a field mouse; nothing to be scared of.'

Melanie was having none of it.

'I'm not coming back in there,' she said, her voice trembling with fear. 'You'll have to do it yourself.'

'It's gone,' I declared, but my pleas fell on deaf ears.

'I don't care,' she protested. 'I am not coming back in there until everything is cleared.

Melanie was adamant; nothing I could say would

change her mind. I would just have to soldier on without her.

It took more than three weeks to create our vegetable plot: four metres wide by ten metres long.

In between times I worked on the marketing for Bob and Janet's house.

'What do you think to *Bon Vista*?' I asked one afternoon.

'What?'

'As a name for Bob and Janet's house,' I replied, '*Casa Bon Vista*.'

'Oh I see.'

'I think it'll be easier to market if it has a name.'

I'd spent a good part of the afternoon trying to think of something suitable. One of my favourites was *Arriba los Carneros* (Up the Rams). As a lifelong Derby County fan (nicknamed the Rams), I thought Bob might appreciate that one. The only problem was that *Casa Arriba los Carneros* seemed a bit longwinded, whereas *Casa Bon Vista* rolled off the tongue.

'*Bon* is French isn't it?'

Melanie had immediately spotted my linguistic gaffe.

'Yes,' I replied, 'but the Spanish *Boa Vista* sounds too much like a snake.'

'You have a point.'

'And after all, it's only a made-up name. It doesn't have to be linguistically correct, does it?'

'I suppose not,' she replied. '*Casa Bon Vista*, yes, I like it. It has a nice ring to it, *Casa Bon Vista*.'

'I'd better run it past Bob and Janet before I start using it. After all, it is their house.'

A few days later, the name had been agreed and *Casa Bon Vista* was born.

While waiting for confirmation, I'd been working on an enticing property description. After numerous attempts I settled on this.

A beautifully renovated 2 bedroom Galician country farmhouse

At the end of a leafy lane you'll find the enchanting Casa Bon Vista. This recently renovated farmhouse provides luxury accommodation for the discerning traveller. Situated 2km from the village of Ferreira de Panton, its location is peaceful and tranquil. Its elevated position provides breathtaking views over the surrounding countryside and distant mountains.

The beautiful living accommodation is situated on the first floor, a typical feature of farmhouses in Galicia. There are 2 bedrooms, 1 double with en-suite shower room and 1 twin bedded room. There is also a separate shower room. The large lounge has a sprung double sofa bed and features a romantic wood-burning fire. The large kitchen/dining room is equipped to the highest standards. Leading off the kitchen is an open terrace with stunning views. Running along the front of the property is a galleria, or enclosed sun terrace, which affords outstanding panoramic views.

'What do you think?' I asked, showing my work to Melanie.

'It sounds lovely. The only thing is …'

'I know what you're going to say.'

At the moment the only views were of derelict outbuildings and a minging courtyard but confidence was high. I had every faith that Manolo would transform our ugly duckling into a beautiful swan, long before the first guests arrived. Until then, I needed to create an appealing photo of the façade. Without it, the chances of securing any bookings seemed doubtful.

I had two major obstacles to overcome. When the house was renovated, the ground floor hadn't been included in the quote. Consequently, the bottom half of the house looked shabby. After discussing the problem with Bob, we decided that the quickest and cheapest way to disguise its unsightly appearance was to build a false wall from one side of the house to the other and clad it with natural stone.

The second problem was slightly more technical. The proximity of the outbuildings to the house made it physically impossible to fit the façade inside the viewfinder. Somehow, I had to find a way to overcome these challenges.

'Why don't you just upload the photos of the interior,' suggested Melanie. 'They're really nice.'

She was right; the photos I'd taken of the inside looked homely and inviting. Perhaps it's my suspicious nature but if I was searching for a rental property and the owner hadn't uploaded a photo of the outside, I'd wonder why. What did they have to hide?

'I know what I can do!' I said.

'What?'

'I'll build a digital wall.'

'You're going to build wall?' asked Melanie.

'A digital wall.'

'What on earth are you babbling on about?'

'If I take a photo of the side of the house, I can digitally cut out a section of the wall and paste it into a photo of the front of the house.'

'Isn't that cheating?'

'No more than airbrushing zits off supermodels,' I replied, 'and besides which, it's only until the real wall is built and then I can replace the photo.'

'I'm not sure,' replied Melanie.

'Just wait and see. It'll be fine.'

Eager to test my theory, we drove up to *Casa Bon Vista* to take a look.

Melanie watched as I snapped away at the side of house.

'That should be enough,' I said after taking twenty or so shots. 'Now, let's have a look inside the courtyard.'

I unlocked the gates and shouldered them open. Over the last few months I'd become quite proficient at wrestling with them.

Standing in the barn, I turned to face the house. Step by step I moved backwards, peering through the viewfinder. No matter how hard I tried, I couldn't squeeze the house inside the glass pane. I walked as far left as I could and then as far right, but wherever I stood or whichever way I held the camera, it simply wouldn't fit.

'All I need is another metre or two,' I said.

'What about taking it from the other side of there?' suggested Melanie, pointing at a window-like opening in the centre of the back wall of the barn.

'That's a great idea.'

Why didn't I think of that?

I rushed out of the courtyard, down the lane and into the field at the back of the barn. Melanie followed. Unfortunately, the field is several feet below the level of the courtyard and the opening was several feet above that. I needed a ladder.

'The next time there's a bright blue sky we'll bring a ladder and I'll give it a go,' I said.

As luck would have it, by lunchtime the following day the early morning clouds had lifted to reveal a bright sunny day with a pastel blue sky. I loaded the folding ladder into the back of the car and we sped off.

The field at the back of the barn is owned by Young José, a quietly spoken chap in his late sixties. We'd christened him Young José as he lives with his father who is also called José. It was obvious from the deep furrows that he had a crop of potatoes growing. I unfolded the ladder, locked it into position and leant it up against the outside wall of the barn.

'Do be careful,' warned Melanie.

The cultivated ground was soft and pliable. As soon as I put my weight on the first rung it sank into the earth, tilting at a precarious angle.

'I can't hold it,' screamed Melanie.

'Don't worry,' I replied.

Quickly I placed my other foot on the next rung and the ladder righted itself, sinking further into the damp earth.

'Do be careful,' she repeated.

After my initial steps the ladder found its own level and felt relatively secure. The view through the opening was perfect. Not only could I get the entire house into the photo but also a tantalising backdrop of the blue sky.

Back home I worked my magic on the photo, cutting out a section of the wall from the side of the house and pasting it seamlessly into the front.

'What do you think?'

'That's brilliant,' remarked Melanie.

That afternoon I uploaded all the photos and house information to four different holiday rental sites. Everything was ready to start taking bookings, everything except the house.

Later that week Melanie had an appointment with the orthopaedic consultant to check on the progress of her physiotherapy. This was her third such consultation during her ten weeks of daily therapy. On each of her previous appointments he'd changed the type of treatment in an attempt to repair her troublesome ligament.

'How did it go?' I asked on her return.

'He's decided to operate; the physio just isn't working.'

Melanie's reply came as quite a shock.

'When?'

'Some time in the new year.'

'How do you feel about that?'

'I'm not sure,' she replied. 'The thing is, it's just not getting any better and I can't carry on as I am.'

'Perhaps it's for the best then,' I said. 'Does this mean you don't have to go to physio any more?'

'Yes.'

At least that was good news. Not that we weren't grateful for the efforts of the medical staff, because we were. However, after spending two hours a day at the hospital, five days a week for the last three months, having a break was a real bonus.

Melanie's news opened the door to an idea I'd been mulling over. During my internet research for marketing *Casa Bon Vista*, I had stumbled across an advert for Iberia Airways. For a limited time period, the airline was offering discounted flights. With Christmas fast approaching, I knew exactly where we could go.

Prior to our move to Spain we had always gone away over the festive period. Our favourite destination was Lanzarote. Out of curiosity, I checked the prices from Madrid–Barajas Airport to Arrecife on Lanzarote. A return ticket price of seventy-eight euros was the only incentive I needed to dig a little deeper. Thoughts drifted back to warm winter breaks and Christmas barbecues, but what about the dog?

Flights from Spain to Lanzarote are classified as internal. This meant that there would be no border to cross and definitely no quarantine, but how much would it cost? A quick check revealed that pets under five kilos could travel in the cabin for free but the last time Jazz weighed so little she was ten weeks old. Pets over five kilos had to travel in the aircraft's hold and were charged as excess baggage. The reference seemed rather cruel but a fee of six euros per kilo helped ease the insult. Perhaps we could spend Christmas on Lanzarote after all.

'How would you like to go away for Christmas?' I asked over dinner.

'Where to?'

'What about Lanzarote?'

'Sounds great but what about Jazz?'

'We'll take her with us.'

'To Lanzarote?'

'Why not?'

I explained my internet findings.

'How much do you think she weighs?' asked Melanie.

'I've no idea. Why don't we find out?'

I wandered through into the bathroom and brought back the weighing scales. Like most females, Jazz seemed reluctant to divulge her weight so I picked her up and plonked her on.

'Sit.'

Jazz was having none of it and walked away in disgust.

'Come here.'

She turned her head and wandered back towards me. I picked her up and tried again.

'Sit!'

Before the scale had come to a stop, she'd hopped off.

'This is no good.'

'Pick her up,' suggested Melanie.

She had no intention of making it that easy for me. She wriggled and squirmed but eventually stayed still long enough to get an accurate reading; her secret was out.

'Twenty-five kilos,' said Melanie, having deducted my weight from the total.

'Twenty-five kilos! No wonder she was reluctant to sit down.'

'That'll cost 150 euros,' said Melanie.

'Each way?' I replied.

'Three hundred euros.'

'You need to go on a diet, young lady,' I said.

Her ears fell limp and her eyes widened.

'Oh, don't be cruel,' replied Melanie. 'Just be grateful she's not a Great Dane.'

'So, what do you think?'

'Let's do it; it's not like we'll be doing it every year.'

Within the week we'd booked the flights and arranged the accommodation. The only thing left to do was buy a travel case for Jazz.

15

Crash Landing

By the end of November, the first winter snowfall had whitewashed the highest peaks of the Galician Massif mountains. Christmas was fast approaching and our trip to Lanzarote beckoned.

Finding a travel case for Jazz proved more difficult than we'd expected. Eventually, we ordered one from our local vet, paying the equivalent of two adult plane fares. The cost of our bargain getaway was starting to mount up.

The case measures one metre long by eighty centimetres tall and seventy-five centimetres wide. The main body is made from two pieces of grey moulded plastic that lock together to form an open ended kennel. Two detachable wire grills, hinged at both ends, ensure that the occupant is safe and secure. As an optional extra, we bought a set of four detachable wheels. This would enable us to pull her along like any other piece of luggage. All we had to do was convince Jazz of the merits of travelling in an upmarket packing case.

In an effort to entice her inside, Melanie knelt at one end holding a tasty treat. I knelt at the other encouraging her to enter.

'Come on lass, in you go,' I said, giving her a little gentle persuasion.

'Good girl, come on,' said Melanie, waggling the treat through the bars of the grill.

Jazz was having none of it and flatly refused to budge.

'Let's try taking the grills off,' I suggested.

Once removed, the case looked like a metre-long ventilated tunnel: a far less intimidating prospect.

Melanie reached through from one end waving the treat in front of Jazz's nose.

'Come on lass,' I said, encouraging her to advance. 'Look what mummy's got.'

Slowly she edged forward, nostrils twitching as she caught scent of the treat. Cautiously, she put her head inside.

'That's it, good girl.'

Without warning, she snatched the treat and scampered off to the other side of the room.

'You're not supposed to give it to her until she's inside,' I said.

'I didn't know she'd taken it,' replied Melanie.

Jazz lay in the corner, nibbling her treat and looking particularly satisfied with herself.

'Let's put her bed inside and see if that makes any difference,' I suggested.

While I stuffed her bed in, Melanie got another treat.

'Come on lass,' I called.

Slowly, she wandered across the room. Melanie knelt down and stretched her arm through the case. As Jazz edged forwards, Melanie withdrew the treat.

'Come on Jazz,' she encouraged.

Cautiously, she put one paw inside and then another. Before she had time to change her mind, I lifted her hindquarters and frogmarched her inside. Realising she had no means of retreat she lurched forward, snatched the chew, and pushed past Melanie to make good her escape.

'You're not supposed to let her out,' I said.

'I wasn't expecting her to walk straight through,' complained Melanie.

At this rate we'd never get to Lanzarote.

Jazz had darted into the corner. She seemed delighted with the new game, hardly surprising given the rewards.

'Come on now, Jazz,' I called. 'Stop messing around.'

Reluctantly, she ambled back towards us.

This time Melanie managed to stop her from escaping. Quickly, we hinged both grills onto the case, trapping her inside. Realising her plight, she turned to face me, eyes wide and ears drooped.

'It's alright,' I said, keeping her calm.

Day after day we lured her into the case until, eventually, she would happily wander inside. Buoyed by our success, we made a start on the next stage of her training.

'Let's attach the wheels and get her used to being dragged around,' I suggested one morning.

'OK.'

'I think it'll be easier if we get her inside before putting the wheels on.'

Jazz wandered into the case, oblivious of our plan.

'I'll lift this end, if you attach the wheels,' I instructed.

As I tilted the case, Jazz became anxious and stood up. Like a half-full barrel, the sudden shift in weight tipped the case, causing me to lose grip and drop it.

'Be careful,' said Melanie.

'I didn't drop it on purpose,' I replied. 'It's not as easy as it looks, you know.'

Jazz seemed none the worse for her crash landing so I tried again. This time I adopted a wider stance. Wheels on, Jazz was ready for her first excursion.

Gently, I pulled the case around the lounge. At first she seemed overwhelmed by the experience, stumbling around to compensate for the movement. Before long she sat down and seemed to quite enjoy it.

'Let's take her outside. There's more room out there.'

'Are you sure?' asked Melanie.

'She's going to have to get used to it,' I replied.

After pulling her around the terrace for ten minutes, Jazz lay down, more in resignation than contentment.

The next hurdle was travelling. The closest experience we could offer to jet travel was a dash through the Galician countryside in the back of the car. Hardly comparable but it would have to do.

'Let's take her for a run in the car,' I said.

'Will it fit in the back?' asked Melanie.

I didn't see why not but it seemed a bit late to be asking now.

'There's only one way to find out.'

We wheeled her around to the back of the car and I opened the tailgate.

'It looks as if it'll fit,' I said. 'You grab that end.'

Melanie bent down, gripped one end of the case and prepared to lift; I took hold of the other.

'After three. One, two, three.'

In synchronous harmony we lifted the case. As soon as we did, Jazz sprang to her feet and the case lurched sideways.

'Hold it, hold it! Jazz, sit down.'

'I can't hold it. I can't hold it!' pleaded Melanie.

'Rest it on the bumper.'

Quickly, we bounced it down onto the bumper.

'Sit down Jazz, there's a good girl.'

Despite my encouragement Jazz was far too disorientated to pay a blind bit of notice.

'Have you got your end?'

'I think so,' replied Melanie.

'Right, let's lift her in. After three. One, two, three.'

In unison we lifted the case off the bumper. As we did it collided with the top of the tailgate.

'It's not going to fit,' screamed Melanie.

With Jazz staggering around, the case had taken on a life of its own and we were battling to keep it aloft.

'It will. Just tilt it forward a bit.'

As we tilted the case, Jazz stumbled sideways, shifting all her weight to one side.

'I can't hold it,' shrieked Melanie.

'We're nearly there. Push it in.'

One final push and the case dropped into the boot.

'There we go. That wasn't too bad, was it?' I said with a sigh of relief.

'You are joking,' complained Melanie. 'It almost broke my wrist.'

'Well it's in now,' I said, lowering the tailgate.

Bump, bump!

'You've got to be kidding me,' said Melanie.

With the wheels on, the case was too tall to shut the tailgate.

'We'll have to take it out.'

Getting it out proved more difficult than lifting it in but eventually we got it back on terra firma. Jazz hadn't a clue what was going on, or what she'd done to deserve such treatment. We carried on regardless.

The second attempt proved equally as difficult and ended with a similar result. Even with the wheels off, the angle of the tailgate was such that closing it proved impossible.

'What now?' asked Melanie.

'Let's take it out again; I'll fold the back seats down and we'll try sliding it in.'

Jazz was up and down like a yoyo. Not so much a Jack-in-the-box as a dog-in-the-box. With the seats folded flat, we eventually managed to squeeze it in and I slammed shut the tailgate. As things turned out, we needn't have worried about her travelling. No sooner had I set off down the lane than she curled into a ball and fell asleep, exactly as she always does.

The week before we were due to travel, we received some very upsetting news. Melanie's brother Charles rang. Their father, Geoff, had collapsed and been rushed into hospital. This was his second such incident within the space of twelve months. The medical staff had decided to keep him in and run a series of tests to try and diagnose the cause. An emotional conversation ended with Charles promising to ring her as soon as he had any news.

Two years earlier, and completely out of the blue, Geoff had lost his hearing, making telephone conversations impossible. Since then, Melanie had been keeping in touch by writing regularly. Following his sudden deafness, he'd suffered a string of health issues including fainting, weight loss, and diabetes. On our last trip to England, we'd been shocked by his gaunt appearance. At the time, he reassured us that he'd been working hard to lose weight but we weren't convinced. The first time he collapsed, he was out shopping. Paramedics were called but he refused to go to hospital. Instead, he went to see his GP who requested a series of X-rays. These highlighted a shadow on his lung but he reassured Melanie that cancer was not the cause.

Later that week, on the 23rd of December, we set off on our three-week holiday to Lanzarote.

Beep, beep, beep, beep!

I'd like to say that the piercing tone of the alarm clock woke me from a deep sleep but I'd been awake for ages. I'm not sure if it's a subconscious fear of missing the flight or the excitement of going away, but I always wake early when we're setting off on holiday.

'Are you awake?' asked Melanie.

'I've been awake for hours,' I replied.

We'd set the alarm for 5:00 am. The flight didn't depart until 12:40 but we had a five-hour drive to Madrid ahead of us and this was our first experience of air travel with a pet. By 5:45 we were up, dressed, and ready for off. Jazz was curled up in her case, blissfully unaware of what lay ahead.

The journey to Madrid passed without a hitch and we quickly found the long stay car park. By now, Melanie and I were old hats at handling the travel case, even one containing an excited pooch. We wheeled her through the car park and waited for the service bus to the airport. Before long we were offloading our cargo and wheeling her into the departure hall. The airport was busy, everyone making their festive escape, and a surprising number with family pets.

We located the check-in desk and waited in line. I watched in horror as the check-in clerk weighed and tagged each passenger's luggage before sending it hurtling along a conveyor. As it travelled onwards, baggage from other desks bounced onto the conveyor and the whole lot bumped and banged its way towards the central handling hall. I hoped Jazz wouldn't suffer such bruising punishment. Before long we were at the head of the queue.

'Passports please?' asked the young lady behind the desk.

We handed them over, along with our tickets.

'You're travelling with a pet?'

'Yes,' I replied, pointing at the travel case.

'Has it been weighed?'

'I thought you'd be doing that.'

'No. Animals get weighed over there,' she said, pointing across to the opposite side of the departure hall.

I looked back at the queue that had built up behind us and wondered if we'd make it in time for the flight.

'You can come straight back to me once it's been weighed,' she added.

At least that was good news.

We pulled her across the hall and waited our turn behind a black Labrador and a chestnut coloured Boxer. After heaving her on and off the scales, we returned to the check-in desk. As we wandered sheepishly to the front of the queue, waiting travellers gave us dirty looks.

Airport staff had electronically transferred her weight details from one side of the hall to the other.

'How does fifteen kilos sound?' asked the girl at the desk in a hushed tone.

Melanie and I glanced at each other and then nodded our agreement. We decided that this was the airline's way of spreading a little festive cheer; either that or Jazz had lost ten kilos since we left home.

'You need to take the dog back to the other desk; they'll take it off you,' she said, handing us our boarding cards.

Thank heavens for that. At least Jazz wouldn't have to fight her way down the conveyor with all the other luggage.

As we said our goodbyes and handed her over to an airline employee, a tear formed in the corner of Melanie's eye. Jazz had no idea what was in store; mind you, neither did we.

'She'll be fine,' I said.

Two and a half hours after boarding, the pilot announced our descent. The flight had been textbook: a smooth ascent and a turbulence-free flight. The landing was less so. As the undercarriage kissed the runway the pilot hit the brakes as if his life, and everyone else's, depended on it. The noise from the engines was deafening as he engaged reverse thrust. The aircraft decelerated so quickly that I felt my bum sliding forward and the seat backs throughout the cabin rattled as the aircraft shuddered to a halt. All I could think of was Jazz. I had visions of her case tumbling along the fuselage closely followed by another 250 suitcases.

'Bloody hell!' I exclaimed.

I glanced at Melanie who looked terrified.

Nervous laughter filled the cabin followed by spontaneous applause.

'Next thing you know they'll be taking up a collection,'

I mumbled under my breath.

We alighted the plane on a tidal wave of impatience and followed the crowd through passport control and into the baggage reclamation area. Wherever Jazz was, she would have to wait. There'd be plenty of time to find her once we had our luggage.

Save for a few excited children, the passengers waited patiently for the luggage carousel to move. As soon as it did, the mood changed. Relaxed holidaymakers transformed into a rabid horde. People shuffled forward towards the moving carousel, marking out their territory with flailing elbows and strategically positioned luggage trolleys. Thou shalt not push in, saith the unwritten rules of baggage collection. Thankfully, after ten minutes of watching nothing but thin air travel around the carousel, territorial tensions eased to a mood of tired impatience. All eyes were focused on the plastic curtain separating us from the luggage handling area.

Da'd'da'd'da'd'da'd'da'd' Da!

Melanie scrambled around in her handbag searching for her mobile phone.

Da'd'da'd'da'd'da'd'da'd' Da!

Nokia's annoying ringtone echoed through the vast hall.

'Hello,' she said quietly, lifting the phone to her ear.

Melanie had been waiting for this call since speaking with her brother three days ago.

'So what are they going to do?' she asked.

She paused, listening to the reply.

'When?'

Woof, woof, woof, woof!

Without warning the first piece of luggage burst through the plastic curtain. Melanie and I couldn't believe it as a crescendo of *AHHH!* filled the vast expanse and Jazz barked her way around the carousel.

Woof, woof, woof, woof!

Her moment in the spotlight was brief as Melanie and I

took centre stage. Surrendering our midpoint position, we dashed towards the travel case.

'The dog's just arrived,' she said to her brother. 'Just a minute.'

Woof, woof, woof, woof!

With the phone wedged between her ear and shoulder, we waited for the case.

'You grab the back and I'll take the front,' I said as it neared.

Woof, woof, woof, woof!

As soon as Jazz clapped eyes on us, her vocal joy hit new heights.

Woof, woof, woof, woof!

Getting her in and out of the car was one thing; taking the case off a moving luggage carousel was quite another. We had one chance: miss it and Jazz would have to complete another circuit.

'Lift!' I called, as soon as we'd grabbed hold.

Our lack of coordination caused Melanie to stumble forwards. As she did, I staggered backwards, and the case tipped onto its side. Dazed and confused, Jazz fell silent and the hall held its breath. Quickly we righted it.

Woof, woof, woof, woof!

The hall breathed a sigh of relief.

'You're alright now,' I reassured her.

Moments later I spotted the suitcases and dragged them off. Throughout our trial, Charles had waited patiently. With everything secure Melanie listened to the news.

The results of Geoff's tests had come through; the diagnosis was lung cancer. To make matters worse, the prognosis was discouraging. The tumour was inoperable. In two days they would begin a course of chemotherapy with the aim of improving the quality of his remaining time. Melanie's devastation was compounded by the fact that, due to his deafness, she couldn't even speak with him.

Pulling Jazz through the airport felt quite surreal and a real head-turner. As always, she'd taken everything in her stride. By the time we'd driven to our holiday villa, she seemed to have forgotten about her adventure on the carousel.

For the first few days, our mood was quite sombre, but life goes on. We booked a flight for Melanie to return to England at the end of January. By then her dad would have completed his treatment and be recovering at home.

On Christmas day we enjoyed a barbecue lunch and an afternoon of sunbathing. That's when I realised exactly how much I'd missed our Christmas getaways to a warm, sunny climate. We'd kept up with some of our seasonal rituals, like Christmas shopping for example. Twenty euros each and as many presents as we can buy one another in under an hour, but alfresco dining in Galicia is a definite no-no at this time of year.

A few days before New Year, we received an unexpected email from Pilar.

From: "Pilar Xxxxx"
To: Craig Briggs
Subject: Happy New Year
Date: Fri, 29 Dec 2005 21:09:00

We wish you a very Happy New Year and all the best for 2006.

We keep moving the papers of the house... i've called yesterday to Lugo and they answered me they are in time, since time expires around the 18th of February... anyway i will write to them a complain letter, since its impossible they take so long to resolve a situation they made. So as soon as i get the answer i will let you know.

Take good care of yourself since i understand there are very low temperatures in the village this winter.

We are going to be there on the 31 and 1ˢᵗ Since its my father in low birthday... yes he is going to be 85.

All the very best for the camming NEW YEAR.

Muchos saludos con nuestros mejores deseos.

Pilar

'What does it mean?' asked Melanie.

'Your guess is as good as mine. She seems to be suggesting that the paperwork for the house isn't ready and she hasn't a clue when it will be.'

We'd been so busy over the last few months that we hadn't given the matter much thought. It wasn't as though we were in a hurry. The wheels of Spanish bureaucracy have their own speed. If Pilar couldn't get them to revolve any faster, I'm damn sure we couldn't.

Powerless to change the situation, we put the matter to the back of our minds to concentrate on more pressing matters. Where to dine on New Year's Eve? After due consideration, we chose the coastal resort of Costa Teguise, a short taxi ride away.

Booking the taxi proved easy; arranging the collection point, a little less so. Neither our villa, nor any other in the village, had a house number, so we chose a well-known landmark close by.

'Do you think he's forgotten?' asked Melanie as we waited on the corner of the street.

I glanced at my watch.

'He's only half an hour late,' I replied. 'We'll give him a bit longer.'

Save for billions of bright pinpricks, the moonless night sky was pitch black. Out of the darkness came the unmistakable glare of headlights, flickering as they sped along bumpy roads.

'I bet this is it,' I said.

The vehicle pulled up alongside. A gleaming white

Mercedes with a tan vinyl roof. We jumped in and the driver sped off.

'Costa Teguise?' he asked, as we hurtled down the road.

'Yes,' I replied, 'the main square.'

Melanie and I buckled up as he sped away, charging round blind corners without a care in the world. Melanie looked across at me, anxiety etched in her face.

'Perhaps he was a racing driver in a former life,' I whispered.

Melanie looked terrified but manage a nervous smile.

Four minutes into a journey that would usually take ten, he screeched to a halt in the heart of the town. I paid the fare and managed to wish him *Feliz Año Nuevo* (Happy New Year) before he raced off to collect his next victims.

'Do you want a drink before dinner?' I asked.

'I think I need one after that.'

We wandered through the narrow streets and alleyways of this manmade resort, searching for a suitable establishment.

'This looks alright,' I said, standing outside a tapas bar.

The bar backed onto a bustling courtyard packed with holidaymakers making the most of a warm Canarian evening. After a quick aperitif we ambled to The Slow Boat Chinese restaurant for our final meal of an eventful year.

On such occasions, it's easy to let one's cravings conquer moderation. We started with a mixed platter: crispy spring rolls, deep fried smoked chicken wontons, honey roasted pork spare ribs, lightly battered deep fried tiger prawns, and prawn toast. The second course was an easy choice. No Chinese meal would be complete without crispy duck pancakes, smothered in plum sauce and stuffed with spring onions. For our main course we chose fillet steak in Cantonese sauce served on a sizzling hotplate and accompanied with egg fried rice. As the waiter removed the stainless steel lid from the hotplate, an aromatic mist of steamy vapour rose from the table while the sauce hissed and spluttered. The entire meal was delicious: a real treat.

'Dessert sir?' asked the waiter after he'd cleared the table.

Melanie and I were absolutely stuffed.

'No thank you,' I replied.

We polished off the wine, paid the bill, and wandered back into town in search of a busy bar in which to see in the New Year.

With seconds to spare, we entered a bar and the countdown began. Ten, nine, eight … one, *Happy New Year!*

The bar we'd stumbled into looked out across a horseshoe-shaped bay, surrounded by hotels and holiday apartments. Bright lights from beachside bars were reflected in the shimmering sea. By one o'clock the crowds had thinned as revellers headed home. Those of us still partying were in for a surprise. On the far shore of the bay, an aerial rocket signalled the start of a spectacular fireworks display. Loud explosions lit up the night sky. Magical pyrotechnics were launched into the sea, exploding on impact, sending a kaleidoscope of fiery starlight cascading over the Atlantic.

Our evening ended as it began, standing on the pavement waiting for a taxi. Thankfully, the ride home was a little more sedate.

A few days into the new year, our friends Aly and Donny invited us to their home for Sunday lunch. We'd met them five years earlier and immediately hit it off. Donny was keen to show me his new toy, a Hyosung GV 650 Aquila. A Korean built cruiser, as much a work of art as a motorcycle. Nestled below a cool grey petrol tank was 650 cubic centimetres of brute force, beautifully configured in a striking V-twin. With its curvaceous styling and polished chrome, it looked a million dollars.

'It's stunning,' I remarked.

'Do you fancy coming for a ride?' he asked, in his broad Scottish accent.

As a former biker, I couldn't resist.

'I'd love to.'

Donny walked off towards the garage and returned carrying two crash helmets.

'Here you go,' he said, handing me one.

I tugged it on and fastened the chin strap. Donny inserted the ignition key and pressed the starter button. A shrill squeak launched a bolt of current to the motor and the beast fired into life. A sharp twist of the throttle sent a booming roar shooting out of the chromium plated exhaust manifold. Donny jumped on and flicked out the pillion foot pegs. I climbed onto the elevated pillion seat.

Before long we were gliding effortlessly down the road. Donny opened her up and the sudden burst of speed threatened to pull me off the back. As the speed increased, a warm wind whistled past my face and blurred images flashed before my eyes. It felt great to be back on a bike, but I have to admit, I much prefer being in the driving seat.

A great day out ended with some fantastic news. As soon as we returned to our holiday home I switched on the computer to check the emails.

'Guess what?' I said excitedly.

'What?'

'Guess?'

'We've had another enquiry wanting to rent Bob and Janet's.'

Since uploading the property details onto the online advertising sites, we'd had three enquires but no confirmed bookings.

'Better than that,' I replied.

'We've got a booking?'

'We have indeed.'

'That's brilliant.'

I was so excited, I emailed Bob straight away.

From: Craig Briggs
To: "Robert Xxxxxx"
Subject: Yipee!!!!!
Date: Sun, 08 Jan 2006 19:56:22

Happy New Year

Just a very quick note to let you know we've taken our first booking today. Last week of June and first week of July.

I'll send the paperwork out over the next few days and wait for the deposit

Love to you both
Craig and Mel

Bob's response was swift.

From: "Robert Xxxxxx"
To: Craig Briggs
Subject: Re: Yipee!!!!!
Date: Tue, 10 Jan 2006 19:41:28

Happy New Year to you both.
Great to get a booking so soon, thought it might take a bit longer than this. Let's hope that this is the first of many.

Hope you are having a good holiday, bet it is a lot warmer and brighter than here. It is not too cold but it is really gloomy and dark nearly all day at the moment. Today it has been pouring with rain all day but at least we have not had any more snow!

Well enjoy the rest of your holiday and hope to hear from you soon. Roll on more bookings!!!

Love Bob and Janet

Three weeks passed far too quickly and before we knew it we were heading back to the airport to catch our flight home. Getting Jazz off the island proved far more difficult than getting her on. According to the manifest, she'd put on ten kilos. The powers that be were reluctant to accept that the airline staff in Madrid could be at fault. Given that the Canary Islands are a favoured European entry point for African drug smugglers and that pets are often used as mules, the airport's concerns were understandable. After protracted administration she was eventually allowed to board.

Although we'd enjoyed our time on the island and looked forward to future festive breaks, something had changed. Three and a half years ago, Lanzarote had topped our list of migration destinations. Revisiting this special place only reaffirmed that we'd made the correct choice by moving to Galicia. It wasn't that the island had changed very much; it hadn't. The people we knew were as friendly and helpful as they'd always been. We were the ones that had changed. Compared to living and working in England, Lanzarote seemed peaceful and relaxed but compared to life it Canabal, it's very busy, almost garish.

Here in the Spanish countryside we stare out across rolling hills and distant mountains; gently flowing rivers meander their way along deep forested valleys as they pass silently through this never ending landscape. Old women sit on drystone walls, knitting colourful cardigans as they watch their flock grazing on rich pasture. The quiet of the day is broken only by the calling of songbirds or the distant barking of a village dog.

Not for the first time since moving to Galicia, I was glad to be home.

16

Bridging the Gap

On our return from Lanzarote, there were two items of mail waiting for us: a late Christmas card and a letter addressed to Melanie.

'This one's for you,' I said, handing it to her. 'I think it's from the hospital.'

Since Melanie had finished her physiotherapy treatment, we'd been expecting to hear from them confirming the date for her knee surgery. She ripped it open and pulled out the letter.

'It's the appointment for my op,' she said.

'When is it?'

Melanie was scheduled to fly back to England this weekend to visit her dad.

'Wednesday, the 8th of February.'

What a relief; she was due to return on the 28th of January. Things couldn't have worked out better.

With the exception of a pile of windswept leaves, decomposing in one corner of the garden, the grounds looked as if we'd never left home. Most of the leaves had fallen from two plane trees growing either side of the front garden. During the summer, the larger of the two provides natural shade across the driveway.

Plane trees are very popular in Galicia. They're often grown in public parks or along river banks. In most cases their growth is carefully managed. Once the trunk reaches a height of between two and three metres, they're trained to grow horizontally. From early spring through to the beginning of autumn, their large-leafed foliage creates a natural parasol. After a winter prune, the remaining branches resemble a Gaudi-like sculpture of a giant spider's web.

The two in our garden had been left to grow naturally but I was determined to change that. Last spring, I pruned the smaller of the two in a way that would encourage it to grow horizontally. Time will tell whether I've done a good job or not. I did learn one thing, however: tackling the other was way above my skillset; it had grown to well over twenty metres. Someone else would have to deal with that giant.

'Who can we get to prune the other tree?' I asked, after checking the garden.

'I've no idea,' replied Melanie.

For jobs like this, we would usually seek the counsel of our neighbour, Meli, but since the death of her son, Jesus, we'd been reluctant to trouble her.

'What about Felipe?' Melanie suggested. 'He'll know someone.'

It had been quite a while since we'd asked Felipe the architect for help. We'd bumped into him a few times in Monforte but since moving into *El Sueño*, we'd managed to sort most things out ourselves. Later that morning, we called to see him. Without hesitation, he picked up the phone and arranged for someone to call round to the house.

'He's a bit busy at the moment, but he'll come and take

a look as soon as he's free,' he said.

On our way home we called to see Manolo. Time was moving on and he still hadn't started work at *Casa Bon Vista*. Since securing our first booking, we'd received a steady stream of enquiries, raising our expectations. One way or another, we had to make sure that the house was ready.

'I have one more job to finish and I'll be straight up there,' he said.

That was great news. We knew from experience that Manolo was a man of his word. Once he started at *Casa Bon Vista*, he'd stay on site until the job was finished.

'How soon will that be?' I asked, keen for a more accurate date.

'About seven or eight weeks, depending on the weather.'

Seven or eight weeks! By my calculation, that meant Manolo wouldn't be starting until the beginning of March at the earliest. Time was slipping away. We would have to cross our fingers and hope for the best. One mistake could spell disaster.

Since returning from holiday, Jazz had taken to sleeping on the sofa. As she'd never done it before, we were a little concerned. Melanie thought it could be separation anxiety resulting from her experience on the flight. A warm sofa and a cold floor might be closer to the mark. Whatever the reason, for the sake of our new leather suite, we wanted to nip it in the bud.

The problem we had was how to stop her from entering the lounge. The living area is arranged in an L shape, with the lounge connected to the kitchen/diner through a metre-wide archway.

'What about a baby gate?' suggested Melanie.

'That's a great idea. I'll have a look on Amazon.'

My search delivered mixed results. The only gates wide enough to bridge the gap required fixing to the wall.

'I don't want it there permanently,' she said, and I agreed.

'I've got an idea.'

'What?'

Before we remodelled the house, the steps leading to the front door were much narrower. Running up both sides were steel banisters. When the builder removed them, I put them to one side just in case.

'Do you remember when we bought the house, there were railings running up to the front door?'

'Were they painted black?'

'That's right,' I replied. 'Well, I've still got them.'

'So what?'

'So, if I cut off a metre-long length and attach some feet to the bottom, we can stand it across the archway.'

'It sounds a bit clumsy. Do you think it will work?'

'Of course it'll work.'

Melanie seemed unconvinced but agreed to go along with my idea. All I needed to do was unearth the railings. I'd put them in one corner of the waste ground at the back of the house, on the opposite side to our newly cultivated *huerta*. They'd been laying there for nigh on two and a half years. During that time, they'd been devoured by a thicket of brambles. After a bruising battle, and a few choice words, I finally managed to free them.

The banister was built in three sections: the handrail at the top, a parallel rail at the bottom, and a series of welded balustrades. Despite its excessive weight, I had every confidence that this would make an ideal baby gate, or in our case, dog guard. Cutting it to the correct length would be easy; working out how to keep it upright, less so. I hauled it over to the shed, plugged in the angle grinder and started cutting.

As I sliced through the steel, sparks flew off the cutting blade like a stationary Catherine wheel on bonfire night. The unmistakable smell of superheated metal filled the air, but that wasn't all. Mixed in with this smoky scent was the whiff of burning fabric; that's when I noticed my trousers, smouldering from the sparks.

'*Arh!*'

Instinctively, I called out, dropped the angle grinder, and frantically patted the fabric around my ankles. Talk about hot pants; mine were on fire. Melanie heard the scream and rushed outside.

'What's matter?'

'Nothing,' I replied, feeling a little embarrassed.

'Do be careful,' she said, before stepping back inside.

At the expense of ruining a pair of work trousers, I'd learnt a valuable lesson. When grinding metal objects, always make sure that the cutting blade is rotating in the opposite direction to your pants.

'What do you think?' I asked, carrying the sawn-off banister into the kitchen.

'Is it long enough?'

I had to admit, it did look a little short.

'Of course it is,' I replied, confidently.

And so it proved.

'We just need some feet now,' I said.

'What sort of feet?'

I hadn't got a clue. Metalwork usually involves welding but as I didn't have a welder, I would have to find another way to attach the feet to the railings.

'I'm not sure but I'll know when I see them,' I replied.

Later that day we drove to BricoKing, a self-service DIY warehouse on the outskirts of Monforte. Surely they would stock something I could use.

Finding what you want in these cathedrals of do-it-yourself consumerism is difficult enough when you know what you're looking for; when you don't, it's almost impossible.

'What about this?' suggested Melanie.

'No, that's no good.'

'Will these do?'

'No, they're no good.'

I could tell from Melanie's expression that my repeated rejection was starting to annoy her.

'What's that?' she asked, as I studied the timber connecting products.

'These might do.'

'The tickets says they're for connecting wood, not metal.'

Melanie clearly didn't understand the concept of bodging.

'I know that but I think they'll work perfectly.'

I'd chosen a packet of timber nail plates. The rectangular alloy plates are used to secure roof joists by nailing them across two interconnecting timbers without the need for a joint. These flat metal plates would provide the ideal platform for my freestanding dog guard.

'I can drill some holes in the bottom of the railings and bolt these to it, one at either end.'

Melanie looked sceptical, but I felt sure it would work.

My confidence was well founded. Within an hour of returning home, I'd secured the plates to the bottom of the railings, creating a custom built dog guard.

That evening, we moved Jazz's bed into the kitchen and put it next to the radiator.

'There you go, lass, you'll be lovely and warm there.'

Jazz gave me a look as if to say, 'Do I have to?'

I lifted the gate into position and admired my handiwork.

'She can't get through that gap, can she?' asked Melanie.

By design, the guard didn't quite fit flush to the wall; the protruding feet saw to that.

'I doubt it,' I replied. 'It's far too heavy.'

We were just nodding off when a strange noise echoed through the house.

Clickety-bang, clickety-bang, clickety-bang, clickety-bang!

'What's that?' asked Melanie.

'I've no idea.'

Clickety-bang, clickety-bang, clickety-bang, clickety-bang!

'There it is again,' she said. 'Someone's in the house.'

Even the clumsiest burglar wouldn't make such a racket.

'Wait here and I'll take a look,' I said.

'Do be careful.'

Wearing nothing but my birthday suit, I headed for the lounge. The sight of me wandering around naked would be enough to scare anyone away. As I grabbed the door handle, it started again.

Clickety-bang, clickety-bang!

I flung it open and caught the culprit in the act. Our midnight prowler was none other than the hound charged with our security. Using her nose, she'd been nudging the guard, rocking it back and forth against the wall in an attempt to get into the lounge. I couldn't believe it; her actions were so out of character.

'What's matter?' I asked, in a calming tone. 'Come on, back to bed.'

I moved the guard to one side and coaxed her back onto her cushion.

'Now you stay there and go to sleep.'

I pulled the guard across the gap and returned to the bedroom.

'What was it?' asked Melanie.

I explained and we went back to sleep.

Clickety-bang, clickety-bang, clickety-bang, clickety-bang!

I rolled over and looked at the clock. Less than fifteen minutes had passed.

Clickety-bang, clickety-bang, clickety-bang, clickety-bang!

'Right, that's it, I've just about had enough. What's matter with her,' I said.

Clickety-bang, clickety-bang, clickety-bang, clickety-bang!

No sooner had I stepped out of bed than an almighty crash echoed through the house followed by an anguished cry. I dashed into the lounge. Jazz was wandering around the dining room.

'What on earth …' I was just about to raise my voice when I spotted the blood.

In her determination to enter the lounge she'd banged the guard so fiercely against the wall that it had toppled backwards and crashed to the floor, quicker than she could retreat. The result was a nasty gash on her toe. Droplets of blood traced her dazed path around the dining room.

'Melanie,' I called.

Melanie dashed into the lounge as naked as I.

'What's happened?' she asked.

The scene was straight out of a horror movie. There was no time for long explanations; Jazz needed attention. Melanie spent the next half an hour cleaning and bandaging the wound while I mopped up the blood. By the time we went back to bed, we were both shattered and Jazz had got her wish.

'Thank heavens we live in the middle of nowhere; can you imagine what the neighbours would have thought?' I said, before switching off the light.

The following morning, we decided to take Jazz to the vet: better safe than sorry. As soon as I pulled into the car park she knew exactly where we were. I lifted her out and she hobbled reluctantly towards the entrance. After a short wait, we were called into the surgery.

'What have you been doing?' asked the vet, directing her question at Jazz.

We did our best to explain but I'm sure she thought we were bonkers.

'Can you hold her?'

I wrapped my arms around Jazz. As she struggled, I tightened my grip and whispered calmly in her ear. I could feel her tiny heart pounding like a clockwork drummer boy. As a precautionary measure, the vet decided to stitch the wound. Her heart rate slowed as the anaesthetic kicked in. As the threaded needle punctured her skin she yelped, instinctively pulling her paw away. My quiet reassurance failed to stop a tear forming in the corner of her eye. Four stitches later and the wound was sealed.

'I'll give her a tetanus injection and write you a prescription for a course of antibiotics. Twice a day,' said the vet, handing Melanie the prescription.

'Does she need a cone?' I asked.

The vet glanced at Jazz who was looking really sorry for herself.

'No, there's no need,' she replied.

Despite her drowsiness, Jazz couldn't wait to leave. Stumbling along the corridor like a barroom drunk.

By the time we got home, the stitches had gone, licked clean by a very determined hound.

'I told you,' I said, having opened the tailgate. 'She needed to be wearing a cone.'

'Well we're not going back,' said Melanie. 'She'll have to make do with a bandage.'

Jazz spent the rest of the day hobbling around the house looking forlorn. She knew exactly how to gain our sympathy.

By the following day, she was almost back to normal. At least it seemed that way. If she caught us watching she would stumble back into a half-hearted limp. As for the do-it-yourself dog guard, that found a home back among the brambles.

By the time I drove Melanie to the airport in Santiago de Compostela for her flight to see her dad, Jazz had made a full recovery. The scar would take a little longer to heal. My sister, Julie, had offered to meet Melanie at Stansted Airport and drive her the 190 miles north to Huddersfield.

During her absence I decided to plant some more grapevines: ten red, of the Mencia variety, and ten Palomino white. This brought our total number of vines to seventy-five.

Given the time of year, I couldn't have asked for better weather. Most days began with a light covering of frost. Morning mist cleared by lunchtime to reveal a cloudless, powder blue sky. Little or no wind made the afternoons feel comfortably warm but as soon as the sun dipped below the horizon, the temperature plummeted.

Every afternoon, Jazz and I would take a walk up the lane into the countryside. The first property we come across is about a mile from home. More often than not, the old man that lives there would be sitting outside, reading a newspaper and warming his frail frame in the afternoon sun. He had a small, wiry-haired dog, similar in appearance to its owner.

'Hola,' he'd call, as we approached.

'*Buenas tardes* (Good afternoon),' I'd reply.

Jazz would wander towards him and he'd offer her an open palm of friendship.

'*Hace frío* (It's cold),' he'd remark.

When it comes to discussing the weather, Galicians are very similar to Yorkshire folk. I'd go as far as to say that climate is the most popular topic of conversation in these parts. If it's cold, it's too cold, wet, too wet, dry and we'll run out of water, and hot, it's stifling. Having exhausted my climatic vocabulary, I'd bid him farewell and we'd head back home.

On one such afternoon, our quiet walk home was interrupted by a spine-tingling wail. It emanated from the dense undergrowth at the side of the lane. Jazz stopped in her tracks, ears pricked and eyes wide. Whatever the source of this terrifying scream, it seemed to be heading in our direction. Seconds later, a scrawny fox dashed out of the scrub, leapt over the drainage ditch and stood in the middle of the lane. Jazz stood motionless, transfixed by its sudden appearance.

The predator stared back at us, looking equally surprised. Its sharp facial features, slim elegant snout and pointed ears gave it an air of intimidating beauty. Lean and mean with a rich, milk chocolate coloured coat and dark, almost black, bushy tail sticking out like a feather duster. Despite its menacing appearance, Jazz's instincts kicked in.

Like a greyhound leaving a trap, she launched herself towards it. I was petrified. A confrontation between a house pet and a bloodthirsty marauder would have one outcome.

'*Jazz!*' I screamed at the top of my voice. '*Come here!*'

My cry stopped her in her tracks and frightened the fox into retreating. For a few seconds it headed down the lane in clear sight before jumping the drainage ditch, clambering over a drystone wall and disappearing into the forest.

Jazz looked confused, torn between my command and her natural instincts. Unable to contain her excitement she charged off again. A second call brought her pursuit to an abrupt end. For me, our pseudo-hunt came to a satisfactory conclusion, although Jazz seemed a little less content.

Our afternoon walks gave me the opportunity to consider Melanie's birthday. Most people in the UK remember 1966 as the year that England's football team won the World Cup or that a bloke from Huddersfield, Harold Wilson, was prime minister. Only a select few remember the year's most significant event. On the 17th of May, Mr and Mrs Kidd gave birth to a baby girl: Melanie Jayne. Forty years on and I felt this momentous occasion deserved to be celebrated in style, but how?

Birthdays in our household have always followed a predictable pattern: a romantic meal for two at one of our favourite eateries. My brain went into overdrive. If only there was an Indian restaurant in the area, but there wasn't. We'd already found out that the closest one is in Vigo, a round trip of over 250 kilometres.

Without warning, my mind leapt out of the box. What about ordering a takeaway?

On reflection, a stone-cold korma, soggy chapattis, and lumpy pilau rice hardly seemed the most fitting way to enter the second age.

What if I had it flown in from Huddersfield? That

would certainly bring a whole new meaning to ordering a 'plane' naan.

Slowly but surely my mind slipped back into the box and then it hit me. What better way to celebrate her fortieth birthday than with family and friends in one of her favourite restaurants? A surprise birthday party at the Naawab Indian restaurant in Huddersfield, England. All I had to do now was realise my epiphany.

17

Ice and a Slice

Initial investigations into celebrating Melanie's birthday in England looked promising. The flight time couldn't have been better, departing Santiago de Compostela at 11:35 am and arriving in Stansted at 12:40. This would give us plenty of time to drive the 190 miles to Huddersfield. We could stop en route for lunch and still avoid the rush hour traffic. I also discovered that Huddersfield's most prestigious accommodation, the George Hotel, was offering an airport special: a one-night stay at very attractive rates.

Just as it seemed that everything was falling into place, I received a most unwanted email.

> **From:** "Mr Xxx Campbell"
> **To:** Craig Briggs
> **Subject:** Owners Direct – Enquiry for property ref: S3337.
> **Date:** Date Thu, 26 Jan 20:00:11
>
> You have been sent an enquiry from Owners Direct:
> Dear Craig

I would like to book Casa Bon Vista for 10 days starting 15 May till 25 May

Look forward to hearing from you.

Mr Xxx Campbell

The one thing I hadn't taken into account was a request to stay at *Casa Bon Vista*, slap-bang in the middle of her birthday. Had it been our property, I would have declined the booking but it wasn't. We'd made a commitment to Bob and Janet and I felt duty bound to honour it.

On reflection, the booking might not be such a bad thing after all. In fact, it could actually work in my favour. What better way to camouflage a surprise birthday party? There'd be plenty of time to prepare the house and greet the guests before flying to England on the 17th. My uninvited party poopers had turned into the life and soul. This perfectly timed reservation ensured that nothing would stand in our way.

Spending a week with Jazz had its advantages but I was looking forward to seeing Melanie again. Despite her concerns, I'd made it through the week without starving to death. I'd even discovered what a marvellous invention the dishwasher is. The same can't be said of the washing machine. Thankfully, my wardrobe lasted the week.

After seven days of unseasonably good weather, I was flabbergasted to open the window shutters on Saturday morning and see tiny snowflakes falling from an overcast and menacing-looking sky. By 10:00 am the entire countryside was covered with a blanket of virgin snow. Hardly ideal weather for driving the hundred kilometres to Santiago Airport. Thankfully, Melanie's flight wasn't due to land until mid-afternoon. Snowfall is quite rare but on every previous occasion it had melted long before lunchtime.

As the morning wore on, the snowfall intensified. The

flakes became larger and the depth thickened. It's bound to stop soon, I thought to myself, but it didn't. Hour after hour it fell, with no sign of stopping.

The journey to the airport usually takes about an hour, so I decided to give myself two. Canabal is situated on the low lying slopes of the Val de Lemos. The only way out of the vale is upward. Driving through the village created virgin tracks in the snow. When I reached the main highway, traffic had made a slushy corridor which disappeared into the distance. From the town of Monforte, the main road climbs steeply out of the vale. The slushy tracks became less visible and the snowfall thickened.

Coming from Yorkshire, I've had plenty of practice driving in snowy conditions. It's vital to keep the vehicle moving, use smooth, gentle movements of the steering wheel, and whatever you do, don't stand on the brakes.

In spite of the conditions, everything was going well until I reached the village of Escairon, eighteen kilometres from home. As I drove past the exit sign, a bright blue glow flashed through the heavy snowfall. Slowly, I lifted off the accelerator and began shifting down through the gears. Positioned across the road was a 4x4, sporting the distinctive white and green livery of the Guardia Civil. With room to spare, I slowed to crawling pace and braked to a halt. An officer jumped out and walked towards me. As he approached I rolled down the window.

'¿*Donde vas* (Where are you going)?' he asked.

'The airport in Santiago,' I replied.

'Do you have some snow chains?'

'No.'

'Then you can't go any further. You'll have to turn round and go back,' he added, pointing to a gap in the central reservation.

Pleading my case seemed futile, so I turned around and headed back towards Monforte. His concerns were understandable; this route to Santiago involves scaling Monte do Faro, a windswept mountain over 1,181 metres above sea level. I had hoped that the snowfall was localised; no such luck. Driving back, I racked my brain for an alternative route. I'd already wasted over half an hour. I found myself in uncharted territory, not knowing which way to turn. There was no time to lose; the weather conditions were deteriorating and Melanie's plane was due to arrive in less than an hour and a half. To make matters worse, when she left for England, she'd forgotten to take her mobile phone.

'I'll use Mum's if I need one,' she'd said.

The only route left open to me was through our provincial capital, Lugo, and then on to Santiago. I'd just have to keep my fingers crossed that the roads were passable.

The road to Lugo is far less dramatic. Rather than driving up and down mountains, the highway rises gently to a plateau before dropping gradually into the city. That said, there was no let-up in the weather and my progress was painfully slow. I lost count of the number of vehicles that had left the road and ended up in a ditch. It took almost two hours to drive to Lugo, a journey that would usually take less than one. By now I was late. All I could do was continue on and hope that Melanie would ring me from the airport. As I neared Santiago the snowfall eased and eventually stopped. Ten kilometres from my destination the phone rang.

'Where are you?' blubbered Melanie.

'I'm nearly there,' I replied. 'You wouldn't believe the journey I've had.'

Melanie cast a forlorn figure as I pulled up outside the arrivals hall. I jumped out of the car and we hugged each other as if our lives depended on it. Now that the snow had stopped, and the roads were beginning to clear, I decided to take the shortest route home.

Unfortunately, we weren't out of the woods yet. By the time I'd given Melanie a blow-by-blow account of my journey, we'd started our ascent of Monte do Faro. The settled snow thickened the higher we climbed but providing we could keep moving, I was confident of reaching the summit. Abandoned vehicles formed an obstacle course, but still we climbed. Eventually, we reached the top.

As I cleared the brow I slowed to walking pace, using first gear to control our speed. In the distance, flashing blue lights pierced the evening gloom. Gently, I applied the brake. The ABS kicked in, sending rapid vibrations shuddering through the steering wheel. All my driver instincts screamed to lift off the brake as our forward momentum propelled us toward the stationary police car but my head countered. Stand on the brake and steer the car. I had a split second to decide. In such a desperate situation there are no half measures. I tightened my grip on the steering wheel and pressed down on the brake pedal, as hard as I could. Still we slid uncontrollably towards the traffic car. Time slowed to a crawl. Had I made the wrong decision? Any second now, we'd have to brace for impact.

Just as a collision seemed inevitable, the car began to respond. My foot was hard down but the car was drifting into the centre of the road. Stopping was impossible; I'd just have to hope that the officer directing traffic got out of the way. Slowly I turned the wheel, coaxing the car around the hazard. With nerves of steel and sophisticated braking technology we avoided a collision.

With the danger passed and my heart rate returning to normal, I decided to embroil Melanie in my birthday scheming.

'I took another booking while you were away,' I said.

'That's good,' she replied.

'Well it is and it isn't.'

'What do you mean?'

'It's for ten nights from the 15th until the 25th of May.' I paused waiting for a response.

'That's alright.'

'You don't mind working over your birthday?'

'Needs must,' she replied.

I decided not to raise the matter again. The last thing I wanted to do was heighten her suspicions.

It had taken three hours to drive to Santiago and another two to get home. We'd had quite an adventure and were delighted to be back at *El Sueño* in one piece.

During her stay in England, Melanie accumulated a vast selection of vegetable and salad seeds the likes of which I'd never seen before. If she managed to propagate them all, I was convinced that we'd have enough vegetables to feed the Five Thousand.

'I don't even like French beans,' I moaned, thumbing through the packets.

'Well you don't have to eat them.'

I ignored her comment and continued flicking through.

'You are joking?'

'What?'

'Lettuce, you've bought a packet of lettuce seeds?'

'They were only ninety-nine pence,' she replied.

It wouldn't surprise me if Galicia grows more lettuce than the rest of the world put together. Throughout summer, neighbours are literally falling over themselves to give them away. Hardly a day goes by when someone from the village doesn't leave a carrier bag stuffed with lettuce hanging over the gate, two, three, even four on occasion.

All those lettuce and we were going to be growing our own. I couldn't believe it. To make matters worse, English lettuce are about as tasty as a glass of water.

'And where are you going to grow all these seeds?'

A few pots of herbs on the kitchen windowsill is one thing but crop cultivation on an industrial scale is quite another.

'I'm going to get a greenhouse.'

'A greenhouse!'

'Just a small one.'

Any suggestion that we might actually save money by growing our own vegetables seemed ridiculous. Within the week, Melanie had bought herself a so-called greenhouse and planted the seeds. It looked more like a clear plastic shoe cupboard with a pitched roof that the slightest breeze would send tumbling down the garden. Its only redeeming feature was its miserly price tag.

Ten days after her return, Melanie went into hospital to get her knee sorted once and for all.

'There's no point in you waiting,' she said, after being admitted to the ward.

Leaving a loved one in the care of hospital staff seems perfectly normal to most UK families, particularly when the procedure is non-life threatening. I'm not sure why but for Spanish families this is unthinkable.

On this occasion I couldn't wait to get away; Melanie's overnight stay was the perfect opportunity to finalise the travel plans for her birthday surprise. I double checked the flight times and hotel availability. Everything was fitting into place perfectly. I was just about to start booking when the phone rang.

Ring ring … Ring ring.

'Hello.'

'It's me,' said Melanie. 'Can you come and pick me up?'

'What?'

'I've just seen the consultant and the first thing he said was, "What are you doing here?" When I showed him my appointment he said that he wasn't going to operate until tomorrow and as I was only having a local anaesthetic, there was no reason to stay overnight.'

'Local anaesthetic!'

I didn't like the sound of that.

'I know,' she replied. 'I don't like the sound of that.'

My scheming would have to wait. I dropped everything and drove into town to pick her up.

The following day we went back to the hospital. This

time I hung around for a while to make sure everything was going to plan. Her operation was scheduled for early afternoon.

'You might as well go,' said Melanie.

'I'll come back this evening about six,' I replied. 'Is there anything you want me to bring?'

'I don't think so.'

I spent the day finalising the birthday plans. Everything was in place and Melanie hadn't a clue. At a quarter to six I jumped in the car and drove back to the hospital. When I arrived, Melanie was sitting up in bed reading a book, looking as though nothing had happened.

'Did they do it?' I asked.

'Oh yes, it's all done.'

'Did you feel anything?'

'Only the injections for the anaesthetic.'

'That's good then. Did you watch?'

'I did not,' she replied. 'Dr Miguéns asked me to take a look at one point but I daren't.'

'How do you feel?'

'Fine,' she replied, 'but he said it might start aching once the anaesthetic wears off.'

'How soon can you come home?'

'He'll see me again in the morning, when he does his rounds. If everything's OK, I should be able to leave straight away.'

That was great news.

'You're in bother though,' she added.

'Me, what have I done?'

Melanie explained that once he'd finished the procedure, he came looking for me. Apparently, it's customary for family members to wait outside the operating theatre to hear the outcome. When he couldn't find me, he was most perturbed.

'Oh well, I'll know better next time.'

'There's not going to be a next time,' replied Melanie.

The following day I returned just before lunch. Dr

Miguéns had given her the all clear.

'Does that mean you can go?'

'I've just got to have an injection.'

A few minutes later a nurse entered the room with Melanie's medication.

'This is an anticoagulant. I'll administer this and you can take these with you. One a day for the next fourteen days,' she said, handing Melanie a white paper bag containing fourteen syringes.

'Will a nurse call at the house?' asked Melanie.

'A nurse?'

'To give me the injection.'

'No,' she smiled, 'you'll have to do that.'

Melanie turned white at the thought of self-administering a hypodermic injection.

'I can't do it,' she said, glancing across at me.

I could see where this was leading, so made my excuses. I hate needles more than Melanie.

'I'll wait outside,' I said, turning to leave.

'Your husband then,' said the nurse, before I'd taken a step.

'I can't do it.'

'You'll have to,' pleaded Melanie.

'There's nothing to worry about,' she said.

That was easy for her to say.

'Come here. I'll show you what to do.'

Hestantly, I shuffled over to the bed. Melanie lifted her nightdress.

'One day here and the next there,' she said, pointing to an area of flesh either side of her navel.

'This is the needle,' she added, tearing open a sealed packet containing a single hypodermic with a pre-measured dose.

'Take a little of this,' she said, moistening a ball of cotton wool with iodine, 'rub here, insert the needle and push the syringe, and that's it: simple.'

I'd been so focused on the ball of cotton wool and

bottle of iodine, I missed the actual injection. Melanie looked surprised and I felt nauseous.

All I could think of was *The Generation Game*: a TV gameshow where contestants had to complete specialist tasks after the briefest instruction by an industry expert. Their attempts to replicate the expert usually ended in disaster, providing hilarious entertainment for the viewer. If only Melanie knew what I was thinking, I doubt she'd find it amusing; I know I didn't.

'You can get dressed now,' she said to Melanie.

Our exit from the hospital proved significantly easier than her first visit, last May. She still couldn't use the crutches but we managed to get back to the car without any problem.

The following day I woke with a sense of dread. After lunch I would have to get straight to the point. All too soon the time to confront my fear arrived. Melanie looked as nervous as me. I thought it important to put on a brave face.

'OK,' I said confidently, 'are you ready?'

'Not really.'

'Don't worry, it'll be fine.'

I unscrewed the cap off the iodine, placed a ball of cotton wool over the top and shook it gently. Melanie's navel stared at me menacingly. Suddenly, the enormity of the task hit home. I stared at her stomach looking for evidence of yesterday's injection with the words "One day here and the next there" ringing in my ears.

'Which side did you have it in yesterday?' I asked.

'I don't know. I wasn't looking; you know how I hate needles. I thought you were meant to be watching.'

'I was, but it all happened so quick.'

My admission did nothing to instil confidence in my patient.

'I think it was this side,' I said, prodding my finger into Melanie's midriff.

Melanie flinched.

'That tickles,' she said, squirming deeper into the mattress.

Gently I rubbed a small area of flesh with the cotton wool.

'That's freezing,' she complained.

We hadn't even got to the sharp end of the business and I was already feeling queasy. Time to set some ground rules.

'Look, Mel, this is difficult enough without you making it any harder. If you want me to do this, you're going to have to remain perfectly still and not say a word.'

'OK, just pass me a book.'

I handed her a paperback. She opened it and pulled it firmly into her chest, hiding everything from view.

The paper bag containing the syringes was on the bedside table. I reached across and took one out. Using both hands I burst the sealed packet and pulled out the hypodermic. A plastic sheath covered the needle. Gently I pulled it off. Just looking at it made me feel weak at the knees.

Pull yourself together, Craig, I thought to myself. Administering this anticoagulant could well save Melanie's life. If I didn't do it, who would? Besides which, I'm sure the novelty of loading the dishwasher will soon wear off.

'Right, don't move an inch,' I instructed.

Having gathered my courage, I prepared to strike. I realised then exactly how ill prepared I was. It had seemed so straightforward when the nurse had done it: in went the needle, down went the plunger and hey presto. I was stuck at first base wondering how to hold the damn thing.

I decided to grip the hypodermic between two fingers with my thumb on top of the plunger. Slowly, I lowered it towards her stomach.

Concentrate, Craig, concentrate, I told myself.

Viewing this area of bronzed flesh as a piece of my beloved Melanie was simply not going to work. I banished all thoughts of human stomachs from my mind and concentrated on one square inch of skin. The needle touched its target but failed to penetrate. A little pressure was called for. Gently, I pushed but as soon as I did, a droplet of liquid squirted from the tip of the needle and dribbled down her stomach.

'Oh!'

'Oh what?' asked Melanie, who up until then had been absent from my thoughts.

'Nothing … nothing, go back to reading your book.'

My hypodermic handling technique required modification. I deliberated for a moment.

I know: Phil "The Power" Taylor.

Phil "The Power" Taylor is probably the greatest professional darts player ever to step up to the oche. His technique was to grip the arrow between index finger and thumb, gently yet firmly. To date, it had helped him secure sixteen world championships. If it was good enough for him, it was good enough for me.

Quickly, I switched my grip and once again lowered the needle onto Melanie's stomach. Gently, yet firmly, I pushed the barrel downward. I couldn't believe it; the needle still wouldn't puncture the skin. It was as if I was pushing my finger into a feather pillow. I pushed a little harder but still nothing. Just my luck to get a blunt needle, I thought to myself.

By now the indentation in Melanie's stomach was almost as deep as her belly button. I was just about to give up when the needle punctured the skin and plunged into her stomach, disappearing from sight. The sudden shock stopped me in my tracks. I certainly wasn't expecting that.

Is it meant to go in that far?

There wasn't time to consider such things. I pressed the plunger and slowly withdrew the needle. I half-expected a jet of blood to shoot out and hit me in the eye; thankfully, it didn't.

'There you go,' I said, with a sigh of relief. 'That didn't hurt, did it?'

'No comment,' said Melanie, buried within the pages of her paperback.

As the week progressed, small bruises developed around her navel. Finding a new entry point became increasingly difficult. After a few days we discovered that relaxation assisted penetration. By the end of the fortnight we were both relieved that this prickly ordeal had come to a satisfactory conclusion.

18

Breaking News

Melanie's convalescence progressed well. Within days of returning home, she'd swapped the bed for the comfort of an armchair. I'd like to say that she'd got to grips with using crutches but I fear the gods of coordination were looking the other way when Melanie was born.

Clang, clang, clang, clang!

Jazz leapt to her feet and dashed to the French doors.

Woof, woof, woof, woof!

'I'll go,' I said, jokingly.

Parked in the lane was a brand new pickup truck and standing at the gates were two unfamiliar faces.

'Who is it?' asked Melanie.

'I've no idea.'

There was only one way to find out.

'Hola,' I called, as I walked towards the gates.

'Hola,' replied the taller of the two.

'Can I help you?' I asked.

He introduced himself as Pepé.

'And this is José,' he added.

I stared at them, still none the wiser.

'Felipe rang me about a tree.'

Like a break in the clouds on a bright sunny day, the purpose of their visit became blindingly apparent.

'Come in,' I said, pulling open the gate. 'This is the tree.'

Pepé and José stood in the middle of the driveway staring at its form.

'It's not worth anything,' said Pepé, shaking his head.

His comment came as quite a surprise. I hadn't expected to be paid for the tree, quite the contrary.

'What do you want to do with it?' he asked.

'I want to train it, like that one.'

I pointed at the smaller tree in the opposite corner. It lacked the finesse and stature of a sculptured Galician tree but they could see what I was trying to achieve. Pepé spoke to José, who nodded his head in agreement.

'José is happy to do it for the timber,' said Pepé. 'He'll call back next weekend if that's OK with you?'

I was more than happy to accept his offer.

A week later José turned up as arranged. His mode of transport was an ageing family hatchback. Had it been a stick of furniture, I would have described it as "shabby chic", only without the chic.

'José's here,' I said, watching him reverse onto the drive.

Clang, clang, clang, clang!

He announced his arrival by yanking the bell chain. The weather over the last few days had been dry but bitterly cold. I wrapped up warm before venturing outside.

'Where do you think you're going?' I asked, as Melanie got to her feet.

'I'm just going to say hello.'

José's arrival coincided with the end of Melanie's official period of convalescence. We were both delighted;

my crash course in amateur abdominal acupuncture was finally at an end.

'Don't overdo it on your first day.'

'Don't worry. I'll be careful.'

With my fleece zipped up I went outside to greet him.

'*Buenas tardes* (Good afternoon),' I called, as I hurried to the gate.

'Hola,' he replied chirpily.

As I opened the gate, José lifted the tailgate of his car and pulled out a red boiler suit. Having dressed for the weather, he struggled to wrestle it on. He rested his backside on the rear of the car and tugged one leg through and then the other before wriggling his arms and torso into the industrial onesie.

'Do you have a ladder?' he asked.

His question came as quite a surprise. I'd assumed he'd bring his own.

'One minute,' I replied, heading off to the shed.

When I returned, José was standing at the foot of the tree staring at the leafless branches. Thankfully, he'd brought his own tools; a pair of loppers, a lumber saw, and a petrol powered chainsaw lay on the driveway.

'Here you are,' I said, handing him the fold-up ladder. 'It's not very tall.'

José seemed unconcerned. He opened it out and leant it up against the tree. It didn't even reach the first bough. After all the effort we'd gone to to get him here, I couldn't believe he hadn't brought his own ladder.

What now, I thought to myself.

Without so much as a second thought, José grabbed his loppers and scampered up the ladder. In one seamless motion, he stepped from the ladder onto the tree and clambered upwards like a chimpanzee. Melanie, who'd been watching from the warmth of the dining room, stepped outside.

'Is it safe?' she asked.

I stared at her for a moment, thinking how to respond.

'He seems to know what he's doing,' I replied.

José had scaled the tree without a care in the world. His nerves of steel had taken him to a lofty height where the branches were at their thinnest. As he climbed, they bent and flexed and looked as if they might snap at any moment. Melanie and I looked on with bated breath.

At some point, José would have to loosen his grip on the tree as loppers are a two handed tool. To my amazement, he wedged his bulky frame between two spindly-looking branches and grabbed his loppers with both hands. Working outward from his position, they sliced through two-inch diameter branches like a hot knife through butter. One after another, long flimsy branches clattered to the ground. Having removed those within reach he changed position and started again, jamming himself into a new vantage point. Every time he moved, I cleared some of the debris.

'*Cuidado* (Look out)!' he called, as he started again.

I moved further back and looked on from a distance. Within fifteen minutes, all the thinner limbs had been severed. The driveway was covered with branches and the tree looked like something you'd expect to see on a battlefield after an artillery barrage. José climbed down, swapped his loppers for the lumber saw and scampered back up.

At least now he could use one hand to hang on with, which was just as well. Unlike loppers, the lumber saw can cut through much thicker and heavier branches. Metre-long lengths of heavy timber crashed to the ground. The effort involved took its toll. His pauses for breath lengthened as the branches thickened. Eventually his fatigue got the better of him.

'Pass me the chainsaw?' he asked.

I don't know why but the word chainsaw conjures up images of severed limbs and blood splatter. Hollywood horror aside, recurrent news headlines of accidental self-decapitation sent a shiver down my spine.

'The chainsaw,' he repeated, pointing at the alligator-toothed mechanical menace.

Eager to hide my terror, I marched across and lifted it off the ground. This was the first time I'd handled a chainsaw and its weight took me by surprise. Cautiously, I climbed the ladder, one rung at a time, and although the motor wasn't running, I took great care to hold it as far away from my leg as possible.

Melanie had been watching from the lounge and came outside to offer her support.

'Do be careful,' she advised.

Gripping the top rung, I lifted it overhead. José stooped as low as he could and took it from me. He steadied himself before handing me the lumber saw. I retreated down the ladder, a hell of a lot quicker than I'd climbed it.

'It's much heavier than it looks,' I said to Melanie, trying to appear composed.

'How is he going to start it from up there?' she asked, staring at José shuffling uncomfortably between the remaining boughs.

That was a good question; I hadn't got a clue.

Once settled, he crouched down hanging the chainsaw as low as he could. With his free arm he reached down, grabbed hold of the starter cord, and gave it an almighty tug. How he managed to keep his balance is anyone's guess. To make matters worse, it failed to start.

'I can't watch,' said Melanie, shielding her eyes.

I knew exactly how she felt. This looked like an accident waiting to happen.

Once again José took up his starting position, stooped low and yanked on the starter cord. With a series of quick sharp tugs, the beast burst into life. Oily blue smoke billowed from the little motor as he revved it repeatedly. Thankfully, he'd managed to stay wedged in the tree.

The chainsaw ate its way through the thicker stumps like a killer whale devouring a penguin. Huge lumps of timber thumped onto the driveway as confetti-like fragments of sawdust floated to the ground.

'Will the driveway be alright?' asked Melanie, as chunk after chunk hammered onto it.

I was just about to answer when catastrophe struck. Without warning, José lost his footing and lurched forward. Instinctively, he dropped the chainsaw, which crashed to the ground with the motor still running. As if in slow motion, he tumbled downwards, bumping against the thick stumps like a bouncing pinball. As quickly as it began, the drama was over. Miraculously, he caught his arm around the lowest bough. Swinging like an orangutan, his trailing feet kicked the ladder to the ground. I rushed across, picked it up and guided his feet onto the rungs.

'Are you alright?' asked Melanie.

José smiled, nodded his head, dusted himself down and, like any self-respecting lumberjack, immediately checked the condition of his tackle.

'Is it alright?' I asked, as José gave it the once-over.

'It's fine,' he replied proudly. 'It's a Stihl. They're the best, you know.'

José's fall hadn't dented his confidence. After a quick breather he climbed back up the ladder and finished the job. By the time he left, his ageing family hatchback was loaded with winter fuel. The tree looked like a three-metre-tall wooden column, and the driveway was full of unwanted kindling.

The saying goes that using wood as fuel warms you three times: once when you cut it, again when you split it, and finally when you burn it. I don't know about that, but on a bitterly cold day in Galicia, tidying up José's mess certainly kept me warm.

Less than a week later, we heard from Bob and Janet.

'Janet's emailed.'

'What does she say?'

'It's probably better if you come and take a look.'

From: "Robert Xxxxxx"
To: Craig Briggs
Subject: Visit to Galicia
Date: Thur, 02 Mar 2006 20:56:39

Hi Craig and Mel

Get prepared to be hit by "The Smith Clan", Janet, Sue and Jennifer plus Bob of course. Isn't he the lucky one!! He will need some support from you Craig with us lot!!! Sue can't wait to see you both again and Jennifer is looking forward to meeting you. And we can't wait to see you both of course.

We have booked to come over on Sunday April 2nd till Wednesday April 5th (Sues ?? birthday). Will you be able to get Ramon to put the heating and water back up for us for then please. As long as we can sleep and shower at our place that will be fine. If the builder is working that is no problem, we will keep out of his way.

Well will close for now, hope to hear from you soon.

Love and best wishes

Janet and Bob xxxx

'Is Jennifer Janet's other sister?' I asked.

'Yes, there's Janet, Jennifer, Steve, Sue, and Simon, in that order.'

'We'd better let Manolo know what's happening and find out when he'll be starting up there,' I suggested.

'And I'll give Ramon a call.'

The following day we drove across to see Manolo to update him on the email and find out when he'd be starting. We knew he'd be at home for lunch; he always is. As luck would have it, he expected to finish the job he was working on by the beginning of next week.

'I should be able to start on Wednesday or Thursday,' he said, 'depending on the weather of course.'

Manolo wasn't a man to make promises he couldn't keep but all the same, I'd wait until he'd actually started to let Bob and Janet know.

'And how long do you think it'll take?'

'Most of the work should be finished by the time the owners arrive but I can always stop for a few days if they want me to.'

'No, no, they won't mind at all if you're working there,' I assured him.

The last thing we needed was a delay; the first paying guests were due to arrive in eight weeks. The margin for error was slimmer than a zero-sized model on hunger strike.

'Here are the keys,' I said, handing them to him. 'You'll need to force the gates; they're a bit difficult to open.'

We apologised for interrupting his lunch and drove home.

'The weather forecast looks favourable,' I said, having checked online.

'That's good,' replied Melanie.

Given the fine weather, I felt confident that Manolo would have started work as promised. On Wednesday afternoon we decided to pop up to *Casa Bon Vista* and check.

'I'll take the camera just in case. If he's started I can send Bob a few photos,' I said, as we readied to leave.

The drive there takes between ten and fifteen minutes. Bob has christened the final kilometre "Cowpat Alley", in reference to the toilet habits of the lane's mainly bovine users. Navigating it cleanly is a task that Olympic slalom skiers would find challenging.

'Do you have to?' complained Melanie as I weaved erratically around freshly deposited cowpats.

As I turned into the track at the top of the lane, my heart sank. I'd expected to see Manolo's van parked outside.

'It doesn't look like he's made it,' I said.

'Hang on a minute,' replied Melanie. 'The gates are open.'

I drove down and stopped opposite the opening. Parked in the courtyard was Manolo's ruby red Renault Express with his trailer hooked on the back.

'Wow! Look at that.'

Less than one day on the job and the results were quite remarkable. Manolo had erected a scaffold platform at the front of the outbuildings and was carefully removing the old terracotta tiles. He'd rigged up an electric winch onto the scaffolding and was lowering the tiles to the courtyard using an oil drum, cut in half to make a large bucket. Removing the tiles had transformed this dark and miserable courtyard into a bright space full of possibilities.

'Hola,' I called.

Manolo was climbing across a wooden roof joist like the star of a high wire act.

'*Muy buenas* (Good to see you),' he replied.

'You managed to open the gates then?' I asked.

Manolo smiled and nodded his head before scampering down the scaffolding to greet us.

'Can they be repaired?' I asked, pointing at the gates.

'They could but it would be cheaper to have some new ones made.'

We stayed just long enough to take a few snaps and prune Bob's grapevines. That night, I emailed him with the news.

From: Craig Briggs
To: "Robert Xxxxxx"
Subject: Great news!
Date: Wed, 08 Mar 2006 19:14:26

Dear Bob and Janet

Great news! (See attached pictures). Manolo has started work.

While we were there, I pruned the two grapevines either

side of the well in readiness for this year's growth. Maybe I can add the grapes to our wine production and we can share in drinking it – hiccup!!! We've already drunk our red wine from last year's harvest.

Now for the bad news. I asked Manolo about the gates, he said that it will cost more to repair them than it will to replace them with new ones. I've asked him to get a quote from the same person who is making the downstairs doors. Once we know how much new ones will cost, we can decide what to do.

That's all for now, see you both soon.

Best wishes
Craig.

Two days later we went back to check on the progress.

Most outbuildings in Galicia are nothing more than giant lean-tos. They tend to be an afterthought rather than a planned structure and are expanded and added to as the need arises. Despite many of them looking like a stiff breeze might flatten them, they seem to have stood the test of time.

The ones at *Casa Bon Vista* were constructed using a series of columns supporting a timber and tiled roof. The position of the columns was dictated by the length of the roof joists which were honed from the tallest and straightest chestnut trees in the forest. The older the barn the more irregular the joists and the more random the columns; the ones here were very old.

The outer columns had been built on top of an existing drystone boundary wall using red bricks as were the taller inner columns. Given their Pisa-like inclination, I guessed the foundations were either shallow or non-existent.

Manolo had been busy; he'd removed all the terracotta roof tiles and stacked them neatly in one corner of the courtyard. Even on an overcast afternoon, the whole area looked light and airy. As well as removing the tiles, he'd taken off half of the timber boards. These boards spanned the gaps between the huge roof joists and supported the tiles. The speed at which the demolition was progressing was extraordinary. Two days earlier, the prospect of the house being ready for our first guests looked doubtful; now I felt confident of success.

As things were going well, we left Manolo to it and didn't visit again until the following Tuesday, six days into the job. The weather couldn't have been better as we slalomed our way up Cowpat Alley en route to *Casa Bon Vista*. Manolo's van was parked in the track opposite the courtyard entrance. I pulled up behind it and we walked towards the gates. As we entered, I couldn't believe my eyes. The outbuildings had been completely demolished. All that remained were a few flimsy-looking partition walls and the brick columns. They reminded me of abandoned skyscrapers in a post-apocalyptic urban landscape. The demolition had also unearthed a huge oak barrel laying on its side in the far corner of the grounds.

Melanie and I had visited the house dozens of times since Bob and Janet decided not to sell and never fully understood why they chose this ruin to restore over all the others on the market. With the outbuildings gone, their reasons were obvious. The views over the surrounding countryside were breathtaking. A panoramic vista of rolling meadows, interspersed with a patchwork of conifer woods and deciduous coppices, framed by distant snow-capped mountains. The view alone made it worth buying. I hadn't realised it at the time but I couldn't have chosen a better name than *Casa Bon Vista*.

'I'll just get the camera,' I said, heading back to the car.

This was one series of snaps I couldn't wait to email.

The views were spectacular but the demolition had left piles of debris. Manolo was sorting through the mess.

'It looks a lot different,' I remarked, and he agreed.

Not wanting to get in his way, I took my photos and we left.

'I think we'd better come up every day from now on; we don't miss anything,' I suggested on our way home.

The following day we decided to pop up a little earlier. The weather forecast hinted at a damp afternoon. A series of fresh, steaming hazards greeted our approach. Dodging them all proved impossible. Manolo had parked his van a little further down the track this morning so we were able to park directly opposite the gates.

'I wonder what Manolo's doing,' I said.

Manolo was lying on his back in the middle of the courtyard. We stepped out of the car and walked in. I didn't quite know what to say so I called 'Hola' in a chirpy manner. That's when I noticed that he was on the phone and sensed that something was wrong. Network coverage in the hamlet wasn't the best in Galicia but this seemed a little extreme.

'Are you alright?' asked Melanie.

'I've broken my leg,' he replied, in a tone of calm resignation.

'Do you need an ambulance?'

'The neighbour, José, has rung them.'

Young José had heard a commotion and come to investigate.

'The Guardia Civil will be coming as well but there's no need to worry, I have all the correct insurance,' he added.

The last thing on our minds was insurance. I looked down at Manolo. Apart from his foot resting at an unnatural angle, I wouldn't have known anything was wrong. Moments later José returned.

'They're on their way,' he said.

Manolo had been trying to ring his wife to let her know what had happened but hadn't been able to get through.

'Is there anything we can do?' I asked.

Manolo wouldn't hear of it.

First on the scene were two officers of the Guardia Civil. Their local headquarters is less than five minutes away. Manolo seemed quite happy to explain what had happened. The ambulance had to travel from Monforte de Lemos, a journey that would take the best part of half an hour. He told the officers that the accident happened while he was using a hand-powered winch to drag the huge roof joists out of the courtyard.

There were eight joists in total, each one measuring over six metres long and weighing considerably more than a metric ton. He'd planned to move them in two stages: from where they'd fallen during the demolition, firstly to the centre of the courtyard, and from there into the lane. The mistake he'd made was to underestimate the weight of the joists, and overestimate the strength of the Pisa-like, brick-built column he'd anchored the winch to. He'd managed to haul five of these great tree trunks into the middle of the courtyard before the inevitable happened. During his attempts to drag the sixth and largest joist, the column had collapsed and fallen on top of him. By sheer luck, he spotted it out of the corner of his eye and managed to move his head out of the way. If not, this five-metre-tall brick-built column could easily have killed him.

Eventually, the ambulance arrived. For the first time, Manolo showed signs of discomfort as the paramedic checked his condition.

'I need to cut your boot off,' said one of the medics.

'I can undo it,' said Manolo, making an effort to get up.

The medic soon put a stop to that.

'Just lay still,' he said, putting his hand on Manolo's shoulder. 'I'll cut it off.'

'Do you have to?' he moaned. 'I haven't had them a week.'

The medic sympathised but stressed that trying to pull it off could potentially make matters worse. Manolo's reluctance quickly faded as the pain of removing it increased. The medics were taking no chances; they tightly bound both his legs together before gently sliding a backboard under him and securing him to it. To add insult to injury they rested his shredded boot on his chest before lifting him up and carrying him to the ambulance.

'Don't worry,' said Manolo as they carried him up the lane. 'I'll be back at work in a fortnight.'

Looking at him now, it was difficult to share his optimism.

'Can you drive my van home?' he asked, as they slid him into the back of the ambulance.

'Of course,' I replied.

I took his keys, wished him all the best, and looked on as the ambulance drove out of sight.

'Are you the owner of this house?' asked one of the officers who'd been monitoring proceedings.

I explained our role in this tragedy. He scribbled down our details and asked us to bring copies of Bob and Janet's passports to the police station. By the time they left, we'd been on site for over an hour. For the first time this morning I felt lost and alone. A chilling breeze blew through the courtyard as I stared out across a mass of rubble and debris.

'Let's go home,' suggested Melanie.

I was in no mood to argue.

Later that afternoon I drove the van across the valley to Manolo's with Melanie following in the car. I hoped for the best but feared the worst. Manolo's wife, Julia, gave us the news.

'He's broken both bones in his lower leg, the tibia and fibula,' she said. 'They are clean breaks but he will have to have an operation to pin the bones with exterior steel.'

Her description of the procedure sounded quite gruesome.

'What about his back?' asked Melanie.

'Only bruised. He was very lucky.'

We were relieved to hear that, in time, the doctor expected him to make a full recovery. We wished them all the best and promised to call round to check on his progress.

Our relief was tempered with the knowledge that we no

longer had a builder and time was running out. What on earth were we going to do?

19

Almost Under Control

Losing the builder was a major setback but wallowing in our misfortune wouldn't get the job done. We'd assured Bob and Janet that the house would be ready by the middle of May; come hell or high water, I was determined to make sure it was.

'Let's go up to *Casa Bon Vista* after breakfast,' I said.

'What for?'

'To figure out exactly what needs doing.'

Melanie looked at me quizzically but agreed.

Half an hour later we were standing in the track outside the house. I unlocked the gates and shoulder-charged them open.

'Well that's one thing that still needs doing,' remarked Melanie.

New gates would have to wait; there were plenty of jobs to do before then. It's funny how even the most depressing sights look that much better with the sun shining on them. In stark contrast to yesterday, thick grey clouds had been replaced by a crisp spring morning: bright and beautiful.

From the entrance, everything looked quite orderly. Immediately in front of us were the five roof joists that Manolo had moved before catastrophe struck. Behind them was a metre-high pile of chestnut planks stacked neatly against the wall and next to that the old roof tiles. As we walked into the courtyard, the landscape changed and the full extent of this demolition disaster came into view. The exterior walls of the outbuildings had collapsed inwards, scattering piles of rubble everywhere. Rising from the debris, like industrial chimney stacks, were four brick-built columns and the half-toppled remnants of another four. Partially demolished interior walls hinted at the buildings' size and layout. Mixed in with the rubble were pieces of timber of various shapes and sizes and resting on top of this chaos were the three remaining roof joists.

'What do you think?' I asked.

'What do I think of what?'

'What do you think about me and you shifting all this?'

'You are joking?'

A rhetorical question if ever I heard one.

'I'm sure it's not as bad as it looks,' I replied.

'What about these?' she asked, pointing at the giant roof joists. 'They nearly killed Manolo.'

She had a point.

I walked over to the nearest one, straddled it, and grabbed one end.

'Do be careful,' she said.

Taking the strain, I lifted. Although heavy, I could at least raise one end off the ground.

'There's no way I'm carrying that out of here,' she added.

I couldn't have agreed more. It would take half a dozen men to carry it out. This challenge could wait for another day.

'We can worry about moving these when we get to

them,' I replied. 'We can easily move the rest of the stuff.'

'What about all the rubble?'

The original plan was to leave the rubble where it fell, smash it into pieces and use it as hard core to level the courtyard. At the moment, it sloped away from the house quite considerably. There seemed no reason to change that part of the plan, although at some point I'd need to get my hands on a sledgehammer.

'Once we've cleared everything else away, I can soon smash it into pieces.'

Melanie gave me one of those "You must be joking" stares, but said nothing.

'So, what do you think?'

'Let's say for argument's sake that we can clear all this rubble away, what then? Who's going to do all the building work?'

'We'll just do the bare essentials and save the rest until the holiday season is over and Manolo is back on his feet.'

'That's all well and good, but who's going to do it?'

Once again, she had a point.

The clock was ticking; in less than eight weeks, a party of four would be arriving expecting to find luxury accommodation for the discerning traveller. At such short notice, any tradesman worth his salt would be busy; those that weren't would be either too expensive or incompetent.

'I could always ask Bill,' I replied.

Bill and his wife, Diana, are an English couple we met about a year ago. He's a bit of a handyman. If he could spare the time, and wanted to earn some extra cash, he'd be just the man to help complete this scaled-down building project.

'It can't harm to ask,' replied Melanie.

Bill's response was positive. He wouldn't be able to start until halfway through April but I felt confident that, with his help, we could complete the necessary work before the first guests arrived.

That evening I emailed Bob with my proposal.

From: Craig Briggs
To: "Robert Xxxxxx"
Subject: I have a plan
Date: Sun, 19 Mar 2006 19:09:36

Dear Bob and Janet

The prognosis regarding Manolo doesn't look encouraging. He's having an operation on Monday to reset his foot and ankle. It would be naïve to think that he'll be back at work in time for the arrival of our first guests. At this late stage, it's going to be impossible to find another builder.

With this in mind I've spoken to Bill. He's the chap that we all went to their house when you were last here. You also bumped into him in Rhonda when you were holidaying on the Costa del Sol. He's willing to help out.

Starting next week, Melanie and I are going to begin tidying the courtyard. The demolition is nearly done so the area is pretty safe to work in. Bill is going to Malaga in 2 days but will be returning sometime between the 12th and 15th of next month. We would only be able to do the basics but sufficient to get the place looking right and most importantly safe. I can discuss the details with you when you are here.

Come hell or high water, the house will be ready for our first guests but regrettably, not for your next visit.

Don't worry about anything, it's almost under control...I mean "it's all under control".

Looking forward to seeing you all soon.

Warmest regards
Craig and Mel

The die was cast. Melanie and I had two weeks to clear the courtyard and clean the house before the Smith clan descended on Galicia. Since offering our help, their mood had changed from resignation to optimism and we were determined to maintain that forward momentum.

'You'd better wrap up warm,' I said, as we readied to leave.

We'd woken to a dense soupy fog. As we climbed the vale to *Casa Bon Vista*, it began to clear. On days like this the panorama is magical. A blanket of pale grey mist stretched out across the Val de Lemos like a vast lake, hemmed in on all sides by a distant horizon of angular mountain peaks. Within this cloudy expanse, tall hilltops broke through the surface like mythical Greek islands.

With the back seats folded down, I'd managed to manoeuvre the wheelbarrow into the back of the car. Other than a pair of thick working gloves, this was all we needed to start the clear-up.

'We'll leave the roof joists for now and make a start on the rest of the timber,' I said.

'Where are we going to put it?' asked Melanie.

'Just follow me,' I replied, picking three planks off the top of the pile.

Melanie grabbed a couple more and followed me through the courtyard.

On the opposite side of the track to the house there's a small parcel of land that was included in the sale. When Bob and Janet first moved here, they went to great lengths to prepare it for planting vegetables. Unfortunately, their dream of living "The Good Life" never materialised and it quickly deteriorated into the overgrown plot they inherited. From our point of view, this patch of scrubland would provide the ideal place to relocate the recycled building materials, at least until Bob decided what he wanted to do with them.

The long grass was damp from the morning's heavy dew. Within an hour, we were soaked up to our knees. By mid-morning, we'd shifted the neat stack of timber. Dragging the rest from the piles of building rubble would be considerably more difficult. It was cold, damp and miserable but we soldiered on throughout the morning. By lunchtime we were ready for a break.

'Let's go home and grab some lunch,' I suggested.

Melanie's eyes lit up for the first time that morning. She didn't need asking twice.

'There's no point in beggaring ourselves up on the first day,' I added.

'No point at all,' she said, opening the car door.

After a warm meal and an hour's rest, I was ready to get cracking again.

'Are you ready then?' I asked.

'Ready for what?'

'To shift a bit more wood.'

'Do we have to?'

Melanie had done enough for one day and if truth be known, so had I. Unfortunately, the weather is too unpredictable at this time of year to let a fine but cold afternoon pass without working. If I could have guaranteed two weeks of favourable weather, I wouldn't have been in such a rush but I couldn't. Besides which, there were jobs to do at home. Only yesterday Meli stopped by to tell Melanie that it was time to start planting her seedlings in the *huerta*. 'It's a good moon', she'd said, and we know better than to go against established wisdom.

By the end of the first day we'd moved all the timber, excluding the roof joists, and made a start on the tiles.

'I can't believe we're shifting roof tiles again,' I said, as we loaded the first wheelbarrow.

'At least we know what we're doing this time.'

'And there's no chance of them falling off the back of a trailer.'

The two of us burst out laughing at the thought of Antonio and his tipsy tractor manoeuvres. An abiding memory from our last property project when we looked on in horror as half a trailer load of roof tiles slid off the back and smashed on the floor.

By the end of the second day we'd shifted everything salvageable, except for the enormous roof joists. At some point, we'd have to move them but for the time being, we could work around them.

Before heading south, Bill leant me his ten-pound sledgehammer. The time had come to put it to good use; smashing the living daylights out of oven-hardened red bricks. There's a certain satisfaction to wielding a ten-pound sledgehammer but after an hour or so, the novelty began to wear off. As the hours rolled by, ten pounds started to feel like twenty.

By the end of the first week Melanie had become redundant, just in time to take full advantage of the "Good Moon". While Melanie planted her seedlings, I cultivated my blisters.

'What's matter?' asked Melanie, as I stepped from the car and hobbled towards the house.

'Oh nothing.'

'What have you done?'

An unforeseen consequence of wielding a heavy hammer is that things don't always go to plan. On more than one occasion I'd smashed a brick with such force that shrapnel from the collision had ricocheted into my shins at terminal velocity. To say it hurt would be an understatement.

'How did the planting go?' I asked, changing the subject.

Melanie had spent the afternoon planting potatoes, onions, and garlic.

'Come and take a look,' she said proudly.

All I wanted to do was sit down and put my feet up but I didn't have the heart to say no. I hobbled into the back garden, limped to the far end and peered over the wall into our newly created vegetable patch.

'There are two rows of potatoes over there,' she said, pointing down one side. 'Next to them are two rows of onions, and over in that corner, four rows of garlic.'

The only visible signs of activity were freshly made footprints.

'Lovely,' I remarked.

'I know it doesn't look like much at the moment, but give it a few months and the place will be bursting with life.'

'What about everything else?'

As well as using the plastic greenhouse, Melanie was propagating a varied selection of vegetables throughout the house. There were peas, French beans, and peppers in the back bedroom and leeks, carrots, parsnips, and cauliflowers in the office. In the kitchen were a number of tomato plants, both cherry and beef, and in the dining room, English cucumbers, and the obligatory lettuce. My contribution to this horticultural experiment was half a dozen strawberry plants, waiting patiently under the dining table.

'If I plant them too early, the frost will kill them,' she replied.

Having fulfilled my marital duty, I hobbled back to the house for a well-deserved rest. Later that evening I shared my thoughts on moving the giant roof joists.

'I've been thinking about these joists,' I said.

'Oh yes,' replied Melanie.

'Yes.'

'And what have you been thinking?'

'Pyramids.'

Melanie looked at me as if I'd gone mad.

'Pyramids? Are you sure it's your shins you banged and not your head?'

'Ha-ha, very funny.'

My plan was based on a vague recollection of a TV documentary. The programme set out to discover how ancient Egyptians constructed the great pyramids at Giza. Engineers and Egyptologists pooled their knowledge to develop a practical theory. The suggestion was that the enormous stone blocks were moved on wooden rollers using three gangs of labourers, one to pull, one to push, and the third to swap the rollers from back to front as the block moved forward. I explained my idea to Melanie.

'But there's only two of us,' she said.

It hadn't taken her long to spot the minor flaw in my otherwise brilliant scheme.

'We can work around that,' I assured her.

'Really. And what about the rollers?'

'I've been thinking about that too.'

Melanie rolled her eyes.

'We can use the roundest joist and saw it into useable sections.'

'We can, can we.'

The following morning, armed with my lumber saw, we headed off to *Casa Bon Vista*.

'That one there looks like the roundest. What do you think?' asked Melanie.

As well as being the roundest, it was also looked like the thickest. Bounding with enthusiasm and determined to prove my theory, I set about sawing through the joist. Within ten minutes I discovered why chestnut is the timber of choice for Spanish construction: the wood is as hard as stone. Back and forth, back and forth, I dragged the saw blade across the joist. Droplets of sweat dripped from my brow, lubricating the cut.

'Chuff me! This wood is like steel.'

I'd intended to cut the whole joist into sections but decided that three would do the job.

'Right,' I said confidently, 'when I lift this end you slip one of the rollers underneath.'

I straddled the great length of timber, took a firm grip and a deep breath, and lifted. The lump weighed a ton, literally.

'Quickly,' I screamed.

Melanie fumbled with the smallest of the three rollers trying to pick it up.

'I can't lift it,' she complained.

Like a hydraulic jack, as I exhaled the joist lowered to the ground.

The three sections that I'd sawn off couldn't have been more than two foot long. If she couldn't lift these my plan seemed destined to fail.

'They're not that heavy,' I said, lifting one off the floor.

'Well they're too heavy for me.'

I carried it to the front of the joist and laid it on the floor at right angles.

'Right, when I lift, you slide it under.'

Once again I straddled the joist, took a firm grip and a deep breath, and lifted. Melanie was struggling to slide the roller underneath but I couldn't give her any encouragement for fear of dropping it. With my body at the limits of endurance, she finally managed to push it under.

'Thank heavens for that,' I sighed.

'It's not easy,' she moaned.

It seemed pointless trying to get another one underneath. My ancient Egyptian method of moving Galician roof joists needed a serious rethink.

What would happen if I picked up the opposite end of the joist and pushed? There was only one way to find out.

'Can you guide it in the right direction if I pick up the other end and push?'

'You are joking?'

'Don't worry, it'll be fine.'

'Do be careful.'

'There is one thing.'

'What?'

'If it looks like it's going to fall off the roller, get out of the way, and quick.'

Melanie looked apprehensive as I took up station at the back of the joist. I bent down and flung my arms around its girth. Taking a deep breath, I lifted. To my surprise, the whole thing felt much lighter with the roller under the other end. Lifting it was one thing; staggering forward and keeping it aloft was quite another. After a few shaky moments, I started to get the hang of it. As the joist neared its fulcrum, Melanie managed to slide a second roller under the front. Miraculously, my plan was working.

By the end of the day we'd moved all eight joists and I'd developed a Quasimodo-like stance. Perhaps that's what they mean by walk like an Egyptian.

By the time Bob, Janet, and her sisters, Sue and Jennifer, arrived at *Casa Bon Vista* on the 2nd of April, I'd managed to smash all the rubble into pieces and level the entire courtyard. Since their last visit the changes were immense, both inside and out. They were overwhelmed by the transformation in the courtyard and blown away by the magic we'd worked on the interior. Seeing their delight made the blisters and bruises all worthwhile.

However, demolishing the outbuildings and clearing the courtyard revealed a potential problem, and one I was keen to discuss with Bob. It was a sensitive issue that required tact and diplomacy, but above all, the right opportunity. A few days into their short stay they invited us for lunch. While the ladies prepared the food, Bob and I made a tour of the courtyard deciding exactly which jobs needed doing before the first guests arrived. Having completed our site survey, I seized the moment and popped the question.

'Did you have any toilet problems while you were living here?'

Bob stared at me with a curious expression rippling across his brow.

'Toilet problems?'

Perhaps my subtle hint lacked clarity.

'Like blockages, for example.'

Bob leered at me. This wasn't quite going to plan.

'Blockages?'

'In the pipes.'

'Ah.'

Finally, the penny had dropped.

'It's funny you should ask that.'

It wasn't meant to be, I thought to myself.

'We did have an issue.' He added, 'The builder came, cleared the blockage and told us that we shouldn't have any more problems. Why do you ask?'

'Well,' I paused for a moment, 'I've found a second manhole that might shed a little light on the previous obstruction.'

When Bob and Janet were last here, he'd pointed out the manhole for the *pozo negro* (black hole) or homemade cesspit. 'Be careful you don't fall down there,' he'd warned. During our clean-up, I'd unearthed a second, smaller manhole topped with an ill-fitting piece of rotten wood. It wasn't until I'd removed the wooden cover that I made an alarming discovery.

When the house was originally built, internal bathrooms were the stuff of dreams. As living standards improved, family conveniences were added as an afterthought and usually housed in the most inconvenient place. At *Casa Bon Vista*, the original toilet was on the ground floor, even though all the living accommodation was on the floor above. The only access was down the outside stone steps. In essence, the facility was little more than an upmarket outside lavvy.

A preliminary inspection of the original sewage system revealed that the waste flowed along an underground channel into the track outside the house. When the *pozo negro* was added later, new pipework was installed. Unfortunately, during the recent renovation work the builder had unwittingly plumbed the new facilities into the old channel. The flow of sewerage from the house was now required to double back on itself while ascending an incline. I'm no expert on the mechanics of human waste disposal but pooh is pooh, and as far as I'm aware, shit rolls downhill.

'Look at this,' I whispered, lifting the wooden cover.

The cause of the previous blockage was clear to see.

'What are we going to do?'

We agreed that the best solution was to renew the underground pipework. My list of jobs had an urgent addition and a new priority.

A week after Bob and Janet's return to England, Bill started work. Two weeks later, we had successfully completed all the tasks; even the new gates had been installed. With two weeks to spare, *Casa Bon Vista* was finally ready to receive guests.

20

Surprise!

Nothing heralds the arrival of spring as vividly as *Genista Hispanica*, or Spanish gorse. It covers the landscape with bright yellow flowers, shimmering in the sunlight like a mythical golden fleece. Deciduous forests develop a green hue as leaf buds begin to open. Closer to home, José's cherry orchard provides a blossoming palette of virgin whites and soft pinks. All too soon, this explosion of pastel shades drifts to earth like bridal confetti. Opposite the house, on the roadside verge, clumps of English Iris have opened. Their delicate purple petals look like exotic birds of paradise as they sway gently in the breeze.

In the beds around the house, dormant bulbs begin to flower. Tulips are among the first to bloom, crimson reds and regal purples. They welcome the sun with open petals and as it sets they slowly close for bedtime prayers. Scattered among the tulips are clusters of narcissus. Creamy white petals surround a deep yellow centre: miniature fried eggs, sunny-side up.

The grapevines circling the house are also beginning to bloom. Lilac and green buds have burst into leaf. Velvety green foliage clings to fragile young shoots. Nestled between the leaves are microscopic bunches of grapes that will soon flower. Small songbirds swoop between the training wires calling out to potential mates.

The allotment too is showing signs of life. Thin spikey onion shoots have forced their way to the surface to bathe in the spring sunshine and parallel rows of fresh leafy potato sprigs have broken to the surface. Unfortunately, we aren't the only ones to notice. A squadron of mischievous magpies entertain themselves by uprooting the tiny onions and scattering them over the plot. Few are eaten and a quick push has them replanted and looking like new.

This botanical explosion is accompanied by much noisier detonations. Loud fireworks signal the start of the fiesta season. The intensity of the blast depends on the party's proximity. The closer the fun, the louder the bang; the louder the bang, the quicker Jazz runs for cover.

The first few months of the year had been nothing if not eventful. The only project that had so far gone to plan was the travel arrangements for Melanie's birthday surprise. At some point I would have to rely on the discretion of others to keep the secret. With less than six weeks to go, that time had come. I decided to ask Melanie's mum, Jennifer, to help with the arrangements; if nothing else, it might go some way to healing old wounds.

Ten years earlier, Melanie and I had married in secret. Jennifer was mortified. It sometimes feels as if I've been paying the price ever since. Ironically, it was Melanie's idea to keep it quiet.

Jennifer accepted my invitation; as for healing old wounds, only time will tell.

My venue of choice was the Nawaab Indian restaurant in Huddersfield's town centre. It had been one of our favourites and was less than 300 metres from the George Hotel. The only potential problem was access. Since Melanie's dad had finished his chemotherapy he'd been confined to a wheelchair; bedsores and a MRSA infection had seen to that. Melanie's granny was also wheelchair bound. Stone steps at the main entrance were an unhelpful obstacle but the restaurant manager was more than happy to let them enter through the kitchen. Invitations had been sent and replies received. Including the birthday girl, twenty of us would celebrate the event. As the date approached, an assortment of cards arrived in the post with instructions not to be opened until the 17th. Everyone was playing their part in my covert operation.

What with flights, car hire, hotels and restaurant, there was little in the kitty for a present but I managed to find a pair of gold earrings worthy of the event. I also had one more surprise up my sleeve. At the last minute, I decided to write an article for the local Huddersfield newspaper in the hope that the editor would publish it on Melanie's birthday.

From: Craig Briggs
To: editorial@examiner.co.uk
Subject: News article submission
Date: Sun, 14 May 2006 14:21:08

Dear Editor

On Wednesday 17 May, my wife Melanie will be 40 years old. To celebrate this milestone, I have arranged a surprise birthday party.

We'll be travelling from our home in Galicia, Spain to Huddersfield. It was an easy choice given Melanie's love of Indian food and that her family and most of her friends live in and around Huddersfield. In addition, Melanie's granny is now in her mid-90s and her dad, Geoffrey, was diagnosed with inoperable cancer over Christmas. His prognosis is poor and it's unlikely he will see Melanie's 41st birthday.

I have written a short article that I am hoping you might publish on the 17th. I'm sure it would be a great thrill for Melanie and her family. For the past two years I've written a weekly column for the online magazine, Open Writing, edited by former Examiner employee, Peter Hinchliffe.

I'm happy for the piece to be edited as you see fit. If you are able to publish the piece would you kindly let me know beforehand?

Yours sincerely
Craig Briggs

After an anxious wait, I received an email confirming its inclusion. I couldn't have been happier.

Two days before our scheduled departure, *Casa Bon Vista* received its first guests. Melanie and I had spent the previous day making sure everything was as perfect as possible. Both inside and out was spotless. I couldn't afford any mistakes. The day after their arrival we went to do our "Meet and Greet", an informal welcome to make sure everything was to their liking and answer any questions they might have.

On the afternoon of the 16th I broke my self-imposed silence; the game was afoot.

'We need to go up to Bill's,' I announced, midway through the afternoon.

'What for?'

'He's agreed to look after Jazz.'

I could see from Melanie's expression that she hadn't a clue what I was talking about.

'Look after Jazz, why?'

'No more questions. It's a surprise.'

Jazz jumped into the back of the car without a care in the world.

'Have a nice time,' said Bill, as we handed her over.

'I would if I knew what we were doing,' replied Melanie.

On our arrival home I revealed a little more of my scheme.

'You'll need to pack a case.'

'Where are we going?'

'It's a secret.'

'Well what am I supposed to take?'

'Whatever you want.'

'How long are we going for?'

'A couple of days,' I replied, trying to be as evasive as possible.

'Will I need a swimming costume?'

Huddersfield in the middle of May! She was more likely to need a raincoat.

'You might do,' I replied. 'Now that's enough questions; just pack what you think you'll need.'

Melanie kept a keen eye on my choices before making her own.

'Save some room for me,' I said, as Melanie began loading the case.

'Are we only taking one case?'

'We're only going for two nights,' I stressed.

Once we'd packed, I pulled the cork on a bottle of vino blanco and we went into the garden for our Teatime Taster. No sooner had we sat down than the phone rang.

Ring ring ... Ring ring!

'I'll go,' said Melanie, rushing inside.

Moments later she stepped back out holding the phone to her ear.

'It's Mum,' she mouthed.

'Well it hasn't come,' she paused, clearly waiting for a response. 'No it won't, it's a public holiday tomorrow.'

Unfortunately for Melanie, her birthday falls on the same day as *Día de las Letras Gallegas*: a public holiday celebrating the Galician language and its literature. Melanie's angry reply was in response to not having received either a birthday card or present from her mum.

I was delighted; Melanie's reaction implied complete

ignorance of her surprise party. Having ended the call, I did my best to placate her mood.

'You know what the post's like,' I said.

'That's not the point. She's known for forty years when my birthday is.'

It wasn't long before the cool wine and setting sun calmed her mood; by this time tomorrow, all would be forgiven.

Over the years, Melanie and I have developed a last-minute approach to airport check-in. I loathe the dehumanising aspect of air travel and airports. Passengers are herded from one place to another like cattle at an abattoir. Today, however, I decided to take a more pragmatic approach. An hour and a half drive to the airport and check-in two hours before departure meant a nine o'clock start and an alarm call for eight.

'It seems strange without Jazz to greet us in the morning,' I said, as we readied to leave.

Melanie agreed. Before long we were heading towards Santiago. I'd decided to take a different road to our normal route, just to keep the mystery alive as long as possible.

'Where are we going?'

'Just wait and see. All will be revealed in due course.'

A text message from her friend, and party guest, Yvonne, wishing her a happy birthday gave no hint of the destination. As we neared the airport, the first part of my surprise revealed itself.

'Are we going to the airport?'

'You'll have to wait and see.'

She'd guessed the first destination but as we pulled into the car park, she would have to wait a little longer for the next.

'Where are we going?'

'Wait and see.'

As we entered the terminal, I checked the departure board for information. Online check-in meant that I could keep the secret for a little longer. The flight was on schedule but hadn't yet been allocated a gate number. The size of Santiago Airport dictates that all its facilities fall under one roof. Its main hub is the cafeteria, where passengers wait for information over a cup of coffee.

'Would you like a coffee?' I asked.

'OK, but where are we going?'

'Over there,' I said, pointing towards the cafeteria.

'Very funny.'

'Just be patient; all will be revealed.'

Soon after taking our seats an announcement came over the personal address system asking for ticket holders on the Stansted flight to make their way to the gate. Melanie stared across the table at me. To throw her off the scent for that bit longer, I ignored the call. A few minutes later I suggested we make a move. Melanie looked confused. I thought it might be fun to wait at the wrong gate once we'd cleared airport security but that would have been a little too cruel.

'Here we are,' I said, taking a seat at gate number two.

'Are we going to back to England?'

'We might be.'

When the final call for Stansted echoed over the PA, I wasn't surprised that the inbound flight hadn't yet landed. Ryanair have a reputation for providing a quick turnaround. It wasn't until the arrivals board changed from on schedule to delayed that my concerns were raised. Thankfully, my plan had plenty of room for manoeuvre. Patiently we waited, and waited, and waited. Five minutes passed, then ten. A quarter of an hour elapsed and then half an hour. At the hour mark I began to feel concerned. I marched up and down the departure hall searching for information but there wasn't any. An hour became an hour and a quarter. As the clock ticked round to one o'clock, the arrivals board changed. Minutes later the aircraft landed. Passengers streamed from the plane clutching their carry-on luggage. Ground crew unloaded a few cases from the hold and members of the cabin crew appeared at the gate. Finally, we were allowed to board.

Any thoughts of a leisurely drive from Stansted to Huddersfield, and stopping en route for a romantic lunch, were well and truly scuppered. After collecting the hire car, it would be pedal to the metal and a sprint up the motorway.

England greeted our arrival in typical style: damp drizzle that was determined to become light rain. By the time we'd picked up the car the dashboard clock read 3:05 pm and the light rain had turned into a shower.

'As soon as we get onto the A1, we'll stop and have a quick snack,' I said as we sped north along the M11 motorway.

'OK.'

Our romantic lunch for two turned into a bacon butty pit stop at a roadside diner. By the time we reached the M18/M1 intersection on the outskirts of Sheffield, the rain was blowing horizontal and the cloud cover was so thick it looked like the middle of the night. To make matters worse, we'd hit this infamous intersection at rush hour. Traffic was nose to tail and moving as fast as a three-legged tortoise. Fortunately, Melanie had no idea of our eight o'clock dinner date. With less than an hour to spare, we reached our destination, the George Hotel, Huddersfield, birthplace of rugby league and Grade II listed building.

'Here we are,' I said as I pulled into the hotel car park.

'Are we staying here?' asked Melanie.

'We are.'

If anything, the rain had worsened the further north we travelled. I grabbed the carry-on out of the back of the car and we sprinted into the hotel. After eleven hours' travelling, we'd made it with fifty minutes to spare.

It would have been nice to have a rest but time was of the essence. I'd asked guests to arrive at the restaurant at 7:50 so that everyone was there when she entered.

'You can use the shower first,' I said, bouncing the carry-on onto the bed.

'Is there a rush?'

'Oh yes.'

'Why, where are we going?'

'It's a surprise.'

Melanie was happy to go along. As she came out of the bathroom, I handed her the earrings.

'Many happy returns,' I said, handing her the gift wrapped present.

Carefully, she removed the packaging and opened the box.

'Thank you, they're beautiful.'

Ten minutes later we were washed, dressed, and ready to leave. We made our way into reception and looked out onto St. George's Square. The rain was belting down, bouncing off the road like glass marbles. Neither of us was dressed for this kind of weather. The only protection I had was a waist length leather jacket and Melanie fared no better.

'We're going to get soaked,' said Melanie.

'Just a minute,' I replied, heading to the reception desk.

'Hello sir, how can I help you?'

'We've just flown in from Spain for my wife's birthday. Unfortunately, our wardrobes didn't come prepared for Huddersfield's wet welcome. You wouldn't have an umbrella we could borrow, would you?'

'I'm sorry sir but the hotel doesn't provide umbrellas,' replied the receptionist.

'Oh dear.'

'Just a minute, let me see if any of the staff can help.'

Seconds later she returned carrying a brolly.

'Here you go, try this.'

Gratefully, I took it and we headed for the exit. As I pulled open the door a gust of bitterly cold wind whistled into the lobby.

'Come on then,' I said.

Melanie clutched my arm as we braved the torrential storm. I wrestled with the brolly as gusting winds threatened to strip it from my grasp. Thinking we were destined for warmer climes, Melanie had packed only summer sandals. As we marched briskly up the street, hiding from the elements behind our flimsy shield, rivers of rainwater lapped over her feet. Even the bronze statue of Huddersfield's Sir Harold Wilson, the former prime minister, seemed to chuckle as we rushed past. As we reached the top of St. George's Street our hard-fought prize came into view: the Nawaab Indian restaurant.

The restaurant is housed in a former bank and dates back to the 1900s. It's Georgian in style with an opulent interior and lavish decorations making it worthy of its name. It proudly boasts the likes of the late Diana, Princess of Wales, cricketing legends Ian Botham, Imran Khan, and Yorkshire umpire Dickie Bird among its former patrons, as well as one-time Heavyweight Champion of the World Frank Bruno. Who knows, it might one day include a damp and windswept Mr and Mrs Briggs on that list.

I held open the door and Melanie entered. By the time I handed the umbrella to the maître d', Melanie had spotted her guests. Overwhelmed with surprise, she burst into tears. In that one instant, all the hard work and effort was realised; the day had been a success.

After catching up with family and friends, and feasting on her favourite food, we went back to the George to continue the celebrations. The night manager proved very amenable and the revelry continued into the early hours.

Before retiring, I made sure to book an alarm call. Despite our exhaustion, there was no way we were going to miss a full English breakfast at Huddersfield's premier hotel. The venue for breakfast was the Victorian conservatory. Sunlight streamed into the room through opaque glass panels. High winds had swept away the rainclouds leaving behind a bright if somewhat breezy morning. Our stay in Huddersfield was brief but before leaving we called to see Melanie's dad, acutely aware that this might be the last time we saw him alive. Conversation proved difficult as emotions were running high.

'Do you have a copy of yesterday's *Examiner*?' I asked.

'Here you go,' said Geoff, handing it to me. 'There's nowt in it, as usual.'

I hoped not. I flicked through searching for the article and there it was, a full page spread.

'What about this?' I said, folding the paper back and handing it to him.

Melanie caught sight of her photo as Geoff took the newspaper. The headline read:

THE SPICE OF LIFE!
Craig curries favour with a surprise birthday trip

WHEN Craig Briggs planned a surprise birthday trip for wife Melanie it was an easy choice.
She loves Indian curries, so a meal out at the Nawaab Tandoori restaurant in Huddersfield was a sure-fire winner.
And the 1,000 miles between Melanie and her favourite dish was not a problem!
Craig, 44, organised a three-day return to their home town for the couple who have made a new life in Spain.
And their flying visit for Melanie's 40th included a meal at the Nawaab, followed by a night in Huddersfield's George Hotel.
"It was an easy choice given Melanie's love of Indian food and the fact that most of our family and friends live in and around Huddersfield," said Craig.
When we moved to Spain in 2002 an Examiner journalist asked her what she'd miss most about England – and the answer was an Indian curry.
"In great secrecy I organised the trip from our home in Galicia back to the UK."
"What better place to enjoy authentic Indian cuisine than the Nawaab, followed by an overnight stay in The George?"
"As well as family and friends still living locally we had other guests travelling from as far afield as London, Nottingham, and Wolverhampton to make this special spicy surprise a night to remember."
The couple then headed off to see relatives in Great Bradfield, Essex before flying back to Spain from Stansted.

'I didn't realise we had family in Great Bradfield,' remarked Geoff, after reading the article.

'That's newspapers for you. They can't even get the facts right when I wrote the article for them,' I replied.

'Did you write this?' asked Geoff.

'Can I have a look?'

Geoff passed Melanie the paper.

'Did you send them the photos as well?' she asked.

'I thought it would be a nice surprise.'

'It is,' she replied, with tears welling in her eyes.

The reference to Great Bradfield was the location of our overnight stay before heading back to Spain. Bucks House is another Grade II listed building. This one was built between 1510 and 1560 right next to the village green. Located less than twelve miles from Stansted Airport, it seemed the ideal location to catch an 08:00 flight.

We'd agreed to take my sister, Julie, with us; her husband, Jeremy, had been on jury service in London and was unable to come to the Nawaab. He'd agreed to meet us in Essex for dinner before they headed back to London.

Bucks House was a charming B&B with one exception, the en suite loo. This modern addition to the Renaissance-built property required a macerator to remove the waste, the noise of which was loud enough to scare the birds during the day and wake the dead at night. The ditty "If it's yellow let it mellow, if it's brown flush it down" springs to mind.

The flight home passed without a hitch. We touched down in Santiago at 10:50 and within two hours we'd collected Jazz and were back home.

21

Cucumber Anyone?

Ten days after flying in to Santiago Airport we were driving back there, this time to collect my sister Julie, and her eldest son Sam. This was Sam's first visit and we were looking forward to seeing him. It hardly seemed possible that in less than a month he'd be celebrating his seventeenth birthday. How time flies.

As usual, Julie had a list of must-do activities which again included visiting Santiago on our way back from the airport. As with most teenagers, Sam mooched along. Given the chance, he would have preferred to laze away the days topping up his tan and swimming in the pool.

On their final evening, he insisted on showing his appreciation by buying a round of drinks at the Parador Hotel in Monforte. We'd been there two nights earlier and he'd taken quite a shine to the cocktail menu. We were delighted to accept his offer.

'To Sam, cheers!'

In the opulent surroundings of the former palace of the

Counts of Lemos, we sipped our drinks and joked about the events of the last few days.

'Can you ask the waiter for the bill?' whispered Sam.

Minutes later the smartly dressed barman placed the tab on the table.

'It's for him,' I said, pointing at Sam.

The waiter smiled and slid it towards him. Sam checked the total and delved into his back pocket, then into his other back pocket, and his front pockets, and finally his jacket. Sheepishly, he turned to his mum.

'Mum, can you lend me some money?'

Through design or oversight, he'd forgotten his wallet. And people wonder why we chose not to have kids.

Later that month, we received an email from Pilar.

> **From:** 'Pilar Xxxxxx'
> **To:** Craig Briggs
> **Subject:** papers are ready...
> **Date:** Mon, 12 Jun 2006 20:31:57
>
> Good afternoon:
>
> I've called you several times, so maybe you are in England.
>
> This is just to tell you that we have papers ready since last week, so we can go to the notary when ever you want.
>
> Please tell me if you are still interested in buying the house.
>
> See you soon.
> Pilar

'You're not going to believe this,' I said, rushing into the lounge.

'What?'

'We've had an email from Pilar.'

'And?'

'And the papers are ready. She wants to meet up at the notary.'

Melanie looked like I felt, dazed and confused. This was the last thing I'd expected to see when I opened my emails this morning.

'I don't believe it. I can't even remember what the place looks like. Can you?' asked Melanie.

'Not really.'

Almost twelve months had passed since we'd walked out of the notary office disappointed that we hadn't been able to buy our next property project. Had it not been for our involvement with *Casa Bon Vista*, we would probably have looked for somewhere else but we didn't.

'I'll write back and tell her that we want to take another look before we go ahead,' I added.

Given its condition the last time we saw it we were keen to make sure it was still standing. Buying a ruin was one thing; buying a pile of stones was quite another. Pilar was happy to oblige providing we could wait a bit longer. She was reluctant to let her father-in-law drive himself to the house.

Don Antonio drives a micro car, a vehicle which, depending on the driver's age, has no requirement for either a driving licence or a test. Pilar would have to arrange for his grandson to take him. Given her concerns, we were happy to wait; another few weeks wouldn't make any difference.

Since Julie and Sam left, we'd enjoyed a spell of unseasonably high temperatures. So much so that for almost a week, our local area enjoyed national prominence as the hottest place in Spain. Temperatures of over 100°F, coupled with 100% humidity, made the slightest physical exertion a rather sweaty affair.

The scorching temperatures took their toll on our kitchen garden. Wilting leaves and sad-looking salads cried in silence for a drink of water. Such extreme conditions usually end with a spectacular storm.

'Did you hear that?' I asked, as we relaxed in the garden.

'It sounds like thunder,' replied Melanie.

Muted atmospheric rumblings rolled in from the southeast and an ominous blanket of dark grey clouds drifted towards us. As it neared, the claps intensified. To the west, the setting sun projected a colourful rainbow, arcing across the sky.

'At least you won't have to water the *huerta* this evening.'

Moments later, huge droplets of rain splattered onto the terrace and a cool wind swept through the garden. Flashes of lightening, illuminating the thick clouds like aerial incendiaries. Melanie and I sheltered under the covered terrace waiting for a dramatic deluge. Some people hate electrical storms; Melanie and I love them. Unfortunately, this summer storm failed to fulfil its early promise and drifted past with hardly a splash.

'It looks like you're going to have to water the garden after all,' I commented.

Despite our disappointment, at least the weather front had replaced the clammy air with a much cooler, fresher environment.

'I think it's about time for a Teatime Taster. What do you think?'

'Sounds good to me,' replied Melanie.

'I'll tell you what, you water the *huerta* and I'll pick some strawberries.'

What better way to end the day: a refreshing glass of chilled white wine, freshly picked, home grown strawberries, a golden sunset, and a chorus of local wildlife.

Our efforts in the *huerta* were finally paying dividends. The monotony of early morning watering was now alleviated with a pre-breakfast nibble of succulently sweet and perfectly formed tiny green peas. The lightest pressure on the pointed pods broke the natural seal of freshness revealing an orderly row of juicy young pearls: delicious. We'd also enjoyed a few early potatoes. The loose, sandy soil has produced a smooth and unblemished creamy white surface that peeled away with the gentlest of rubs. In another bed, delicately thin French beans were hanging from their stalks like deep green icicles.

In the salad beds, various lettuce varieties provided a colourful leafy collage of greens, cherry reds, and royal purples. Several had bolted adding a miniature alpine landscape to a sea of leafy lettuce. Spring onions and baby carrots added strong flavours and vibrant colours to our lunchtime salads.

The award for most exciting plant went to the humble cauliflower. Large waxy leaves cradled a creamy white heart. Pale veins spread across the dark green leaves like forked lightning and perfectly formed florets grew larger every day.

The prize for the most productive crop was unquestionably the cucumber. Earlier research indicated that one plant was capable of providing sufficient fruit to feed a family of four for an entire summer. With that in mind we decided to propagate four seeds assuming that half would probably fail. If two survived, we'd have something to trade when it came to inter-neighbour crop swapping. Not only did all four survive but they flourished. Within days of the bright yellow flowers falling from the tips of pencil-sized cucumbers, they'd grown to eighteen inches long and were as thick as table legs. At this rate we'd be able to supply every household in the parish, never mind the village.

June is that time of year when the promise of spring is realised and the intensity of summer is still to come. This year, the beginning of summer had a special significance. A favourable viewing of Don Antonio's ruin had the potential to set our lives on a new path. When we began our search for another property project we were undecided what to do with it. Looking after *Casa Bon Vista* had focused our minds and given us the confidence to try property rental. If things didn't work out, we could always sell it.

When we arrived for the viewing, the house looked as charming as ever. Don Antonio insisted we take another look inside; little had changed. The holes in the roof looked that bit bigger and last winter's rain had made the floorboards a little less safe but none of that mattered. All we were interested in was the integrity of the shell; everything else could, and would, be changed.

'OK,' I said, as Don Antonio's grandson locked the front door, 'how soon can we go to the notary?'

'You'll have to speak with Pilar,' replied Don Antonio.

That evening I emailed her.

From: Craig Briggs
To: 'Pilar Xxxxx'
Subject: Happy to proceed
Date: Sun, 02 Jul 2006 16:23:42

Dear Pilar

We would like to proceed with buying your father-in-law's house. Could you let me know if there is anything Melanie and I need to do?

I look forward to hearing from you in due course.

Best wishes

Craig

At times it seemed as if this day would never come. Pilar's reply made me think it might not. Last year, her husband, José, had taken a tumble off his scooter and broken both of his ankles. Unfortunately, the natural healing process was not altogether successful. To rectify this, clinicians had recommended resetting one of the breaks and pinning it. José was scheduled to undergo the procedure this week and would be incapacitated for up to eight. Pilar's first responsibility was to him; visiting Monforte to conclude the paperwork would have to wait.

'You're not going to believe this.'

'What?' asked Melanie.

'I've had a reply from Pilar and we're going to have to wait a bit longer.'

I explained the reason and we resigned ourselves to the delay.

If I was superstitious, which I'm not, I might have had seconds thoughts about going ahead with the deal; every time we got within striking distance, the goal posts moved.

Almost seven weeks passed before we finally managed to get to the notary office. By then, the excitement of owning a new house and the prospect of renovating it had long since waned. Our appointment coincided with Monforte's annual fiesta.

Thinking the town might be busy, we left home early. To our surprise, everywhere was eerily quiet. Rows of market stalls, covered with sun-bleached tarpaulins, lined the street in front of the college. Stacks of tables and chairs cluttered the pavements where bar staff had hurriedly cleared them away in the early hours. In the car park opposite, covered fairground rides looked like statues waiting to be unveiled.

Roadside parking had been commandeered by an assortment of caravans and campers: temporary homes for nomadic traders. This shortage of roadside parking had rippled into the surrounding areas. Eventually, we found a parking space in a dry dusty field on the outskirts of town.

Having parked, we headed towards the centre. Save for the odd dog walker and those searching for a morning paper, the streets were abandoned. Closer to the centre, road sweepers were clearing up from the previous night's festivities in readiness for another day of celebration.

First stop the bank, to collect the money. I stuffed the bundles of used notes into my briefcase before we walked next door to the notary office. As expected, Don Antonio and his entourage hadn't yet arrived. Our wait was short. Pilar was first to appear, pushing open the heavy door of the waiting room for her husband, José. He swung through on crutches with one foot in a plaster cast; Don Antonio brought up the rear.

Before long we were ushered into the *notario's* office by Enriqueta, the office administrator. As we entered, the *notario*, Don Arturo, looked at us and smiled. Hardly surprising given the number of times he'd seen us over the last four years. As always his personal appearance mirrored his meticulously organised office. He greeted us warmly and invited us all to take a seat. With everyone sitting comfortably he turned to Don Antonio, checked his identity and outlined the contract. Then it was our turn, only this time in English. Almost thirteen months to the day since we first came here to buy the house, we signed the contract, handed over the cash, and took possession of our very own Galician ruin.

'What have we done?' commented Melanie, as we strolled back to the car.

'Bought a ruin,' I replied.

'I thought so.'

That evening, over a glass of wine, we discussed our plans for the new house.

'I think we ought to manage this project ourselves.'

'What about drawing up plans?'

'Let's go up to the house tomorrow, measure up, and take it from there,' I suggested.

Having employed Felipe to design *El Sueño*, I felt confident that we could take the knowledge we'd gained and use it to our advantage. It seems to me that the most common mistakes people make when designing their own home are perspective and proportion. They inevitably end up with bathrooms the size of billiard halls or kitchens no bigger than a cupboard.

The following day we woke to an uncharacteristically damp and overcast August morning. Armed with nothing more than a vivid imagination, a tape measure, and a notepad and pencil, we ventured off on our next adventure.

Twenty minutes later, we were trundling through the narrow lanes of Vilatan, location of our latest acquisition. It seemed fitting that the first person we bumped into was Pablo, wandering through the village. His attire mirrored the weather: a pair of faded jeans, a torn T-shirt, and an old green cardigan that was obviously his favourite. On seeing us, he wrapped the open sides of his cardie around himself like an old blanket. I stopped the car and wound down the window.

'Hola, how are you?'

'Better than the weather,' he remarked. 'Have you bought the house?'

'Yesterday morning,' I replied.

I sensed from his manner that he was hankering after an invitation. Given the help he'd given us, it seemed rude not to ask.

'We're just going to have a look and take some measurements. Would you like to join us?'

His face lit up.

'I'll follow you round,' he replied.

Slowly, I moved off; Pablo followed. I drove round the corner and parked in the narrow entrance. Ten metres from the lane were a pair of rusting gates, held together with a loop of twisted wire.

'If you want to widen the track, the owner of this field will probably let you move that wall,' he said, pointing at a row of stones marking the boundary of the adjacent field.

It seemed a strange comment to make but something to bear in mind. At the moment, we were more concerned with mapping out what we already owned rather than adding to it.

The gates did little more than mark the limits of our plot. I opened them by untwisting the wire and manhandling them to one side. The meadow in front of the house was a sea of knee-high, straw-like grasses save for a narrow pathway that we'd flattened on our last visit. In line, we walked across the field to the house and climbed the stone steps to the door. In exchange for a wad of used notes, Don Antonio had handed me four keys. The first I tried slipped easily into the lock but wouldn't turn.

'It must be this one,' I said, picking the only other key that might fit.

The second key was much tighter. I wiggled it up and down and pushed it into the lock.

Clunk, clunk!

I turned to Melanie and smiled.

'Hurry up,' she said.

I lowered the door handle and pushed but it didn't budge.

'It won't open.'

'You need to pull the cord,' chirped Pablo.

I'd forgotten about Don Antonio's security mechanism: a length of frayed nylon cord dangling inside of the door and accessed through a neatly drilled hole. I slipped my forefinger through, hooked the cord and pulled. As I pushed, the bottom of the door scraped along the stone threshold.

Nothing had changed since our last visit, seven weeks earlier. The interior was dark and dusty but felt refreshingly cool. Worn old rugs and offcuts of threadbare carpets partially covered the irregular-shaped floorboards and scraps of lino had been strategically placed below holes in the roof where rainwater had leaked in. We began by measuring the length of the house along the central corridor. Calculating the width proved a little more difficult but we got there in the end. Room by room we mapped out the internal space, taking every conceivable measurement and a few more besides.

'That should do for now,' I said, winding in the tape measure.

'I know a builder if you want a quote,' said Pablo.

'As soon as we've decided what we want to do, I'll let you know,' I replied.

Pablo seemed as keen as us to see this derelict property restored. Having decided to manage the project it felt reassuring to know that if we needed to, we could call on him for help.

That afternoon, I set about converting all the measurements we'd taken into a scaled floor plan. I had a blank sheet of paper and endless possibilities. Originally, the house was half its current size but had been extended many years ago. Along with the external walls this central dividing wall would have to stay but everything else could go. By the end of the day I'd settled on a two-bedroom, two-bathroom home with a large kitchen diner and a comfortable lounge. All the living accommodation would be on the first floor but, finances permitting, we'd add an internal staircase leading to a downstairs lobby and laundry room.

'What do you think?' I asked proudly.

'What's that?' asked Melanie.

'That's the staircase.'

'But there isn't a staircase.'

'There will be when we've finished.'

Melanie paused, looking carefully at the proposal.

'Well?' I asked, impatient to know what she thought.

'It looks expensive.'

'Everything is dependent on cost but what do you think of the layout?'

'I like it.'

The day had started dull and overcast, a fair reflection of our mood, but ended with a renewed sense of excitement at the prospect of converting this tired ruin into a luxury farmhouse rental.

22

The English Inquisition

The holiday season at *Casa Bon Vista* was a little shorter than we'd hoped. Overall we were very pleased with how the first year had gone and so were Bob and Janet.

From initial enquiry until the morning of departure, we worked hard to ensure that everyone had an enjoyable experience and a stress-free holiday. This began by providing clear instructions on how to find the property, including written directions and a map of local roads. The keys were left in a safe and secure location and visitors could arrive at any time after 4:00 pm.

On the day of their arrival, guests could settle in at their leisure, acquaint themselves with the area, and have a good snoop around. The following morning, we popped in for the official, Meet and Greet, to welcome them personally and answer any questions. On the morning of their departure, we asked them to vacate the house by 10:00 am. This gave us plenty of time to make sure that *Casa Bon Vista* always looked its best for the next arrivals.

As well as the keys, we also left a welcome letter.

Welcome to Casa Bon Vista

Dear Guest

Please feel free to leave your car in the lane outside the gates. It's perfectly safe and doesn't disturb the neighbours.

To open the front door, insert the key and turn anticlockwise until the door opens.

The key can only be removed in the horizontal position.

From outside, the door can only be opened with the key.

Please remember to take the key with you every time you leave the house, even to go into the garden. You cannot access the house without the key.

If you have any problems my telephone number is: 123 456 789.

We will call tomorrow morning at about 10:30 to welcome you properly and answer any questions that you might have.

We hope you have a wonderful stay and return to see us soon.

Best wishes
Craig and Melanie

The inaugural guests were the Campbells, a party of four from Ayrshire in Scotland. Although their stay clashed with Melanie's surprise birthday party, everything went to plan and they were none the wiser about our absence.

Second to arrive at the house were the Strankmüllers, a couple from Germany with a young daughter. We quickly discovered that each party would leave their individual stamp on the place. In this case, it came in the form of sticky little handprints scattered throughout the house and cute little footprints on every glass pane in the *galleria*. Needless to say we had our work cut out ensuring that everywhere was spick and span for the next guests. Kids, who'd 'ave 'em?

Those minor workarounds paled into insignificance when compared to our third booking. Call it intuition, or a sixth sense, but right from the start I suspected we'd have our work cut out with this married couple from the UK. My suspicions were first raised by the probing nature of their initial enquiry.

From: 'Mrs Xxxxx Crockford'
To: Craig Briggs
Subject: An enquiry from Holiday-rentals.com
Date: Tue, 3 Jan 2006 21:09:13

Arrival date: 24 Jun 2006 Departure date: 8 Jul 2006
Total no in party: 2 No of children: 0

Please could you tell me:
1.   How far off the road is the villa and is the drive a made/unmade road?
2.   The size of the double bed?
3.   How large is the village and is the villa in it, on the edge of it, or outside it?
4.   How large is the garden and which direction does it face?

Many thanks.
Mrs Crockford

'Come and look at this,' I said, as I entered the lounge.
'What?'

'An enquiry for *Casa Bon Vista*,' I replied.

I could see from Melanie's expression that I'd pricked her curiosity. She sat at the computer and read the email.

'The villa ... what villa?

'The farmhouse "villa", I presume, but what about the next question?'

'What size is the double bed?' Melanie paused for a moment. 'Let me guess. That wouldn't be double, would it?'

In fairness to Mrs Crockford, I assumed her questions were based on past experiences. We knew from our own trials that not all property descriptions are as accurate and honest as ours.

Imagine arriving at your destination to find that the only access to your dream holiday home is fifteen miles down an unmade track, or discovering that the previous owner of the "double bed" was Baby Bear, and Goldilocks was nowhere to be seen. Or worse still, finding out that the reference to "village" should have been prefixed with the word Greenwich, and the south-facing garden backed on to a tower block.

With this in mind I did my utmost to reassure her with a detailed and accurate reply. My attention to detail and forthright honesty seemed to encourage even more inquiry.

From: 'Mrs Xxxxx Crockford'
To: Craig Briggs
Subject: Re: An enquiry from Holiday-rentals.com
Date: Sat, 7 Jan 2006 02:09:42

Dear Mr Briggs

Many thanks for your detailed response. We would like to book your house for the aforementioned dates and look forward to your instructions regarding deposit, etc.

I am assuming the twin beds are 3 ft ones and not bunk size?

We would like all the beds to be provided with enough linen for 2 weeks as my husband is tall and we are used to a 6' wide bed. Usually this means that, like Goldilocks, we sleep in all beds in turn to see which ones suit us best. Would this be a problem?

Kindest regards
Mrs Crockford

Once again I replied in a timely manner. To confirm the reservation, we required a deposit of twenty-five percent and the return of a completed booking form. We waited, and waited, but nothing arrived in the post. Towards the end of the month, I asked for clarification and received this response.

From: 'Mrs Xxxxx Crockford'
To: Craig Briggs
Subject: Re: Rental of Casa Bon Vista
Date: Wed, 1 Feb 2006 15:37:29

Dear Craig

I have scanned and attached a copy of the booking form. If you still have not received the cheque by the w/e, I will transfer the money to your account on Monday (it takes 3 or 4 working days as it is not the same bank as mine), and cancel the original cheque. No-one has cashed it yet, so I guess it is 'missing in the post'!

Many thanks for your flexibility in this matter and hope to hear from you soon

Regards
Mrs Crockford

Given the unusual nature of our correspondences, I began to question the authenticity of her enquiry but surely no one would go to such lengths just to amuse themselves, would they?

Two days later my concerns were allayed when their deposit payment and booking form arrived in the post. Unfortunately, their payment difficulties didn't end there. When the outstanding balance became due, ten weeks prior to their arrival, Mrs Crockford emailed again. She'd misplaced our address and asked if I could send it again. I duly obliged and their final payment arrived soon after.

In the end, I spent more time organising this booking than all the others put together but I wasn't finished yet. Mrs Crockford's thirst for knowledge showed no bounds.

From: 'Mrs Xxxxx Crockford'
To: Craig Briggs
Subject: Supermarkets
Date: Sun, 28 May 2006 13:40:33

Dear Craig

I am sorry to bother you and I hope you do not mind, but as our holiday draws near I have a few questions that I hope you can answer.

Firstly, approximately how long do you think it will take to drive from Bilbao to Casa Bon Vista, bearing in mind it will be for the first time?

Secondly, is there a large supermarket on the way to Casa Bon Vista that we can stop at for a 'weekend' shop? We thought about shopping in Bilbao, but will have no means of keeping 'coolbag' things cool if it is a long journey. I am a coeliac and although I will bring all my gluten-free food with me, filling up with ordinary meat/veg/dairy/groceries is also very important for us.

Thirdly, as I presume local shops will be closed on Sunday, my Spanish is almost non-existent and we will not eat out very much, I would be most grateful if you could also give us directions to the nearest, reasonably-sized supermarket to the house, in whichever direction.

I hope the above is not too onerous and look forward to receiving your reply. We are looking forward to Galicia and getting away from the atrocious weather we are having over here at the moment!

Kindest regards
Mrs Crockford

Onerous – how could she suggest such a thing?

Her first question was by far the most difficult to answer. It reminded me of the conundrum "How long is a piece of string?" and threw up more questions than answers. Is Mr Crockford a Sunday afternoon driver, a medium paced driver, a racing driver, or a complete lunatic? Do they intend to take the most direct route, the coastal route, the toll free route, or the quickest route? Will they stop for fuel or refreshments, and if so, how many times and for how long? The permutations were endless so I decided to avoid that question and concentrate my efforts on the second and third. I should have known better.

From: 'Mrs Xxxxx Crockford'
To: Craig Briggs
Subject: Re: Supermarkets
Date: Sun, 28 May 2006 15:10:20

Dear Craig

Thank you very much indeed for your detailed instructions, I will now go away and look in the Michelin map. However, just one query still. Approx. how long will it take from Bilbao? Not normally being early-risers on holiday, we want to know when we have to leave the hotel! Will we need a 6am wake-up call?

Many thanks and best wishes
Mrs Crockford

Oh well, I guess it was time to put my head on the

block. In the end I settled for between six and seven hours. Nine days before they were due to arrive, I received another email.

From: 'Mrs Xxxxx Crockford'
To: Craig Briggs
Subject: Hello
Date: Thur, 15 Jun 2006 13:05:43

Dear Craig

Hope you do not mind, but have just a few last minute queries. Does the house have an iron and deckchairs/recliners? Is the tap water drinkable?

Looking forward to setting off on Wed and to meeting you soon.

Regards,
Mrs Crockford

'You'll never guess who I've had an email from?'
'Don't tell me, Mrs Crockford,' replied Melanie.
'You've got it.'
'I don't believe it. What now?'
'More questions.'

After months of written interrogation, I would soon come face to face with my inquisitor.

On the morning of their Meet and Greet, we left home feeling a little apprehensive.

'I wonder what questions she'll have?' remarked Melanie, as we slalomed up Cowpat Alley.

When speaking with someone on the phone it's easy to conjure up an image of the caller, even if it turns out to be completely wrong. Communicating by email is very different. When we pulled up outside *Casa Bon Vista*, we had no idea who we might encounter.

We rang the bell, pushed open the new gates and strolled into the courtyard. As we did the front door opened. Standing at the top of the steps was a tall man in his mid-fifties.

'Good morning. Welcome to your home. Please come in,' he said, gesturing us to enter.

We climbed the steps and walked into the kitchen. Mrs Crockford was sitting at the table thumbing through a guide book.

'Good morning,' she said, as we entered.

As expected, she did have some questions, a long list of them, but her immediate concern was over the number of towels we'd supplied.

'I contracted an eye infection just before we left England and it seems to be getting worse. Could we have some extra towels to reduce the chance of cross infection?' she asked.

We were happy to help and returned later that day with another set.

'If there's anything else you need, anything at all, don't hesitate to phone,' I said as we left.

Ring ring ... Ring ring!

'Who's that at this time in the morning?' moaned Melanie, as she dashed to the phone.

I listened from the bedroom.

'Oh hello.'

Her response left me in no doubt as to the identity of our early bird caller.

'It's in Monforte,' I heard her say.

'If you can wait an hour we'd be happy to take you.'

That sounded ominous.

'It's no problem at all, don't you worry.'

Big softie, I thought to myself as she replaced the receiver.

'Guess who that was?'

'Let me think ... It wasn't Mrs Crockford by any chance?'

'You've got it.'

Her eye infection had worsened overnight to such a degree that she felt it warranted medical intervention. She'd asked for directions to the nearest hospital. Unwilling to see a traveller in distress, Melanie had offered our assistance.

'I couldn't leave them to it; neither of them speak a word of Spanish.'

'You did the right thing, love.'

As things turned out, they were fortunate we'd offered to help. It's not every day that the staff at Monforte Hospital are presented with an English printed holiday insurance certificate.

'What's this?' asked the receptionist, holding the certificate as if it was a blood-soaked handkerchief.

We did our best to explain but she was having none of it.

'Do you have a health card?' she asked, directing her question at Melanie.

'Yes,' she replied, pulling it from her purse.

'That'll do.'

With the eccentricities of Spanish bureaucracy appeased, treatment could begin. A few hours later, we called at a pharmacy to fill the doctor's prescription and drove them home.

'Thank you so much,' said Mrs Crockford. 'I don't know what we'd have done without you.'

Their sincere appreciation made our efforts worthwhile and their parting gift of a bottle of Lepanto's finest brandy was a nice touch.

By the time the Crockfords left *Casa Bon Vista*, our changeover day cleaning routine was running as smoothly as a well-oiled machine. Melanie would start inside the house while I spruced up the outside.

'I'm just going to check the *pozo*,' I said, having finished in the courtyard.

'OK,' called Melanie.

Since Bill and I re-plumbed the soil pipe, I hadn't had chance to see if the *pozo negro* (septic tank) was working properly. We'd tested it at the time but there's no substitute for regular daily use. To dissuade visitors from taking a peek, we'd placed a planter on top of the manhole cover. It wasn't heavy but the spiky *berberis* had so far proved an adequate deterrent.

Carefully, I lifted the planter to one side, slipped a large screwdriver down the edge of the manhole cover and prised it upwards. What greeted me was a scene of impending doom and a feeling of inevitable resignation. The *pozo* was full to the brim with sewage, so much so that effluent was backing up the new soil pipe.

'*Melanie!*' I screamed from the garden.

'What?' she called, rushing to the front door.

'Look at this,' I said, pointing into the *pozo*.

'I'd rather not.'

She walked down the stone steps and across the courtyard, held her nose, and stared into the abyss.

'Oh my God. What are you going to do?'

With one short sentence, Melanie shifted the burden of responsibility fairly and squarely onto my shoulders.

'What do you mean, what am *I* going to do?'

'Well you can't leave it like that,' she replied.

'*We'll* have to get it emptied.'

'How?'

That was a very good question.

One of the many benefits of living at *El Sueño* is a connection to the mains sewerage system. Getting a septic tank emptied was a whole new challenge.

'Don't they use one of those farmyard slurry spreaders to suck it out?' I said.

Melanie retched at the suggestion.

'I don't know,' she replied, 'and I don't want to.'

'Well someone must know.'

'Why don't you go and ask Carmeña?'

Carmeña and her husband, Andres, live in the manor

house at the top of the track. They own a large estate and would certainly know how to empty a *pozo negro* and probably have the equipment to do it.

'That's a good idea,' I replied.

Purposefully, I marched out of the courtyard and up the track. As I approached the entrance to their driveway, my pace slowed. In a little over three hours, new guests would be arriving at *Casa Bon Vista*. Between now and then, I had to persuade someone to empty an overflowing pit of human effluent and dispose of it. Asking someone's advice on the matter was bad enough; pleading with them to empty it was another thing altogether. When we agreed to help Bob and Janet, this was not what I'd envisaged doing but what choice did I have?

The gates to the manor were open so I walked warily up the drive. My approach lacked sufficient stealth to avoid the attention of their five snoozing dogs. Without warning they leapt to their feet and came charging over, barking at me like a pack of hungry hounds.

'Good dogs,' I said in a calming tone. 'Good dogs.'

Thankfully, their barks were far worse than their bites and by the time I'd strolled to the front door, all but one had returned to lie in the shade.

'I haven't got anything,' I said to the other, offering it an open palm.

Disappointed, it mooched off and laid down.

Standing at the front door, I rang the bell and waited. Seconds later a first floor window opened.

'Hola,' called Carmeña, hanging out of the window.

'Hola,' I replied.

'What do you want?' she asked, in a friendly yet typically direct manner.

Sounding as helpless and pathetic as I could, I threw myself at her mercy and explained the welling problem.

'Andres can do it tomorrow,' she replied. 'He's out in the fields at the moment.'

As generous as her offer appeared, tomorrow was no

good. I thanked her and walked forlornly back to the house.

'Andres can't do it until tomorrow,' I said.

Melanie was busy cleaning the kitchen.

'What about Bill?' she suggested. 'Perhaps one of his neighbours can help.'

Bill lives in the next village. With no time to spare, I hopped in the car and sped off down the lane. Fortunately, he was at home.

'Perhaps Arturo can help,' he suggested.

Arturo and his wife, Matilde, live opposite. We strolled across the lane and I knocked on the door. Given the subject matter, Bill was happy for me to lead; besides which, his Spanish was limited to please and thank you, one large beer, and a curious version of good day.

After a short wait, an upstairs window opened and Matilde leant out.

'What do you want?' she asked.

I stepped into the middle of the lane and announced my dilemma to anyone within earshot.

'One minute,' she said, before disappearing from view.

Seconds later she returned.

'No problem,' she said, 'Arturo can call round tomorrow afternoon.'

My hopes had been raised only to be dashed. I thanked her for their generous offer but explained that time was of the essence.

'Try Manolo,' she added, as we turned to leave. 'He might be able to help.'

The pair of us trouped off in search of Manolo. He was working in the stable, preparing feed for his cows. Once again I explained the mess we were in.

'No problem,' he said, 'I'll call round later this afternoon.'

'Is there any chance you can come straight away?' I asked sheepishly.

'Right now?'

I pleaded my case.

'No problem,' he replied.

My heart skipped a beat. I'd found our saviour.

'You lead the way,' he said, climbing onto his tractor.

The urge to hit the accelerator and race back was overwhelming but I managed to curb my enthusiasm. Manolo did his best to keep up but an ageing tractor towing a filthy slurry spreader is hardly the speediest mode of transport. As we approached *Casa Bon Vista* I parked, allowing him to expertly reverse his tractor and trailer down the track. In one continuous movement he turned the slurry spreader into the courtyard and stopped. Melanie came rushing to the front door.

'Hola,' she called to Manolo.

Manolo acknowledged her greeting.

'You found someone then,' she added.

Slowly and methodically, Manolo coupled a long flexible hose to the back of the slurry spreader and hauled the pipe to the open manhole. He lowered the tube into the mire and ambled back towards the spreader.

'It's not very deep,' he remarked.

I wasn't sure whether he was referring to the *pozo*, or its contents, so I nodded my head and smiled at him nervously. Back at the tractor, he flicked a switch and the pump burst into life. A disgusting gurgling sound accompanied the noise of the motor as a combination of liquids and solids shot up the tube and hurtled into the spreader. Manolo rushed back to the manhole, picked up the tube and started swirling it around, vacuuming everything in sight. In less than two minutes the job was done. He switched off the pump and pulled the tube out of the *pozo*. Without thinking I bent down, grabbed the tube with both hands and helped haul it out. No sooner had I taken hold than I realised what I'd done. Human effluent ran between my fingers and down my hands. But for a strong constitution I could easily have barfed. Instead, I held my breath and swallowed.

Shaking Manolo's hand seemed a little inappropriate. As for the final destination of our domestic effluent, that was anyone's guess. Later that day we returned with a bottle of whisky. A small token of our appreciation and one which he humbly accepted.

When our next guests arrived, they were none the wiser. The Benoit family had driven from France. They'd chosen to holiday in Galicia believing summer temperatures would be favourable for rambling. Their surprise verged on disappointment.

A party of four, plus one, were next to arrive, from Hong Kong of all places. It's difficult to imagine a more cosmopolitan family. Father and husband, Russell, was born in England. His wife, Alexandra, is Belgian, their eldest child, Tristan, was born in Italy and daughter, Madeline, delivered in Hong Kong. Their Meet and Greet was by far the most interesting of the season.

'Good morning,' I announced, as a young woman opened the door holding a toddler in one arm.

'Do come in. I'm Alex,' she said, sounding decidedly flustered.

'Is everything alright?' asked Melanie.

'The house is beautiful,' she replied. 'It's just I've had quite a stressful time getting here.'

Sitting at the kitchen table was her husband Russell and their son Tristan.

'Hello,' said Russell, as we entered. 'Say hello Tristan.'

The young boy was tucking in to a bowl of cereal but managed to mumble a greeting.

'We're sorry you've had a difficult journey. What's happened?' I asked.

Their stay in Galicia was the final fortnight of a month-long holiday for Alexandra and the kids. Having left Hong Kong, they'd flown to Belgium to spend time with her mum and dad. From there they flew to England to spend time with Russell's parents before travelling to Spain. Due to work commitments, Russell missed the first part of their trip and had flown here direct from Hong Kong.

Since landing in Belgium, Alexandra had suffered a torrid time. It began when the plus one absconded.

'Absconded!' said Melanie.

The plus one was the family's Filipino maid who was travelling to Europe for the first time. Shortly after receiving her monthly salary, she'd asked permission to go sightseeing on her day off. Alexandra thought nothing of letting her go out alone. Unfortunately, that was the last she saw of her. After reporting the disappearance to the Belgian authorities, she was shocked to discover that holidaying with an employer is one of the most common ways that Far Eastern women illegally enter Europe. Alexandra's unaccompanied travels had proved traumatic. It was clear that they had their hands full so we answered their questions and left.

'We'll call back next Saturday at about this time to change the linen,' said Melanie. 'Don't worry if you're not here; we have spare keys.'

When we returned the following Saturday, Russell was keen to quiz me. It seemed that their motives for visiting Galicia were not confined to a relaxing holiday.

'Do you know anything about the estate agents in the area?' he asked.

I can say with confidence that if I'm ever invited to take part in the quiz show *Mastermind*, I could do a lot worse than choose property viewing in Galicia as my specialist subject.

'A little,' I replied.

Two hours later, Russell was still asking questions and I was doing my best to answer them.

'Let me buy you both lunch as a thank you,' he suggested.

'There's no need for that,' I replied, but he insisted.

After lunch we said our farewells; we probably wouldn't see them again before they left.

'If you have any more questions, anything at all, just ask,' I said.

Four days later, the phone rang.

Ring ring … Ring ring!

'Hello.'

'Hi Craig, this is Russell.'

'How can I help you?'

'We have a small problem.'

Without realising it, they'd managed to do the one thing we'd warned guests not to do: lock themselves out.

'Don't worry,' I said. 'If you look under the planter with the dwarf conifer in it, you'll find a spare key.'

It seemed inevitable that someone would lock themselves out so we'd taken the precaution of hiding a second key. How did we know this? Melanie and I did exactly the same thing on a holiday to Lanzarote, and the owners of that property had also hidden a key.

'OK, thanks. I'll put it back when we're in,' he replied, before hanging up.

'Who was that?' asked Melanie.

'Russell. They've locked themselves out.'

'It was bound to happen to someone.'

Ring ring … Ring ring!

'Hello.'

'Hi Craig, it's me again. Is there a knack to opening the door?'

'A knack?'

'The key doesn't seem to fit.'

Blood drained from my face as the realisation of what they'd done dawned on me.

'Was the first key in the lock when the door closed?' I asked.

'I think so.'

With the key in the lock on the inside, it's impossible to insert another from outside. Russell had inadvertently locked everyone out.

'OK, wait there and I'll be right up,' I said, confidently.

I explained what had happened to Melanie.

'What are you going to do?'

I thought for a moment.

'Perhaps they've left a window open.'

'Did he say they had?'

'I didn't ask. He caught me by surprise.'

'What if there isn't a window open?'

My mind went blank.

'What if …'

'I know what you said, just let me think for a minute.' I racked my brain for a solution. 'We'll have to break in.'

'Break in!'

'Come on, I'll fetch the ladder if you carry the hammer.'

'Hammer!'

'If there isn't a window open, I'm going to have to open one.'

'With a hammer?'

I loaded the ladder into the back of the car and we raced off.

Slap! Slap! Slap!

Freshly dropped cow muck struck the underside of the car as we sped up Cowpat Alley.

'All the side windows are closed,' said Melanie, as I drove down the track.

Apologetic parents greeted our arrival.

'One of the kids pulled it closed by accident,' said Russell.

'Not to worry, these things happen. You didn't leave a window open by any chance did you?'

'Unfortunately not; that was the first thing I checked.'

I surveyed the house deciding which pane would be the least expensive to replace.

'Kitchen window looks favourite,' I said to Melanie.

The breakfast terrace leading off the kitchen would give me somewhere stable to stand while wielding the hammer. I leant the ladder up to the terrace and climbed up.

'You'd better stand back,' I said to the assembled audience.

I pulled on some gardening gloves and prepared to strike. My first whack was a rather reluctant effort resulting in the hammer bouncing off the double glazed unit. Undeterred, I readied myself again. This time I swung with considerably more force, turning my head at the last second. Once again the hammer bounced off the glass like a drumstick off a snare. I hit it again with a little more force but it still didn't break. By now I was feeling a little isolated and a bit foolish; all eyes were focused on me. I hit it again, and again, and again.

'Do be careful,' called Melanie, sensing my mounting frustration.

With malice running through my veins I swung the hammer with all the force I could muster.

Smash!

Shards of glass cascaded onto the kitchen floor. After a quick sweep up we called the local carpenter who sent one of his lads to board up the hole.

That was the last we saw of Russell, Alex, and family; as for the whereabouts of the plus one, that remains a mystery.

When the next guests arrived, we were still waiting for a replacement unit. Two young couples had driven here from Murcia on the Mediterranean coast. Their stay passed without incident and after the Meet and Greet we didn't see them again. Given the number of condoms floating on top of the *pozo*, we presumed they'd enjoyed their stay.

The final guests of the summer season were a family of three from France, mother, grandmother, and son. On their Meet and Greet they invited us to join them for wine and tapas; we were delighted to accept.

Our first season as hosts had been full of surprises. We'd enjoyed meeting our guests and from the comments written in the Visitors' Book, they'd enjoyed staying at *Casa Bon Vista*. It seemed appropriate that after everything we'd learnt, one guest should have the final say.

'You're not going to believe this,' I said, walking into the lounge.

'What?'

'Mrs Crockford has emailed. Come and take a look.'

From: 'Mrs Xxxxx Crockford'
To: Craig Briggs
Subject: Thank you
Date: Sun, 1 Oct 2006 15:56:06

Dear Melanie and Craig

Apologies for my tardiness but we wanted (very belatedly) to thank you for all your help during our holiday at Casa Bon Vista. It was very much appreciated. We had a lovely stay there and learned so much about the region.

The only thing we did not find out and forgot to ask you is: "What were the short, round, tiled 'towers' in some fields in the area?" Obviously they may be feed or machinery stores nowadays but were they originally built for any other purpose like shepherd's huts, water stores, winter animal shelters, siege towers? If you know, we would be very interested in the answer please.

Anyway, I have taken up enough of your time on a relaxing Sunday after changeover day! I hope you had a good first season and that next year will be even better. You both deserve it.

Kind regards
Mrs Crockford.

'That's lovely. It makes all the hard work worthwhile,' said Melanie. 'And one more question to add to the list. By the way, what are those towers?'

'Dovecotes,' I replied.

Our foray into the holiday rental business reinforced our belief that we'd made the right decision buying our

Galician ruin. All we had to do now was convert it into a dream holiday home. What could possibly go wrong?

HASTA PRONTO

About the Author

Craig left full-time education aged eighteen and began a career in retail. At the age of twenty-eight, he found his true vocation after buying into a small printing business. After thirteen years of blood, sweat, and holding back the tears, he sold up to pursue his dream.

In May 2002, two months before his fortieth birthday, Craig, his wife Melanie and their pet dog Jazz squeezed all their worldly goods into their ageing executive saloon and headed off to Spain. Not for them the tourist-packed Costas of the Mediterranean coast or the hills of Andalusia, no, they headed for Galicia, a remote and little known region in the northwest corner of Spain.

Craig began writing a weekly column for an online magazine in 2004. Over the last few years he has written a number of articles for the Trinity Mirror Group and online publications such as: CNN, My Destination, and Insiders Abroad.

In 2013 he published his first travel memoir *Journey To A Dream*. It tells the story of a turbulent first twelve months in Galicia. Two years later he published his second book, *Beyond Imagination*.

His latest book, *Endless Possibilities*, continues the adventure.

As well as writing, Craig and his wife Melanie own a traditional Galician farmhouse which they rent to tourists from around the world. He's also an enthusiastic winemaker and owns a small vineyard.

Printed in Great Britain
by Amazon